El Salvador
The Face of Revolution

Robert Armstrong
and
Janet Shenk

SOUTH END PRESS   BOSTON

Preface

San Salvador, July 1982. Handkerchiefs pressed to our faces, we visit a clandestine cemetery that everyone knows about, several miles from the capital at El Playón. White skulls stand poised on a bed of black lava that stretches from the road to the green hills in the distance. Some of the bones still have flesh clinging to them; a fresh load of bodies had been dumped the day before.

At a refugee camp run by the Catholic Church, two thousand women, children and elderly men are crammed into a schoolyard now filled with makeshift tents. They describe the military campaigns that forced them to flee the northern provinces of Chalatenango, Cabañas and Morazán; they tell of their young sons and daughters whose whereabouts are now unknown; and some speak in soft tones about their hopes vested in *"los muchachos,"* the guerrillas. Meanwhile, the refugees learn to read and write for the first time, take turns in the communal kitchens, and wait for the war to end.

At night, in the capital, firefights can be heard in the distance but they last only a few short rounds. The black-outs are more disconcerting. They happen nearly every night and

iii

seem to last longer each time. The guerrillas can blow up generators and powerlines much faster than the U.S. aid dollars arrive to replace them. But aside from these inconveniences, the war is barely felt in the capital; only the despair of the mothers of the disappeared, who tell their stories over an awkward cup of coffee at our hotel; or the priest from a working-class *barrio*, where ninety percent of the parishioners have had a family member killed or disappeared; or the businessman whose factory has been idled for over a year and whose family waits nervously in Miami for the signal to return. There's no end to the war in sight, they all agree, but differ on where to place the blame.

Only at the American embassy is there a mood of cautious optimism, but even there it is conditional. "Democracy can take root here," says the political officer, if only Congress is patient, the right-wing parties behave, and the army takes our advice and supports the reforms. "We can reduce the guerrillas to banditry in five years," says the military attaché. And, again, if only we can get the army to go out on night ambushes and small-unit patrols; if only the aid keeps coming. Then a note of uncertainty and resentment at the kind of support he can expect from back home: "$100 million is zero. Less than the traffic fines in New York City." That's no way to fight a war.

* * * * * *

Washington D.C., July 1982. In unusually cautious language, the State Department declares that El Salvador's new government is making "a significant and concerted effort" to curb human rights abuses and promote economic reforms. The civilian murder rate has declined "somewhat"—"according to available statistics"; things could be worse and they are slowly improving. This is the second time that the administration has had to follow this disagreeable procedure—imposed by Congress—in order to "certify" El Salvador as a proper recipient of U.S. aid. The storm of criticism that followed the first certification has tempered the administration's arrogance.

"It was a close call," says Elliott Abrams, Assistant Secretary of State for Human Rights, with a candor intended to bolster his credibility in the eyes of Congress. But in reality, certification was a foregone conclusion long before the State

Department made its "findings" public. For only with this stamp of approval can the President ask Congress for more military and economic aid. And only with more military hardware, advisers, training and millions in cold cash, can the Salvadorean army expect to hold its own in a civil war raging since 1980.

Ronald Reagan is not about to let the Salvadorean government fall to forces that he insists are controlled by foreign powers. He is not about to let the conditions imposed by Congress stand in the way of aiding an ally in its battle against "Communist subversion." Hopes for a quick and easy victory in El Salvador—a strong signal to the Russians—have been dashed over the last two years. But El Salvador is still a "place to draw the line," in the words of ex-Secretary Haig, and certification is just another battle in the war.

For its part, the Salvadorean government does its best to look presentable. In the weeks preceding certification, peasants that had been evicted from their newly acquired lands are reinstated by soldiers swearing to uphold the agrarian reform. For a time, the civilian death count drops sharply. And Roberto D'Aubuisson, the president of El Salvador's new Constituent Assembly, keeps a low profile so as not to alarm those in Washington who remember his days as leader of the death squads.

But no sooner than certification is over and done, with a few squawks from Congress, do the headless bodies reappear on the streets of San Salvador, and the death count rises to levels reminiscent of the worst periods of violence. New civilian massacres are reported in the foreign press, and denied by the Salvadorean High Command or chalked up to the dirty business of war.

In the embassy and in Washington, officials begin to worry about the next certification in early 1983: How to make sure the body count drops in time to note a "significant improvement" with respect to human rights; how to make it plausible that things can improve and still remain so bad.

*   *   *   *   *   *

Several years ago, when we first started writing on El Salvador for the North American Congress on Latin America, few people knew or cared about this tiny country—seventy miles across at its widest point—where priests and peasants, teachers and students, were being killed by an army in power for fifty years. El Salvador was only one country among many vying for the attention of human rights organizations, activists and writers, in a hemisphere dominated by dictatorial regimes. Even the Carter Administration, with its pronounced emphasis on human rights, paid El Salvador little heed—until the Sandinistas in Nicaragua awoke Washington to an isthmus on fire.

How did El Salvador take center stage in a drama that threatens to envelop all of Central America, and the United States, in a long and bloody war? Who are the actors in this drama, behind the facile labels of left, right and center? And why is a country so long ignored by the United States now considered "vital" to our national security? This book is an attempt to contribute to an understanding of these questions, by exploring the history of El Salvador, its relations with the United States and its role in the region.

Our focus is El Salvador, not the East-West struggle that dominates official rhetoric, because we believe that meaningful debate must begin with an intimate knowledge of the facts, and an acceptance of the uniqueness of each nation's history and culture.

Back in 1932, long before the world had heard of Fidel Castro, El Salvador was the site of the first communist uprising in the hemisphere, a rebellion that cost the lives of 30,000. Unless we understand the roots of that rebellion, its lasting impact on every sector of society, we can never understand the war in El Salvador today.

In the 1960s, El Salvador was called the "showcase of development" in Central America—the pride of Kennedy's Alliance for Progress and the proof that capitalism could work for poor countries. Investors, both domestic and foreign, praised the industriousness of the Savadorean worker: "Tell a Salvadorean to plant rocks and harvest more rocks," said a Chamber of Commerce brochure, "and he'll do it." How, then, and why, did that stubborn determination of a people turn toward the task of revolution? And why did millions of dollars in U.S. aid and investment fail to achieve their goal?

A new phenomenon appeared on the political scene in the 1970s. "Popular organizations," as they called themselves, mobilized tens of thousands of people in acts of civil disobedience and street demonstrations, demanding basic democratic and economic rights. They eluded all labels by including Marxists and Catholics, peasants and professionals, slumdwellers and market women. And in October 1979, their strength prompted a military coup that sought to preempt revolution by promising reforms. How did these organizations arise beneath the boot of military rule? And why did each successive junta fail to carry out its promises of reform?

These questions and many others illustrate the complexity of the war that consumes the people of El Salvador today. We are not impartial observers of this conflict. El Salvador is a small country. Coming to know it means, inevitably, meeting people who will eventually be tortured or killed by the security forces: Enrique Alvarez, the first president of El Salvador's Democratic Revolutionary Front, a millionaire dairy farmer who gave his life for the poor; Ernesto Barrera, a priest who worked in the slum communities of Quiñónez and La Chacra, and who died in a gun battle with the police; Iride Beltrán, a graduate of Mt. Holyoke College, who was "disappeared" by the security forces, along with her infant son. It is our hope that by writing a history of El Salvador with them in mind, we will have given human face to a conflict so coldly labeled the work of shadow puppet-masters, by those who would have us forget the stories of those involved.

* * * * * *

This book builds on the efforts of the North American Congress on Latin America, over the last fifteen years, to explore the realities of Latin America and analyze the impact of U.S. policy on the hemisphere. We owe a great debt to our compañeros at NACLA for their research assistance and criticisms, and most of all for their patience and cooperation in allowing us to write this book while they shouldered the extra responsibilities of NACLA's ongoing work. Our thanks to America Badillo-Veiga, Judy Butler, Martha Doggett, Eric Feinberg, Paul Horowitz, Nathan Locks and Steven Volk of the NACLA staff.

Long before El Salvador made headlines in the United States, many people were researching and writing on the subject, and struggling for greater public awareness of conditions there. They have been an essential community of friendship, knowledge and support during the years of silent indifference. There were also many people who listened patiently to what at times must have seemed an obsession, asked good questions and just were there when we needed them. We thank them all, and especially Cindy Arnson, Philippe Bourgois, Esmeralda Brown, Roger Burbach, Roberto Cuellar, Elmo Doig, Heather Foote, Guillermo Galvan, Grid Hall, Marc Herold, Bob Hilliard, Beverly Keene, Michael Klare, Natasha Krinitzky, O. A. Magaña, David Mancia, John McAward, Marc Mihaly, German Montoya, Anne Nelson, Gene Palumbo, Julia Preston, Arnoldo Ramos, A. G. Rodríguez, Posie Roth, Orlando Sandoval, Mario Salgado, John Scholefield, Helen Shapiro, George Shenk, Margaret Shenk, Otto Shenk, Jon Snow, Heidi Tarver, Doug Walker, Phil Wheaton, Bill Wipfler and Jody Zacharias.

Countless people in El Salvador shared their lives with us, their memories and their hopes. They can only be thanked by name once their struggle has been won.

Finally, our special thanks to Karen Judd, for her skill as an editor and patience as an arbiter; to Liz Mestres for cover and photographic design; and to John Schall of South End Press for twisting our arms to undertake this project in the first place, and for helping us see it through.

Contents

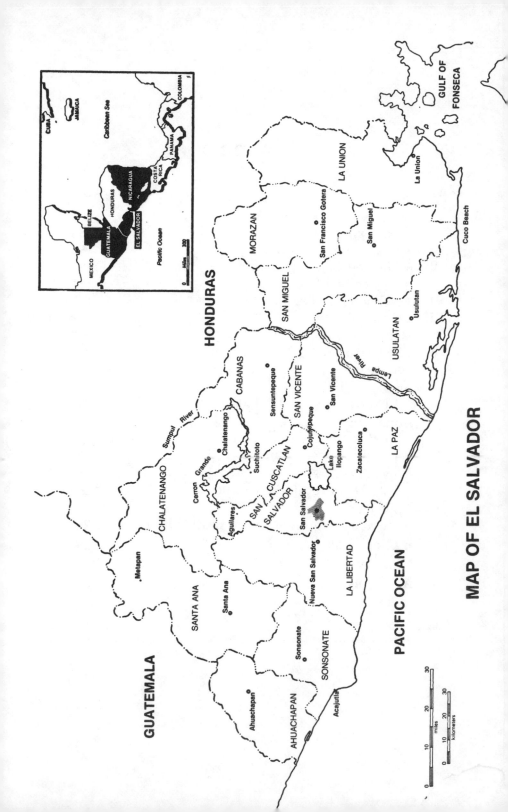

MAP OF EL SALVADOR

CHAPTER I

Where Coffee Is King

Near the top of the steep hill a man pushes a plow. His forearms bulge as he drives its steel head through the rocky soil. Into the open furrow a woman—his compañera—pokes a stick and drops a seed. From the seed will come the corn, *maiz.* Across the valley, smoke rises from another field as its farmer burns away the stalks of last season's harvest.

The sequence is an ancient ritual: the rude plow, the planting stick, the preparation of the corn field, the *milpa.* Before colonization, before the Spanish, it was a communal rite. The land belonged to all. And the corn was sacred. Mayans called that tall, leafy stalk "Your grace," and thought it the supreme gift that the gods had given to humankind, the sustenance of life. The gods of creation were in each plant, so to eat the plant was to share communion with the source of being.

A Spanish friar, traveling through Central America in the mid-eighteenth century, marveled at the people's respect for the corn they cultivated: "Everything they did and said so concerned maize that they almost regarded it as a god.

1

The enchantment and rapture with which they look upon their *milpas* is such that on their account they forget children, wife and any other pleasure, as though the *milpa* were their final purpose in life and source of their felicity."[1]

As the sun crosses the sky, the woman and man could turn and follow its trip across the 240 miles from the scrubby mountains of Morazán in the east to Lake Guija on the Guatemalan border in the west. From left to right, east to west, the grandeur of the volcanoes defines the landscape. El Salvador is a land of volcanoes, their mouths open to the sky, while the coffee trees flow like deep green lava down their slopes. And between them the long valleys, the smoky golden light tinting their green with beige. To the west, Izalco—the volcano at whose feet the Indians grew the cacao, maize, and squash in peace with the land. Moving east, Coatepeque, a lake in the crater of a volcano. San Salvador, its lights a halo in the night sky, then Lake Ilopango, and the Lempa River directly below. This silver snake slides down from the north, dropping toward the sea and passing Chichontepec Volcano, guardian of the verdant Jiboa Valley. And there, to the east of the river, the volcanic cluster of Chaparristique, Tecapa, and Usulután. Finally, the mirror of the Gulf of Fonseca and, beyond, Nicaragua or, north of the Gulf, Honduras. The eye retraces its path, but now 60 miles south along the coastal plain, the strip of sand and the Pacific that with a lifted glance becomes the sky.

But the man and the woman do not look up. Hunger and the ancestral obsession fix their attention on the *pedacito de terreno* which most certainly is not theirs; a rump-end lot on a cattle ranch or coffee *finca*, rented for the season for one-third of its harvest. So worthless the land, so uncultivable, that only a campesino family—one of the thousands without land or home—would want it.

And were they to look up from their work, look south from the hill, would they be able to see the beauty of this land? Or has the numbing struggle for their daily bread blinded them to the majesty that sustained their Indian forebearers? The ancient prayer, is it still uttered?

> O god, my grandfather, my grandmother, god of the hills, god of the valleys, my holy god. I make to you my offering with all my soul.

Be patient with me in what I am doing . . . It is need-
ful that you give me . . . all I am going to sow here
where I have my work, my *milpa*.

Watch it for me, guard it for me, let nothing happen
to it from the time I sow until I harvest it.[2]

El Salvador. A rich land, a fertile land. When the Span-
iards came, they found its peoples growing beans, pumpkins,
chilis, avocados, elderberries, guavas, papayas, tomatoes, cocoa, cotton, tobacco, henequen, indigo, maguey, and corn.
Today, the plantation crops—coffee, sugarcane, cotton—
dominate the land. Their rich harvests are sold for export.
The majority of the people in a country which is the third
largest producer of coffee in the world can drink only instant,
and basic foods are imported.

There are almost 5 million people here: 550 persons per
square mile, the highest population density in the hemisphere, ten times that of neighboring Nicaragua; and for
most, the land yields just bare subsistence, its bounty the
exclusive domain of the 2 percent of the population which
owns 60 percent of the land.[3]

From May to October, the rains come. After that the
dry season, which leaves a four-inch blanket of dust on every
country road. The children bound through it, tan dust socks
on their bare legs. The socks wash off quickly as they stand
in the stream, waiting while their mothers beat the clothes
on its rocks.

Who is that couple high on the hillside, their children
with them in the tiny field? Were they able to trace their
histories, they would reach back to the Mayans—Pipil,
Pokomam and Lenca peoples—who numbered between
116,000 and 130,000 at the eve of the Conquest. Over the
next 300 years the Spanish changed that history forever;
some peoples, their labor coerced, their religion crushed,
their culture perverted, still fought to preserve—or rede-
fine—their customs and communities. Others, driven from
their lands, fled into the highlands to cultivate their *milpas,*
and leave their Indian ways.

In the sixteenth century, the Spanish Crown reorganized
the Mayan economy to satisfy its need for raw materials. Yet
reluctant to let the local conquistadors get too powerful, it

kept some land from their grasp—preserving it for subsistence cultivation. Thus communities and towns were established: Crown-protected lands on which the population could collectively grow their daily produce.

But the Crown was chronically short of money—and when it couldn't reward its servants, they joined forces with the wealthy settlers to wrest first labor and later land from the Indian communities. Initially, they were content to let the Indians own the land—so long as they controlled what the Indians produced. Cocoa and balsam were products that were in much demand within the Spanish empire. In the late eighteenth century the rise of textile production that resulted from the industrial revolution, together with the increased number of uniformed soldiers as other European nations joined the race for empire, greatly augmented the demand for dyes. Indigo production flourished in El Salvador. To exploit it more profitably, the settlers realized that they needed to control not only labor but the land as well. The large plantations, haciendas, were few, but unlike most of Spanish America, where they were relatively independent of the growing European markets, in Central America, those that existed were based on production for a competitive European market. Slowly, but increasingly, the number of haciendas grew and the land came under the private control of those who sold its bounty across the seas.

In 1821, when Central America was granted its independence from Spain, these elites and their armies fought each other. When they called a stop in 1842, those who had the most land moved to create national governments in order to secure their gains. From then on, in El Salvador, the same names appear and reappear on laws and decrees: Alfaro, Palomo, Regalado, Orellana, Escalón, Prado, Menéndez, names that even today mean the power and privilege of the oligarchic "Fourteen Families."

In the mid-nineteenth century, as England and France outpaced Spain in trade and commerce and coffee houses became popular among the rich, *hacendados* in El Salvador began to switch from indigo to coffee production. Immigrants from Europe and the Middle East sought their fortunes in the coffee production of the New World. Many opened stores; the more far-sighted staked out a claim in the export-import sector. Still others, along with several of the older families and English bankers, financed the commercial development of coffee. Their names resonate today in the corridors of power: Hill, De Sola, Sol, Parker, Schonenberg, Dalton, Deinninger, Duke. These immigrants and the founding elite are the seeds of the oligarchy.[4]

Coffee production grew dramatically. But it made immediate and insistent demands on the land and its use. Indigo required little tending, grew everywhere, and seldom interfered with local subsistence farming. But coffee was different. Not only was demand greater, requiring more land and more labor, but coffee also needed constant tending and hundreds of people to harvest its red berries. Moreover, the crop grew best on the higher slopes of the volcanoes, and much of that land, especially in the west, comprised the communal and subsistence plots of the campesino populations.

The history of modern El Salvador begins in a cup of coffee. A new elite of exporters and bankers were determined to make their country the coffee center of Central America, and with the election of one of their own, President Zaldívar, in 1876, they began in earnest. On the grounds that neither the Indian communities nor the country's municipalities were making efficient use of their common lands, the would-be coffee magnates pressured the government to eliminate all forms of landholding that were not in private hands. The governor of San Vicente province wrote in 1879: "The majority of these farmers do not wish to change their way of life or to make progress because of the deep-rooted customs, their lack of financial resources and their ignorance about the great advantages of coffee cultivation."[5]

Shortly thereafter, in 1881, the government simply decreed that the common lands, which had endured throughout the colonial period and after, would be no more. It passed legislation to control and recruit the dispossessed for work on the coffee *fincas,* appointed agricultural judges who kept lists of day workers on the estates, and ordered their capture if they left before they completed their duties.

New laws permitted landowners to evict squatters, forcing them to rent or wander landless. On most estates the landlords kept a few workers—*colonos*—to tend the farms between harvests, sometimes for pay, sometimes for room and board.

But so radical a change in so short a time risked upheaval. Campesino revolts broke out in 1880, 1885, and 1898. To ensure their control the coffee barons urged the buildup of the army. In 1900 a military training school was opened. In 1912 the government created a special security force exclusively to maintain order and to enforce the landlord's law in the rural areas, the *Guardia Nacional* (National Guard).

With the dawn of the new century, the communal lands were but a memory and the Guard-imposed peace reigned throughout the land. A public relations tract on El Salvador in 1916 proclaimed:

> One of the great obstacles that our agriculture was confronted with was the deplorable system under which the national land was divided into *ejidos* and *tierras comunales* [communal lands], which caused land and labour to remain unused . . . . now the landscape presents to the traveller a scene similar to a vast chessboard where the various products of the fertile land may be admired; from the highest peaks to the beautiful valleys and plains, Salvador presents a view that reminds us of a large and well-kept garden, with every available piece of land being under cultivation.[6]

Six decades later, here are some facts about life in the "large and well-kept garden":

- 2 percent of the population controls 60 percent of the land
- 96.3 percent of the rural population has twelve acres of land or less
- In 1975, 58 percent of the population earned $10/month or less
- 70 percent of the children under five years of age are malnourished

- The per capita calorie consumption rate is the lowest in the western hemisphere
- Illiteracy affects 42.9 percent of the population
- The infant mortality rate is 60/1000 births (compared to 25/1000 in Cuba)
- 64 percent of the urban population lacks sewage facilities
- 45 percent of the population has no drinking water on a regular basis
- The per capita income in El Salvador is the lowest in Central America
- 8 percent of the population receives 50 percent of the national income
- Most of the rural population has work for only one-third of a year
- Unemployment and underemployment in the rural areas is a permanent 45 percent.[7]

To Frighten the Night

It is the harvest. Coffee, cotton and cane. The rains have stopped and on the plateaus and in the highlands, a chill bites the December night.

Children, women and men mill around the plaza. They have come to Sonzacate from all over the country, from Chalatenango in the northwest, Morazán in the northeast; from San Vicente and Sonsonate. The city dwellers, residents of the shantytown communities of San Salvador and the *mesones* of Santa Ana, wait there too.

Soon the trucks will carry them to the coffee *fincas*. In the towns to the south where cotton is grown, elsewhere near the cane fields, it will be the same.

They pile in: the men in their white shirts, their machetes hung like cutlasses from their belts; the women holding children by the hand, carrying the smallest in their arms; *los cipotes*, the children, running here and there, balancing on their heads the woven bags which hold the family's possessions.

This annual search for seasonal work is a necessity for most of El Salvador's rural population. For those lucky enough to have small plots—too small, though, to feed a family year round—it means a chance for a few months' security and perhaps a few treats; for the totally landless— 40 percent of the rural population in 1975—it means literally a chance to avoid starvation, *si Dios quiere*, God willing. To them, the plantation workers, the *colonos*, seem fortunate; they at least have some security.

On the sidewalks of the plaza, the vendors sell fruit drinks, *refrescos*, hats, oranges and young corn, *elote*. National Guardsmen prowl the streets, watching the throng, ever alert for "subversives."

The trucks arrive. The trip is short. Soon they will be climbing the hillsides to crawl under the tent-like trees, picking the bright coffee berries; or bending under the endless sun to gather the cotton balls; or swinging their machetes against the green cane. Lunchtime brings two tortillas and a spoonful of refried beans. Night and enough work bring three to five dollars for each member of the family.

Christmas comes during the harvest season. The extra *centavos* go to buy the little plastic toy that the vendors sell along the sidewalks. A strange harmony comes over the land. But it lasts less than a week. With the approach of New Year's Eve, the annual explosion is at hand.

In San Salvador, the sound of fireworks begins at 7:00 in the evening, incessant almost until dawn. By midnight the city is shrouded in smoke.

Throughout the rest of the country where 98 percent of the population lives—in the *tugurios*, the *mesones*, the rural *cantones*—jars of *chicha*—home-brew liquor—*aguardiente*, and among the better off, bottles of Chepe Toño, a white cane liquor, appear on the tables. Glasses will be raised to toast the New Year and forget, no, bury the old.

But the alcohol releases fury. Perhaps 100 will die this night in useless brawls, hands cut off with machetes in fratricidal frustration at their shared hunger and that of the children, the old.

Out of this dark night comes a man, his face ghost white, his eyes blood-shot red and his lips full and bleeding. He has fallen and lain in the dust, his face now a macabre mask. The machete that he waves is an extension of his arm and his rage. He staggers up the path and then attacks, first that house, then the next, driving the blade into the wood of the door and scarring the lime of the walls. He screams with each blow.

On the other side of town a statue of Jesus Christ, his arms outstretched, balancing himself on a tiny globe, stands high above a little park. He is surrounded by a shopping center, an automobile showroom and McDonald's Hamburgers. *El Salvador del Mundo:* the Saviour of the World.

El Salvador. It means the Saviour. The eyes of the statue look east toward the rest of the city, toward San Miguel, toward Honduras. Christ on the ball, the gringos call it.

Under the shadow of El Salvador del Mundo
One sees the face of the exploiters.
Their grand residences
With windows that sing the night
Illuminated
To kiss a blonde in a Cadillac.

There in the rest of the country,
A great pain
Nightly:
There are the exploited
And I with them.
Those of us that have nothing
Except a scream,
Universal and loud
To frighten the night.

—Oswaldo Escobar Velado,
Salvadorean poet

The Two Percent

Time magazine first called them the Fourteen Families. Actually there are about 250 of them, if you count all of the branches and all of the intermarriages. Their wealth comes from coffee: growing it, processing it, exporting it, financing it.

In everyday discourse, these families are the "oligarchy." They even refer to themselves by that name. Some liken them to feudal lords, but there is nothing feudal about the way that they get rich. Theirs is a highly efficient, capitalist operation. Virtually all of their land is in use with almost none available for speculation. Every last acre is planted; the most modern techniques and best fertilizers are employed to produce the most bountiful harvests. How else could a country as small as El Salvador have become one of the world's major coffee producers? And unlike neighboring Honduras, these Salvadorean entrepreneurs have done it themselves, and they are proud of it. No United Fruit, no U.S. money, it has come from the sweat of "our brow," they say. Or more accurately, the sweat of the campesino.

On the coffee *fincas,* in the cotton and cane fields, workers, owning only their muscle power and their time, sell those to these capitalist landowners for a daily wage. The difference between what they produce and what they and the owner need to survive is invested in enterprises from which the Salvadorean businessman expects a minimum return of 25 percent.

Among the grand old families, there is little social distinction between those who have land and those who have investments in industry and commerce. All of them have holdings in each of the vital sectors of the economy.

There are petty differences. The old, old families, descendants of the "founding fathers"—the Palomos, the Regalados, the Guirolas, the Dueñas, the Alfaros—these can claim the classiest credentials in the social pecking order. The immigrant families—the Hills, the Dukes, the Sols, the Deinningers, the De Solas—perhaps have slightly less prestige, but their wealth and power erase the difference. The merchants—the Lebanese, the Palestinians, most of the Jews— are on a lower social rung: "Turcos" (Turks), with their own clubs and social life.

Yet all share a culture of genteel mediocrity, insulated from all but the most crass of twentieth-century consumerism. Their sons and daughters, sent to the United States for a college degree, rarely aspire beyond the expensive "party school," ending up in second-rate provincial colleges far from the mainstream of contemporary thought. The exceptions who study at Harvard or Yale must confront that mediocrity when they come back.

Returning home, these young oligarchs can look forward to marriage, hopefully to a member of one of the "families" and, if a man, a place in one of the family businesses. If a woman, then there is the joy of babies and pampering by her husband and the servants. The periodic trip to Miami is the occasion for the revival of romance.

There is the country house. There is the beach house. There is the city house in the San Benito or Escalón sections of San Salvador, the capital. The Mercedes is parked in the driveway; the strains of Montovani waft through the night air and the ice tinkles in the glass of imported scotch.

Of an evening one might go to the Cine Presidente to see the latest Hollywood extravaganza or to the Cine Vieytez for the latest in European fare. The Club Campestre offers a game of polo or a dip in the pool. Or there is night at one of the six restaurants in the country where "our set" might go.

In San Salvador
in the year 1965
the best sellers
of the three most important
book stores
were:
The Protocols of the Elders of Zion;
a few old books by
diarrhetic Somerset Maugham;
a book of disagreeably
obvious poems
by a lady with a European name
who nonetheless writes in Spanish about our
country
and a collection of
Reader's Digest condensed novels.

—"San Salvador," Roque Dalton
(translated by Edward Baker)

It may not be much by jet set standards, but it is theirs. And no one, not even the government of the United States, is going to tell them what to do with it. The rest of the country—the lazy, the drunken, the worthless, the "Indios"— they are there to make them money. And they are to stay in their place.

"Look at how they live," a wealthy woman said. "They live like pigs; they have children with different men; their houses are made of cardboard. And, you know, look at all the television sets. Why don't they spend that money to get an education?"[8]

La chusma: the rabble. They lie begging on the streets of San Salvador, mothers with their babies sleeping in cardboard boxes; one-eyed old men, gangrenous stumps protruding onto the sidewalks. Shoeshine boys at every outdoor cafe, newspaper vendors, sellers of lottery tickets. Old women with arthritic fingers offering a home-made candy from their baskets; drunken campesinos wildly waving their machetes and firing pistols into the night; a maybe-rabid dog snarling and foaming on a country road; a man urinating on the street corner. On the Avenida Independencia, women clustered behind the bars of the window. Only five *colones!* At the bordellos, El Recreo, Punta del Este. Focky, focky?

The toothless, the crippled, the degenerate, the lazy, the drunken, the mad, less than animals! *La chusma:* the rabble.

On the clean streets of San Benito, the neighborhood where the wealthiest live, only the obsequious maid and the well-mannered gardener can be seen. Yet the world laps at their shoes. There is a little chapel. It faces onto a tree-lined street, elegant, quiet. Behind the church there lies a courtyard and a wall. A door stands in the wall.

Behind it are the cardboard and mud huts of *El Manguito,* one of the oldest of the shantytowns of San Salvador. Through that door come the charitable ladies of San Benito. Moving quickly, tensely, they distribute their gifts, the requisite embrace, imparted to the bright-eyed little boy done up in his only white shirt. Then rapidly, but with studied calm, they pass back through the wall to the other side. The door is closed. Back to the gossip, the parties, the romances. Safe again.

They are afraid. Their husbands, their lovers, their children, all are afraid. Somewhere they know that the wall is just made of brick; they know that the *chusma* neither forgets nor forgives. And it is now—and always was—too late and too hard to do anything about it. Get what is yours while you can, before the communists ruin it. If only those communists were eliminated, those communists who demand that the starving be fed, the naked clothed and the homeless housed.

The oligarchy, pathetic, savage creatures. Their greed, their fear, their insularity, their stupidity blind them to the essential lesson that every ruling class which hopes to survive must learn: "Things must change a little if they are to remain the same."

Dogs at the Gate

Instead, the oligarchs protect themselves with the armed forces. The price—to quiet the fear of the *chusma*—is bribes and payoffs, invitations for drinks at the Club Campestre to the cloddish colonels, and occasional sacrifices to the soldierly beasts.

In 1977 a story was told in hushed and angry tones among the oligarchs. A beautiful young woman was being pursued by an army officer. She was of an important family; her wealth, her beauty, her charm guaranteed her a good match. The officer was valiant in his chase, but she found him pompous, overbearing and a bit foolish. Definitely not of her class. And she threw him over.

One night at one of the social clubs favored by the oligarchy, they met again. He wanted to talk. They ambled toward the parking lot. He tore off her dress and beat her until blood ran from her nose and mouth. And he raped her in the back seat of an unlocked car.

The hauteur of the oligarchy changed to rage. The master had been bitten by his own dog. The family prepared to press charges.

But the officer corps countered that the young man was a good soldier with a promising future. Soon, one heard rumors of reprisals if charges were brought. What would be the effect if all of this came out in the newspapers?

In time her wounds will heal, the colonels said. And that young hothead, why let's send him abroad.

Her wounds did heal and the officer became the ambassador to a very important Salvadorean ally in the Middle East. The end.

Since 1931, the soldiers have run the government and organized the political game. For a young man, if he can endure the training, it is one of the few sure ways to get ahead. There is money, there is security. The work is not that difficult. And even if he does not enjoy the respect of the population, he has its fear.

For a noncommissioned soldier, it is one way to get three meals a day and a warm place to sleep. The pay isn't great; but after he's out, they remember him. Among the security forces—the National Police, the National Guard, the Customs Police and the Treasury Police—the perquisites come from extortion, intimidation, theft. Advancement comes from how good he is at killing. "Already López Mejía is a sergeant! He must have killed a lot of people."

When there are not enough recruits, the trucks of the armed forces roll into the villages, rounding up young men in forced conscription. Upon discharge, there will be places for them in the territorial guard or ORDEN, paramilitary organizations that keep watch while the National Guard sleeps.

It is a web of fear: the oligarchs, the army, ORDEN— each dependent on the other, each trying to extort from the other some margin of safety against the fear. And behind it, in the entrepreneurial paradise that it maintains, is one more group—the gringos.

The Hidden Presence

The U.S. strategic view of Central America as its backyard seems to have been taken literally by many of its citizens. The gringos. Latecomers in El Salvador, their spirit is now everywhere. It is a small country, and it takes little to create a presence. Colgate toothpaste, Dustin Hoffman movies, Johnnie Walker Red. In the United States 90 percent of the population has never heard of El Salvador. In El Salvador, one cannot avoid the United States. Its embassy, once a quaint Spanish colonial structure, now occupies a city block, a fortress, with aerials and antennae on the roof and a marine at the door. Turn on the television, and there is "Dallas"; the radio, rock 'n roll. In the cities, U.S. fashions are sold to the middle classes, and fast food is dished out to everyone.

Outside the cities, in the provinces of Morazán, Cabañas, Chalatenango, the gringos are no more than their cultural trappings; their myth is their only substance. Save for a few Peace Corps volunteers and the ever-wandering Mormon missionary, the gringos do not leave the cities.

Wearing the invisible shield of the "American abroad," they live in a world of their own, insulated from the fear and oblivious to the daily violence. They have servants. Their children go to the American school where classes are taught in English, the junior prom has its queen and a date is a trip to McDonald's. At the supermarkets on the Boulevard de los Heroes, they can find the same cellophane-wrapped cuts of meat that are sold back home. Kid Creole and the Coconuts are broadcast over local radio stations. Their social circles are small, confined to each other or a few of the internationalized oligarchs. They have their clubs, trips to the beach and the eternal sun.

The gringos are nags. Always telling the Salvadoreans what to do, how to do it. "Back home we have . . . back home we do. . . ." Their advisers at the embassy remind the oligarchs and the colonels that they cannot rely exclusively on agriculture to survive. They push land reform and insist that, religious and cultural principles or not, a country with an annual birth rate of 3 percent needs some kind of family planning. The businessmen go on at them about the money to be made in the world market with the burgeoning garment industry and the electronic assembly plants.

The greed and intransigence of the oligarchs and the corruption and crudity of the military repel and attract the gringos. The arrogance of the gringo offends and intimidates the Salvadoreans. But there is money to be made by all, and they share a deep bond of hatred for "communism" and "communists."

The embassy officials, the investment experts, the heads of the corporate subsidiaries stand metaphorically on the parapets of the embassy, keeping watch. They venture back and forth, helping this faction of the business community, promoting that colonel's interests, looking for new business.

These guardians of the empire can see the web of fear sprung around them. A few others, also. The rest live their suburban lives, blind to the vulture circling there in the sky.

The Beginning and the End: 1932

In 1932 the oligarchs handed the direction of their political destinies to the armed forces, this *parvenu* class, the sons of small farmers, artisans, failed professionals. For in that year the people of El Salvador rebelled against the tyranny of the oligarchs. Hundreds of poor campesinos took up their hoes, their machetes and a few crude rifles to take over their country. Within hours they were crushed. El Salvador's president, General Maximiliano Hernández Martínez, ordered the slaughter of all who participated, or might have participated, or merely did not protest. The death toll echoes down the decades: 30,000 people.

One of the organizers of the revolt—a shoemaker, Miguel Mármol, who survived a firing squad, wrote:

> I believe that the drama of 1932 is for El Salvador what the Nazi barbarity was for Europe, what the North American barbarity was for Viet Nam—a phenomenon that completely changed—in the negative sense—the face of a nation. . . . Since that evil year all of us are other people and I believe that since then El Salvador is another country. Above all else, El Salvador is today the work of that barbarity.[9]

Some call it the first communist uprising in the western hemisphere. For all Salvadoreans, oligarch, worker or peasant, it is a shadow and a ghost. Afterwards, nothing was the same; everything before, gone. The beginning and the end.

Before 1932 is to mark history like B.C. and A.D. 1932 is A.M.: Anno Militaris—in the year of the military. How did it happen and why?

Viva la Civilización: El Salvador's Golden Age

The roots of the *matanza* of 1932 are found in the delicate civilization that the coffee moguls set out to create at the turn of the century. It was a fairy tale world, a world of Pierce Arrow motor cars, concerts in Bolívar Park, dreams of Central American unity, and the strange "duck races," where men on horseback played football with a live duck.

To the north, in Mexico, it was the same. The ruling elites were oblivious to the rest of the world—the Indian peasants they scorned and the Yanquis they ignored. Porfirio Diaz appeared to be guaranteed an eternal rule, blind to the anguish and frustration that in less than ten years would rend Mexico with the cries of campesinos following Zapata and Villa.

Teddy Roosevelt, his spectacles shaking, sat in the White House. It was the dawn of the age of empire, and the hero of San Juan Hill sent a White Fleet around the world to announce the birth of a new imperial power.

In 1898 Cuba had fought to throw off the last shackles of Spanish domination in the hemisphere. The United States, despite popular protest, sent troops to "help" the Cubans and wound up the proud possessor of two full-fledged colonies, Puerto Rico and the Philippines, and a virtual protectorate, Cuba. The young empire had joined England, France and Germany in the mad scramble for colonies and the hunt for resources and markets to feed the engine of their burgeoning economies. Leaving Africa and Asia to its European rivals, the United States asserted its authority under its self-proclaimed Monroe Doctrine to dominate the western hemisphere.

How ephemeral and short-lived those times, the twilight of the genteel gods. The opulence of the few was built on the impoverishment of the many, who now listened seriously to those who talked of the day when the workers would take power and run things for the majority. Capitalists soon swallowed up other capitalists; rivalry among the wealthy opened rifts; and government was often their arena of struggle. The prize of rule would go to those who both helped business and prevented workers from threatening profits and the rule of the business class.

In San Salvador, the oligarchy and the growing class of professionals who serviced them fed that civilization with coffee and nourished themselves on its money and the accoutrements of its culture: western civilization circa 1900, *a lo salvadoreño.*

> Long live Civilization
> Long live the Honorable Government
> Viva Boquerón Volcano and the tourists
> Viva the Central American Union
> Long live the National Theatre and the
> Civil Company which inaugurated it
> with the play, the Positive Ones, one of
> the best flowers of the modern Spanish theatre.
> Viva the Ministry of Public Instruction
> Long live Bolívar Park and the Band of the High
> Powers
> Long live the Peace with Guatemala
> Viva the Director of the Police, Mr. Charles Fitch,
> inventor of new tortures
> Long live the insurrection of the market women
> Long live the duck races
> Long live the Orphan's Lottery,
> Viva the devil's lodge, viva the Day of the Cross
> Long live Srta. Coronada Peña, Srta. Jesús Galana
> Señorita Balbina Calero, Señorita Ramona Choriego
> Viva the Srta. Dolores Arauz
> student of the Normal School,
> good application, average conduct
> Noteworthy in Geography and Social History
> Very good
> In reading, writing, piano and manual labors
> average in Morality and Urbanity.
>> —"You can say what you wish,
>> the best thing about a coun-
>> try are its girls"
>> Roque Dalton, 1975

It was a golden age for the new elite. But serpents were to slip into their large and well-kept garden, dividing one from another.

When the coffee barons first built their power they found the needed capital at the Bank of England. England had outpaced Spain not only in capitalist development at home but as an imperial power in the region. And England was the land from which many of the coffee planters came.

But by the turn of the twentieth century England was losing ground to its former colony. Roosevelt recognized that colonies were not enough to guarantee supremacy in the hemisphere; economic competition with European rivals required regional stability—the catchword for domination. In 1904 President Roosevelt proposed a corollary to the Monroe Doctrine that would permit the United States to intervene in Central America and the Caribbean whenever it detected independence rearing its head.[10]

Over the next three decades, U.S. Marines were dispatched to Cuba, the Dominican Republic, Haiti and Nicaragua, on the pretext that governments of the area were "inefficient" or "unstable." U.S. "dollar diplomacy" encouraged business investment and loans to local governments under terms that gave U.S. bankers increased control over the neighboring economies.

In El Salvador, a sector of the oligarchy had grown restless. A little group—immigrants, many—lacking ties to British bankers, concentrated on the export side of the coffee business and then gradually expanded their activities to include the processing of the little red berry. They attracted to their number many of the large growers. But their desire to modernize was blocked by other, usually smaller, producers and their conservative British bankers. Fortunately for these early modernizers, they found eager—and rich—new allies in U.S. investors. With visions of *colones* and dollars dancing in their heads, this clique within the oligarchy saw in dollar diplomacy a way to consolidate their power and reorganize the economy—through the control of the national government. In 1913 they backed the presidency of Carlos Meléndez, the first installment of what became known as the

Meléndez-Quiñónez dynasty (1914-1927). With the power to legislate and with control of the machinery of state, they pushed to diversify and industrialize the economy, experimenting in henequen, cotton and textile production.[11]

Throughout the 1920s, disagreement festered within the oligarchy between those associated with the Meléndez-Quiñónez succession and an unorganized potpourri of medium-sized growers, anglophile capitalists newly subordinate to U.S. money and on-the-outs professionals. The most astute of the dynasty, President Alfonso Quiñónez, fearing that internal division might appear to the United States as "instability" and anxious to neutralize his opposition, began to hunt out allies among the artisans and campesinos. He encouraged the creation of the Red League in 1918, a mass organization which pushed for broader popular participation and better working conditions. The League was designed not only to thwart Quiñónez' political enemies, but to quiet popular discontent.

For internal differences were not the only flaw in the idyllic vision. With prosperity limited to a tiny handful, the vast majority of the population struggled for survival, oblivious to the internecine quarrels of the oligarchs. New industrialization schemes and an expanding economy increased the number of unskilled workers while skilled crafts workers declined. The first trade union federation was organized in 1918.

Soon after, Quiñónez repressed the first sign of discontent within the Red League, while independent forces, drawn primarily from artisans, railroad and utility workers, grew strong in a nascent workers' movement. In 1925 they formed the Regional Federation of Salvadorean Workers (FRTS), within which reformist currents contended with the more militant anarchist and Marxist ideas now increasingly audible in the union movement. By 1932, 10.6 percent of the economically active population were members of the Regional.[12]

Organizers of the Regional worked surreptitiously in remote areas of the country. They took their inspiration from the fierce resistance in Nicaragua to domination by U.S. "dollar imperialism"—backed by marines—a resistance led by a man who quickly became a legend in Central America and whose name means triumph in Nicaragua today, Augusto César Sandino. These organizers were especially active in the western regions of El Salvador, where the Indian population remained bitter over the expropriation of communal lands.

From 1925 to 1928, the Regional was the special project of a man who would play a key role in the events of 1932. Known to his friends as El Negro Martí—the Black Martí—for his dark skin, Agustín Farabundo Martí had been a revolutionary of sorts since his university days; for hours he read the works of the anarchists and Marxists that filled a little shelf in the library of the law school. The son of a farmer with a medium-sized holding in La Libertad province, in 1920 Martí was arrested in a student rally in downtown San Salvador. Exiled, he moved to Guatemala where in 1925 he joined other Central American intellectuals to found the Central American Socialist Party.[13]

Later that year he returned to El Salvador to do organizing work with the Regional. During the next two years, the Regional attracted more unions, set out a national program of land reform and struggled for an eight-hour day. Its most interesting project was the People's University, which taught literacy and political economy to workers and peasants.

In 1927, when Sandino declined to submit to the occupation of Nicaragua by the U.S. Marines and formed a small band of guerrilla fighters, the Regional decided to send a contingent to support Sandino's struggle, and Martí was soon a colonel in his army. But by then Martí was a Marxist, and Sandino's movement was more narrowly anti-imperialist. Ideological differences between the two Central American heroes were too great, and Martí left Sandino's ranks.

Prelude to Revolution

In 1929 Martí again returned to El Salvador, now as a representative of International Red Aid (*Socorro Rojo*), a solidarity organization to support the communist workers' movement. He found his country in economic crisis, the oligarchy divided and the military growing in importance along with the workers and peasants.

With the Great Depression, the coffee market collapsed. In 1928, the average price of coffee was $15.75 for a hundred kilograms. By 1929, it dropped to $13.21; in 1930, to $7.50; in 1931, to $7.31; and in 1932, $5.97.[14] The power of the Meléndez-Quiñónez dynasty crumbled with the international market. In the vacuum, a half dozen new political parties sprang to life to compete in the first and last free election in El Salvador's history—in 1931.

The oligarchy divided their support among three different candidates. But El Salvador's armed forces, numbering about 3,000 men, had transformed themselves from a rag-tag troop into a modern army whose leaders had political ambitions of their own. Two generals entered the contest.

A sixth candidate talked of reforms: Alberto Araujo. An engineer who hoped to build a labor party like that in England, Araujo enjoyed the counsel of El Salvador's most prominent intellectual, Alberto Masferrer. Throughout the 1920s Masferrer had lectured the oligarchy on its duties to share their immense wealth with the rest of the country and scolded the poor campesinos on the evils of drink and machete brawls. His program for providing the "vital minimum" to each Salvadorean became the basis for Araujo's campaign platform.

Araujo's promises and the vigor of his electoral campaign made him the clear favorite. To the dismay of the oligarchy, he built an unheard-of alliance of workers, peasants, students, professionals and intellectuals. As the election approached, there were rumors of an army coup if Araujo won. But when he polled over 100,000 votes to 62,000 for his nearest competitor, the garrisons stayed quiet and Araujo took power.

That silence may have been explained by the unexpected withdrawal late in the campaign of one of the army's two generals, a decidedly unconventional man: General Maximiliano Hernández Martínez. After Araujo's election was ratified in the legislative assembly, the new president named Martínez as his vice-president.

Araujo's nine-month regime started badly. Two days after he was inaugurated, thousands of workers and peasants besieged his offices to demand the land reform promised in his campaign. When he appeared on the balcony to calm the crowd, they would not listen and only shouted louder. They camped below his window for three days.[15]

The new president also faced the problem of who was to run the government. The oligarchy regarded his ascendancy to power with horror and withdrew from the government both themselves and their professional minions. That left the administration solely in the hands of Araujo's fledgling Labor Party, few of whom had any experience. The party lacked discipline, and soon its cadres fell to dividing up the spoils.

The blatant corruption of Araujo's followers caused Alberto Masferrer to turn against the new president. Masferrer appealed to him from the floor of the National Assembly: "Don Arturo, listen to the voices of your friends and not to the voices of flatterers who surround you. Do not see as white that which some of us see as black. Don Arturo, don't be dragged into the mud, don't soil your reputation."[16]

But the most serious threat was the growing resistance in the *campo*. Araujo had reason to worry. Farabundo Martí was back in El Salvador; the Regional's organizers were concentrating on the rural areas; and a few months before the 1931 election, on the shores of Lake Ilopango, a small group of workers and intellectuals formed the Communist Party of El Salvador.

After the Bolshevik Revolution of 1917, communist parties were forming everywhere in the world. The thirty-five or so people who gathered on the shores of the lake had worked for the previous five years in the Regional and had helped run the popular universities. Now they would form a party and look for affiliation from the Third International in Moscow. But El Salvador was far away and tiny; links with Moscow were extremely tenuous.

The membership of the Communist Party was small, but its influence went far beyond its size. Worsening economic conditions and the years of work with the popular universities gave it an eager audience and willing followers. In the 1931 election the party was too recently formed to influence the outcome. Its cadres, however, were gearing up for the municipal elections in January 1932.

The party's organizing was concentrated in the coffee-growing areas of the west, where the Indian communities remembered that not-so-distant time when they shared their lives through the communal lands. In Izalco village, at the base of one of the country's most famous volcanoes, the Indian *cacique*, José Feliciano Ama, who had supported one of the oligarchic parties in the election, was drawn by the goals of those who talked a new ideology—communism. For people in the *campo* and the tiny working class in San Salvador, these people held out the hope of real change: a thirty-six hour week, the right to unionize, the right of rural workers to strike, social and unemployment security, a minimum wage, progressive taxes, free and universal education, state ownership of transportation, equal opportunities for women and an end to discrimination against Indians.

Organizers from the Regional, Martí's Red Aid, and the new Communist Party talked of the new workers' state in the Soviet Union and linked the growing poverty in El Salvador to world capitalism and the Great Depression. Their success was extraordinary. Many of the communists' arguments made sense. The Indians were old enough to remember another system; they knew they had been treated badly and remembered who were responsible. How readily the listeners appreciated the links with "world capitalism" one can never know. José Feliciano Ama seemed to understand. When his former *patrón* asked that he abandon the foolishness of his new ideas, the old *cacique* responded: "I do not want to have correspondence with an arrogant and exploitative bourgeois."[17]

The protests of Araujo's first days in office did not die. On March 21, 1931, peasants and workers staged a huge demonstration in Parque Barrios in front of the National Palace. Araujo called out the troops to disperse the crowd. The next day the scene was repeated in Santa Ana, the second largest city in the country. Determined to root out the discontent at what he saw as its source, Araujo cracked down on leftist organizations. Farabundo Martí led a march on

Araujo's house to denounce the repression, and for that he was imprisoned together with his chief lieutenant, Rafael Bondanza, on April 9. The Araujo government in turn denounced a supposed "alliance of communists and politicos" for plotting a coup d'état.

In the Central Penitentiary, Martí began a hunger strike that lasted almost a month. When the government finally capitulated to mass protest and freed him, he emerged a popular hero and a national symbol of opposition to the Araujo government..

More disturbances. In May, police fired on demonstrators near Sonsonate, killing workers and peasants. Protesting campesinos marched into Sonsonate and more blood flowed. Then in Zaragoza, to the south of San Salvador, twelve people were killed in a battle between police and demonstrators.

The government chased Martí throughout the countryside, identifying him with the causes of the dissension. Meanwhile, coffee prices continued to fall. On October 7, Araujo prohibited the export of gold, and bankers retaliated by cutting credit to coffee growers. By the November harvest, there were few jobs for the thousands of peasants who needed the harvest to sustain their incomes. Those who worked received barely enough to survive. After the National Guard killed a dozen people in Asuchiyo, Martí surfaced again to lead the protest.

The Winter of the Patriarch

On December 21, 1931, a small group of military officers ended the Araujo experiment. Heading the new government was that uncommon general, Martínez, the man Araujo had made his vice president. Martínez' role in the coup is a matter of great debate. Salvadorean historian Rafael Guidos Véjar suggests that the conspirators may have been followers of Masferrer, who hoped to restore the program of reform lost so early in the Araujo administration. If they were, their choice of General Martínez to head the provisional government was a mistake. Martínez looms so large in Salvadorean history that it is hard to imagine him as an insignificant actor in the events that brought him to power. A more sinister interpretation is that he engineered the coup himself. In an interview in 1968, Araujo, who came to see his vice-president as the Iago of his downfall, was convinced of it.[18]

Martínez is a figure of folkloric dimension, the patriarch of García Márquez' novel. Madness and bloodlust haunt his image and his reign. On the surface, Martínez was typical of the new army. Of middle-class origins, he saw it as a way to move up in the world and was active throughout the 1920s in developing the military as a self-conscious caste. In 1922 he founded the *Círculo Militar* to stimulate the intellectual, moral, physical and economic betterment of the armed forces.

His own intellectual tastes, however, were exotic. A student of theosophy, he dabbled in the occult, often turning the presidential palace into a site for seances. *El Brujo*—the warlock—he was called. After the *matanza* of 1932, when safely in power, Martínez regularly shared his vision with the Salvadorean people over the radio:

> Biologists have only discovered five senses. But in reality there are ten. Hunger, thirst, procreation, urination, and bowel movements are the senses not included in the list of biologists.

> It is good that children go barefoot. That way they can better receive the beneficial effluvia of the planet, the vibrations of the earth. Plants and animals don't use shoes.

> It is a greater crime to kill an ant than a man, because a man who dies is reincarnated while an ant dies forever.[19]

The Volcano Erupts

Writing some twenty days after the Martínez coup, Major A.R. Harris, U.S. attaché to Central America, described his visit to El Salvador:

> About the first thing one observes when he goes to San Salvador is the number of expensive auto-

mobiles on the streets. There seems to be nothing but Packards and Pierce Arrows about. There appears to be nothing between these high priced cars and the ox cart with its bare-footed attendant. There is practically no middle class between the very rich and the very poor . . . .

I imagine the situation in El Salvador today is very much like France was before its revolution, Russia before its revolution and Mexico before its revolution. The situation is ripe for communism and the communists seem to have found that out. On the first of December 1931, there was in the Post Office in San Salvador over 3,000 pounds of communist literature emanating from New York City, which had been confiscated by the postal authorities during the previous month.

The authorities seem to realize that the situation is dangerous and are quite alert in their fight against communistic influences. One thing in their favor is that the people never go hungry. The poor can always get fruit and vegetables for nothing and they can steal fire wood. . . . Also, since they never had anything, they do not feel the want very acutely of things they have never had. . . .

A socialistic or communistic revolution in El Salvador may be delayed for several years, ten or even twenty, but when it comes it will be a bloody one.[20]

The people of El Salvador went hungry too often; they were tired of the scramble for survival. Despite the coup, Martínez decided to go ahead with the municipal elections in January. The communists hoped that the discontent would give them a big electoral victory. Many thousands signed the electoral rolls as supporters of the communists, and a surprising number of their candidates won.

But the Martínez government refused to certify their victories. Angry, frustrated and aware of the increasing expectations of the poor, the Communist Party debated what should be done next. One faction argued strongly that unless it prepared for insurrection, there would be a spontaneous uprising that would be crushed. Another faction argued that the time was not right, that the party was too weak to lead a revolution.

Looking back, it may be that both sides were right. In any case the voice of caution was overruled and an insurrection was planned. January 22 was chosen as the date. The campesinos would march on the town halls in their communities; officers sympathetic to the communists would lead a rebellion in the garrisons; the workers would strike.

But somehow word of the insurrection got out. On January 18, Martí was arrested; that night and the next, the hoped-for barracks revolt was aborted. Mass arrests began. The Communist Party tried to countermand the order for the uprising, but it was too late.

On the night of the insurrection, a strange thing happened. The volcanoes of neighboring Guatemala erupted. As the earth shook, the campesinos of the western provinces marched, machetes in hand, toward the towns. In El Salvador, Izalco volcano joined the doomed chorus, and a fine ash hung in the air.

The revolt was primarily centered in the western coffee regions, especially the villages of Juayua, Izalco and Nahuizalco. In Ahuachapan, near Tacuba, torches also lit the night sky. In Santa Tecla, not far from San Salvador, rebels attacked the telegraph office crying *Viva la República Soviética.*

A principal target was Sonsonate, a town of 20,000 and commercial center for the coffee region. Armed with machetes and a few rifles, the "reds" reached the city shortly after dawn. They were met in the square by the army, who despite their greater fire power could not hold them. The soldiers fled to the town fort. The rebels repeatedly attacked the doors of the fortress only to be driven back by the rifles and machine guns. By 10:00 a.m., the rebels withdrew. They retreated to a nearby town and gathered there, some 5,000 strong, led by a woman called "Red Julia."

In the explosion of hatred, there were doubtless atrocities; later, tales would be told of rape and pillage by the Indians. But the most systematic chronicler of the *matanza,*

Thomas Anderson, believes that 100 people, civilian and military, were killed by the rebels.[21] This was nothing compared to what followed.

Martínez mobilized to crush the rebellion. Besides the army, he ordered the creation of Civic Guards, composed of civilians, primarily from the upper classes, to quell the uprising. All forces moved toward Sonsonate. The rebels abandoned the encampment and the army closed in on Izalco. The peasants fled into the bullets of the soldiers. Seeing the bodies falling, the old *cacique*, José Feliciano Ama, ordered his troops to retreat.

Battles continued for several days. In Ahuachapan province, a Lieutenant Flores described the attack: "Major Cortéz attacked from the east side of town, along a place known as Las Piramides. It was not possible to go by the access road to Tacuba because it was barricaded by the communists. There was an enormous slaughter and the bands of communists attacked in wave on wave, crying savagely."[22]

Then came the *matanza*. Outraged at the challenge to their rule, terrified by the threat to their continuing domination, the ruling class wanted a blind and bloody vengeance. In Izalco, groups of fifty men were tied together by the thumbs and led to the wall of the Church of the Assumption where they were shot down. Victims were forced to dig mass graves for themselves as a machine gun dropped them into the hole.

The roadways were littered with bodies as the National Guard killed anyone they met. Some who were shot down survived, like Miguel Mármol, one of the leaders of the Communist Party. He crawled out of a mass grave and hid behind an altar in his mother's house until he could flee the country. Mármol later wrote of the experience:

> General Ochoa . . . made everyone who had been captured crawl on their knees to where he was seated in a chair in the courtyard of the fort and he said to them: "Come here and smell my gun." The prisoners pleaded with him in the name of God and their children, having heard the sound of intermittent shots before entering the courtyard.

But the general insisted: "If you don't smell my pistol then you are a communist and afraid. He who is without sin knows no fear."

The campesino smelled the barrel of the gun, and in that instant, the general would put a bullet in his face.

"Bring the next one in," he said.[23]

The Communist Party was almost wiped out. Using the electoral rolls from the January municipal elections, the army systematically killed virtually all of its members and sympathizers. Farabundo Martí died before a firing squad on February 1, 1932. His name was erased from history; his gravesite covered with weeds.

José Feliciano Ama was jailed. But a mob led by the local landlords dragged him out while his guards looked the other way. Legend has it that children were let out of school to watch the old chief hang in the town square.

And so it went. As in the days after the Paris Commune, the good burghers of El Salvador wreaked their vengeance on those who dared or might have dared to oppose them. How many died? The figures vary. Some say only 4,000; others say 50,000. But 30,000 has come to be the accepted number: two percent of the population. Had such a massacre been carried out in the United States on the same scale, 4,400,000 people would have lost their lives.

For the wealthy, 1932 was the dark night of their worst fears. Henceforth, the oligarchy would cede the responsibility for governing El Salvador to the armed forces. And during the next twelve years, General Martínez would consolidate that power.

For workers and peasants, 1932 was an evil memory that dared not speak its existence. In the Indian communities of the western coffee areas—the scene of the uprising—the traditional ways were abandoned; the traditional garb discarded and Nahuatl no longer spoken in public. Even in the late 1960s, in the cities and countryside the young rarely knew what happened and the old were afraid to talk about it. And today, the area of least commitment to the FMLN/FDR is the region of the *matanza*.

Legends grew up around 1932, ghost stories to frighten the rich and poor alike:

> In that time no one ate pork. First because the pigs and the vultures and the insects took charge of eating the bodies of the campesinos who had fallen, and second, more than one person was sure that unscrupulous vendors were selling human flesh, especially in the western areas where there was so much hunger, passing it off as pork.

> No one was tortured? That is false. They tortured every day. Everyone who was captured died after horrible beatings, machete wounds, their eyes pulled out, hung from trees . . . the army used bayonets. When a campesino resisted, four of them would grab him by the arms and legs and throw him into the air and catch him on their bayonets.[24]

So began the era of Martínez, a dark and sinister time that lasted for twelve more years.

As the fascists rose to power in Europe, Martínez flirted with them and their ideas. He prohibited the immigration to El Salvador of all Arabs, Hindus, Chinese and blacks. Even before Hitler and Mussolini, Martínez recognized the new government of Francisco Franco in Spain. He brought a Prussian general to run the military school and shared U.S. tactical plans with the German chiefs of staff.

Determined to destroy the alliance of workers and peasants that lay behind the January uprising, Martínez passed laws discouraging further industrialization. He ordered everyone in the country to carry an identification card. All print shops were placed under government supervision. "On the occasion of the outbreak of a measles epidemic in El Salvador, General Maximiliano Hernández Martínez refused to put into practice any of the modern measures for controlling epidemics or to accept the aid of international health organizations. He simply ordered that the street lights be wrapped in colored cellophane, concluding that the multicolored light would be enough to purify the air and wipe out the pestilence."[25]

All of us were born half-dead in 1932
We survived but half-alive
Each one with an interest bearing account of 30,000
dead compounded daily
That continues today to charge with death those
who continue being born
Half-dead
Half-alive.

All of us were born half-dead in 1932.

To be a Salvadorean is to be half-dead.
That which still moves
Is that half of life they left us
And as all of *us* are the half-dead
The murderers presume not only that they are alive
But also immortal.
But they too are half-dead
Living only by halves.

Let us unite the half-dead who are this country
"That we may be worthy of calling ourselves your
children"
In the name of the murdered
Let us unite against the murderers of all
Against the murderers of the dead and half-dead
All of us together
Have more death than they
But all of us together
Have more life than they.

The all-powerful union of our half-lives
Of the half-lives of all of us born half dead in 1932.

—"Todos"
Roque Dalton

CHAPTER II

Great Expectations

A *Time* magazine correspondent, William Krehm, arrived in San Salvador at Easter time, 1944—twelve years after the *matanza*. "The figures of Christ bearing His Cross, paraded through the city, were poignant in their symbolism," he wrote. "You could sense the taut nerves of the people who swarmed in the streets; the women wore black, even those with no relatives of their own to mourn. An eight o'clock curfew had been clapped on and each morning there were telltale pools of blood on the pavements. The nights were hideously staccato with rifle fire. Platoons of heavily armed police patrolled the city. Prisoners were rounded up and herded to the police station, from which grisly tales of tortures emerged."[1]

By 1944 the power born of brutality and repression was eroding, and Martínez had drowned a coup attempt in the blood of its plotters. When asked by the archbishop of San Salvador in the name of God to halt their execution, he replied: "In El Salvador I am God."[2]

And so it had been since 1932. But in the first years

33

Martínez had shown the oligarchy that he was good for more than killing. Initially many of them had been uncertain. The problems of the country were complex. But he had surprised them by taking strong measures to protect their economic interests and stabilize the economy. He passed legislation to discourage further industrialization and turned the economy back to the coffee growers, declaring a moratorium on all debt and making agricultural credit easy to obtain.

Despite his flirtation with the fascists, Martínez joined the Allied side after Pearl Harbor in 1941. The war forced the economy to rely on local resources. Cotton was planted along the Pacific Coast and a tiny textile industry found dispensation from the anti-industry decrees. Martínez established a central bank to regulate currency and a mortgage bank to finance housing construction. At the military school, an officer from the United States replaced the Prussian. And the United States welcomed its new ally by sending lend-lease planes, tanks and automatic weapons until, in the words of a U.S. army officer formerly stationed there, "Salvador became per square mile one of the most heavily armed nations of the world."[3]

But Martínez was clumsy and eccentric. He proclaimed that "democracy is love," but many of his former defenders began to realize the high price they were paying for "national order." Younger officers chafed ambitiously in El Brujo's shadow, and a new generation of professionals were inspired by the Allied war effort and the Four Freedoms espoused by Roosevelt and Churchill. The oligarchs began to resent the erosion of their personal fiefdoms, as government became more centralized, and the subversion of the country's intellectual aspirations to the vagaries of the "master," as Martínez liked to be called. In private, the oligarchs called him "that crack-pot little Indian." Early in 1944, when the general sought to alter the constitution to prolong his term of office, his opponents consolidated and the struggle for power began.

A coup d'état was to be the quick way out, but Martínez outsmarted the conspirators and punished them brutally. Yet to his amazement, opposition did not end. William Krehm describes the primitive leaflets that circulated in the capital, with the request that each reader make ten copies to pass on. "Children flaunted the seditious sheets before the police and dared them to make an arrest. At first the police obliged, but they tired of the game soon enough. It was a groundswell of popular indignation that dwarfed anything ever hatched by politicians. Suddenly, no one knew at whose prompting or how, it broke as a general strike. The people, who from time immemorial had served as a doormat for hob-nailed military boots, now reared, fierce, towering, and a bit incredulous of their new might."

The strike officially began on April 19, 1944. Students padlocked the doors of the university; primary and secondary school students followed suit; then the nascent trade union movement lent its support. Doctors closed their offices and opened emergency clinics, donating the proceeds to the strike fund. "Bank employees marched out, and only the central bank maintained nominal operations in the shadow of machine guns. The strikers had difficulty persuading some of the smaller food shops to stay open to supply the population with essentials; students volunteered to bake bread. Justices of the peace and most government employees failed to show up at their offices. Parodying Martínez' famed definition of democracy, the strikers sported 'The strike is love' on their placards."

For three weeks, a permanent vigil was maintained in front of the National Palace, where a growing crowd stood silently, occasionally singing the National Anthem. Martínez arrested the movement's leaders as the country braced for a replay of 1932.

Then on May 7, an agent of the National Police killed a young student, José Wright Alcaine, the son of a wealthy immigrant from the United States (today El Salvador's cotton king). Two days later, with the economy paralyzed and the U.S. ambassador demanding an explanation for young Wright's death, the "master" resigned and quietly fled the country.

The Nervous Oligarchs

The Patriarch Generals—Anastasio Somoza in Nicaragua; Hernández Martínez in El Salvador; Carías Andino in

Honduras, and Jorge Ubico in Guatemala. They controlled the destinies of Central America throughout the 1930s and early 1940s, and inspired the pages of García Márquez and others who sought to capture the bizarre eccentricities of life in *nuestra América*. After Martínez, the others began to teeter and fall, their graves dug by greed and cruelty, the desperation of a lone assassin or the organized despair of the poor. But as in the vision of García Márquez, nothing really changed. Except in Guatemala, for a time.

In Guatemala a middle-class revolution in 1944 ousted dictator Jorge Ubico, in power since 1931, and led to what have been called the "freest" elections that country had ever had. A moderate reformer, Juan José Arévalo, was elected president, succeeded in 1952 by Jacobo Arbenz. Arbenz did the unthinkable: he passed an agrarian reform law through Congress that expropriated idle lands—including lands owned by United Fruit—for redistribution to the landless.

To El Salvador's elite, the revolution in Guatemala was like a fire next door. It permitted free elections, gave land to the peasants and allowed the growth of a militant trade union movement. There was already a smoldering in El Salvador. Might it not spread?

Already the ghosts of 1932 had come back to haunt the nervous oligarchs. In the days after Martínez' fall the first strikes in twelve years broke out. The middle-class leaders who had led the movement to replace Martínez sought out the tiny National Workers Union to support their proposed reforms. Anxiously, the pro-Martínez forces rallied. El Brujo was finished, they reasoned; yet "order" had to be restored. When their new man, General Salvador Castañeda Castro, was "elected" president in 1945, many labor leaders had already been jailed and reformers exiled.

Martínez' anti-industry laws had worked; the industrial working class was still very small. But it was a new, hopeful generation for whom the *matanza* was a childhood memory. The few surviving members of the Salvadorean Communist Party came out of hiding to offer these younger men and women their advice and experience.

A group known as the Coordinating Committee organized artisans and workers in small manufacturing plants in and around San Salvador. Largely through the efforts of this group, a more self-conscious workers' movement took form. Frustrated reformers increasingly looked to it for leadership. In October 1946, in the hopes of toppling Castañeda, a general strike was called, led by the bakers' union and workers from a textile factory. It flashed bright, but quickly turned to ashes. Two hundred workers were arrested and the union movement was forced underground.

There a trade union organizing committee, CROSS, was formed in 1947. This time there would be no dramatic gestures, only slow, careful organizing. CROSS rallied support around its demands for the right to collective bargaining, an eight-hour day, the right to strike and civil liberties for all.

In December 1948 General Castañeda Castro was deposed in a coup d'état. The divisions within the oligarchy which had plagued the country since 1944 had to be resolved. Consistently high coffee prices during the tumultuous postwar period had prevented chaos. But the more visionary elements of El Salvador's elite knew that some things would have to change if things were to remain the same.

The small schism that had developed within the oligarchy in the 1920s opened once again: on the one hand the modernizing oligarchs, intent on diversifying their own wealth and the country's economic base; and on the other the entrenched landowning families—the "agro-front"—committed not to change but to stability. No clear-cut lines of separation existed between the two. All of the "Fourteen Families" had investments in industry. And commerce. And banking. All of their fortunes were rooted in the agro-export economy and none of them favored tampering with that pillar of the country's wealth. But in the 1950s, different notions began to circulate concerning the political and economic means of holding onto that wealth.

The modernizers, in their search for allies, courted a new breed of young military officers, many of them trained in the United States. These soldiers were professionals and technocrats, instead of epauletted generals. They shared the modernizers' zeal for shaking El Salvador loose from its dependency on a single crop, and they wanted the army to contribute more than massacres to the country's glory.

In the 1948 coup led by Colonel Oscar Osorio, the modernizers came to power. Two years later Osorio was elected president. He was the perfect symbol of the new era, his closely cropped crew cut suggesting the modern soldier-cum-technocrat. And his ideas were grandiose. Size was no obstacle: El Salvador could become the Belgium of Central America, pouring coffee profits into industry, building roads and dams and generators. It was to be a revolution, many said, and even the Communist Party of El Salvador described it as such: "the beginning of the bourgeois-democratic era, the triumph of the capitalist class over the feudal and semi-feudal landowning oligarchy. The bourgeoisie finally had come to power."[4]

The Revolution of 1950

The Osorio government gradually developed a three-pronged strategy that would remain the framework of rule in El Salvador for decades to come: *developmentalism*—the creation of conditions to permit the expansion and modernization of the economy; *reformism*—the policy of adjusting existing political and social structures to keep the system one step ahead of its own contradictions; and *repression*—reserved for those who could not be coopted and wanted more than ameliorative change.

As the first order of business, Osorio repealed the anti-industry laws of the Martínez era and replaced them with strong incentives to invest in new sectors. The power and size of the state bureaucracy was greatly expanded, as new offices were set up to coordinate the development of commerce, industry and mining, and taxes were imposed on coffee exports to feed new areas of investment.

A modern infrastructure began to take shape, with the building of the giant Fifth of November dam on the Lempa River, to provide cheap electrical power to the cities. And a highway running the length of the Pacific coast opened new lands to the production of cotton and cattle. The peasants displaced by these new activities were a source of cheap labor to industry, bent on competing with imported manufactured goods for the small national market.

But as plans for industrializing the country got under way, the modernizers retained the memory of 1932—of the alliance of workers and peasants that channeled discontent into organized rebellion. The labor movement in El Salvador was alive and growing, and CROSS had become a force that the Osorio government set out to tame.

The Constitution of 1950 reflected both the strength of the working class and the government's attempt to coopt it. The new constitution granted, at least on paper, the right to organize unions within very strict limits; the right to strike; the right to a minimum wage, social security benefits and subsidized housing. None of these rights were extended to the rural sector, which remained unchanged in every respect. That was part of the deal with the agro-front, the price for their support of modernization.

Later, with the aid of the AFL-CIO and its regional workers' organization, the ORIT, the government also tried to encourage a new style of unionism that would shake members away from more radical approaches. Based on a concept of harmonious cooperation between labor and capital, and boosted by government favors, a new federation was established by 1958, called the General Confederation of Salvadorean Unions (CGS). This was intended to compete with the more radical General Workers Confederation (CGTS) formed a year earlier.

Electoral Schemes

The process of modernization gradually created more layers between the very rich and the very poor in El Salvador. The rapid expansion of the state bureaucracy stimulated the growth of a middle class; industrial growth began to enlarge the small, still mainly artisan working class. The modernizers needed a vehicle to legitimize their rule and integrate these new sectors of society into their "revolution."

Colonel Osorio had lived in Mexico and admired the

Right: the National Guard on patrol in a barrio of San Salvador.

Facing page: Las Vueltas, a small town in Chalatenango province.

Meiselas

H.E. Mattison

Left: caskets of 21 members of LP-28, massacred during a demonstration on October 29, 1979.

Facing page: soldiers opened fire on the unity march of the popular organizations, January 22, 1980.

Meiselas

Above: a member of ANDES, the teachers' union, marches for "Education for Liberty."

Right: Archbishop Oscar Arnulfo Romero

ability of the PRI (Mexico's Institutional Revolutionary Party) in drawing diverse sectors into its ranks. El Salvador's PRUD—the Revolutionary Party of Democratic Unification—was Osorio's brainchild. He made it the political vehicle of the modernizing alliance, running military candidates for president and using the military command structure as a political machine.[5]

Osorio and the modernizers also proceeded to replace the decades-long reign of tyrants with the stability of a single-term presidency and smooth succession every five years. They allowed small opposition parties to emerge, representing dissident factions of the oligarchy that wanted a return to civilian rule.[6] But they were no match for the massive machinery of the PRUD. In 1956 Osorio's hand-picked successor, Colonel José María Lemus, was elected on the PRUD ticket by an overwhelming margin.

Repression and a Brief Respite

The small reforms of the modernizers never replaced the need for repression. In 1952 Colonel Osorio outlawed the CROSS after brief and unsuccessful efforts to coopt its leadership. But the repression in this period was still subtle and selective. It was always justified by "a great conspiracy, a communist coup discovered in the nick of time," wrote one of its victims, the baker and labor leader, Salvador Cayetano Carpio, arrested and tortured in 1952.[7]

But Colonel Lemus was less sophisticated and more corrupt than Osorio. His term coincided with a sharp downturn in the economy: worldwide recession reached El Salvador in the late 1950s, sending coffee prices to rock bottom and disappointing the popular hopes inflated by the fanfare of 1950. And then came Cuba—that unexpected island of revolution that burst upon the scene in 1959. Castro's victory provoked demands for harsher measures from the oligarchy and more militant forms of struggle from the opposition. The Communist Party of El Salvador took its first steps toward armed struggle, forming "action groups" within the trade unions and universities. And even within the army, the notorious corruption of the Lemus government caused rumblings of needed change.

Soon the jails were packed with political prisoners. Student demonstrations were fired upon; the National University, its autonomy theoretically protected by the constitution, was invaded by army troops; and political opponents of many persuasions, including former Justice Minister Roberto Canessa, were arrested, beaten and tortured.[8] Even the U.S. press suggested that Lemus had "pushed too far" in reacting to his growing isolation.[9]

On October 26, 1960, Colonel José María Lemus was informed by army couriers that his presence no longer served the national interest. Junior officers had decided to act, in the tradition of the officers who ousted Martínez in 1944, to preserve the integrity of the military as an institution.

The economy was in crisis.

The streets belonged to protesting students and workers, although the opposition was still weak from prolonged clandestinity and repression.

The oligarchy had been caught off guard. And the stage was set for a brief interlude in Salvadorean history—when it became acceptable to talk about more than cosmetic reforms; when free elections seemed possible and corruption a disease that could be cured.

It lasted barely three months, but remained engraved in the minds of many Salvadoreans as an intensive course in the foreign policy of the United States, and a lesson in the fragility of power unprotected by military strength.

Free, But Not Too Free

The new junta that replaced the regime of Colonel Lemus combined junior army officers and independent professionals linked to the university.[10] It committed itself to prompt and free elections, and proposed a massive literacy drive in the cities and countryside. It enjoyed broad popular support. But none of this impressed the U.S. government—still burned by Castro's "betrayal" and unwilling to risk another loose link in its chain of domination.

Years later, Fabio Castillo, a doctor and civilian member of the junta, would recall the role of the U.S. embassy in San Salvador during that brief respite from oligarchic rule: "Accompanied by Mr. Ricardo Quiñónez, a well-known financier of conservative views, he [the chargé d'affaires of the U.S. embassy] said that the U.S. embassy did not agree with the holding of free elections and that he supposed that we were not talking seriously. He . . . added that the embassy would agree to a 'free election' held with two candidates previously approved by them. Of course, I rejected the proposal. Thereupon, the two visitors immediately got up, and Mr. Quiñónez, unable to control his anger, turned to the chargé d'affaires and said, 'You see, they are Communists; we have to go ahead.' "[11]

On January 25, 1961, the interlude ended—despite the protests of hundreds who took to the streets to hold onto the promise of reform. A clique of colonels, led by Julio Adalberto Rivera, enlisted the support of three token civilians and established the *Directorio*—a new junta to undo the work of the old. It was recognized with embarrassing speed by the newly inaugurated government of John F. Kennedy, who announced immediate plans to send economic aid. Tiny El Salvador now took on an importance well beyond its size in the setting of U.S. policy toward the hemisphere. Alongside the modernizing oligarchy and the technocratic colonels, the U.S. government was preparing to make El Salvador its showcase.

Cold War in the Americas

Guatemala's short-lived revolution in the mid-1940s had alerted Washington to the need to pay more attention to the hemisphere. By 1954 a CIA-sponsored coup had eliminated Arbenz and the nationalist experiment that dared to expropriate United Fruit.[12] The lands were returned; the generals were back in power. But Cuba's stubborn survival, in tantalizing contrast to the pervasive misery of its neighbors, posed a new challenge to U.S. hegemony in the region.

In 1960, when El Salvador dared to flirt with reforms independent of Washington's designs, it was taken as added proof that the Cold War had to be fought in Latin America as well. John F. Kennedy brought a certain sophistication to the effort. In 1961 he announced the opening of a new stage in U.S.-Latin American relations, summarized by a slogan and program called the Alliance for Progress.

The Alliance preached that certain reforms were necessary in Latin America if Castroite revolutions were to be contained. The disparities between rich and poor were too glaring; tax, land and labor reforms could help bridge the gap and give more people a stake in the status quo. Electoral contests could provide channels for discontent.

But to buy time for such efforts in the impatient sixties, the Alliance also had its military side: the armies of Latin America were trained in the latest techniques of counter-insurgency warfare, to be used against current and expected guerrilla threats. Local police forces took courses in interrogation methods and intelligence. And in Central America, military cooperation was encouraged among the five republics. In 1964 the Central American Defense Council (CONDECA) was formed at U.S. insistence, to assure regional stability by enabling one army to aid another.

El Salvador, ruled by a modernizing elite since 1950, was a perfect "testing ground for U.S. policies"—in the words of the *Wall Street Journal*.[13] And John F. Kennedy couldn't have been more pleased with the new *Directorio*: "[G]overnments of the civil-military type of El Salvador," he said, "are the most effective in containing communist penetration in Latin America."[14]

There was no guerrilla movement in El Salvador in the 1960s, so the military side of the Alliance for Progress could be modest, albeit still out of proportion to any existing threat.[15] But the soft side of the Alliance was everywhere: schools and clinics bore the message of American largesse; labor unions and rural workers' organizations were molded in the image of the AFL-CIO; and a dramatic increase in U.S. investment toward the mid-1960s lent new steam to the stalled industrialization scheme.

The Alliance represented a major shift for El Salvador,

where U.S. influence and investment had been modest. And even after the Cold War began in earnest the U.S. presence there was small compared to the ubiquitous presence of United Fruit in Guatemala, Honduras and Costa Rica; or to the umbilical cord joining Washington and the Somozas in Nicaragua. El Salvador's oligarchs were still proud of their self-reliance in the 1960s, and many disagreed profoundly with Washington's stress on reforms. But the military aid was reassuring; the business contacts were lucrative; and as for the reforms—well, the oligarchs were not about to be pushed around.

The Land Must Not Be Touched

El Salvador's president was the perfect partner in this new Alliance with the United States. Colonel Julio Rivera, leader of the coup that installed the *Directorio,* ran a one-candidate race for president in 1962—and won. He was vigorous, charming and charismatic. He was John Kennedy, *a lo latino* and in uniform, touring the countryside on motorcycle, inaugurating schools and irrigation projects, and spreading hope to the rural poor.

No other leader in the hemisphere embraced the Alliance for Progress with such gusto. Rivera created a new official party to replace the moribund PRUD of Osorio and Lemus. He called it the Party of National Conciliation (PCN) and chose the clasped-hands logo of the Alliance as its symbol. And he allowed an electoral opposition to reemerge in the early 1960s, embodied first in the Christian Democratic Party and later in a variety of reformist parties. Rivera was confident and the country was buoyant with hopes that El Salvador would become a showcase of development.

But there were problems and obstacles as well. Industrialization since the 1950s had been based on import substitution—replacing manufactured imports with goods produced at home. But the concentration of wealth in so few hands meant that only a tiny fraction of the population could afford to buy the soaps and jellies and canned hams now processed inside the country. El Salvador's large peasantry was far removed from the market economy, subsisting on small rented plots or buying the bare minimum of rice and beans from 70 cents-a-day wages. Industrialization faced a constant threat of stagnation because El Salvador's internal market was too small to sustain it.

One obvious remedy was land reform—breaking up the large estates to create a class of small farmers or cooperatives with the purchasing power to consume manufactured goods. This was the remedy favored by the Alliance for Progress. But land reform was beyond the political pale in El Salvador; it would violate a tacit agreement between the modernizers and the agro-front: the land must not be touched.

The oligarchs stubbornly ignored Washington's insistent pleas, encouraged by the waning influence of the Alliance with John Kennedy's assassination and Johnson's near-total absorption in Vietnam. In El Salvador, the Alliance for Progress became a set of stop-gap measures to raise production in the countryside and contain the stirrings of unrest. The U.S. Agency for International Development (AID) zeroed in on the rural poor with money, birth control, public health clinics, and—a Peace Corps favorite—basketball courts. But all were targeted at the symptoms, not the causes, of the still silent crisis.

The terror of 1932 still hung over the countryside. It was quiet, smoldering in its misery, watched over vigilantly by the National Guard. The U.S. embassy saw rural poverty as El Salvador's Achilles' heel. It worried and nagged, but the oligarchs had their minds on other matters. The optimism of the Rivera presidency was pervasive, and the oligarchs—living up to their reputation as aggressive entrepreneurs—were hatching new schemes to overcome the barrier of inadequate demand. Without touching the land, they could expand their markets by going beyond El Salvador's narrow borders.

A Way Out: The Common Market

El Salvador, Nicaragua, Guatemala, Honduras and Costa Rica—all of them shared the same pattern of concentrated wealth. All were loath to change it. But in unity there was the potential to sustain industrial growth by amalgamating their separate markets.

The United Nations Economic Commission on Latin America (ECLA) had been pushing the idea of regional integration since the early 1950s. ECLA argued for planned, balanced development within the region, with specific industries assigned to each country to avoid competition and duplication of capacity. It encouraged limited foreign investment in these countries, carefully regulated to allow national industries to develop.

The idea of a free trade zone, allowing the unrestricted flow of goods, capital and people among the five republics, was particularly appealing to the two most developed countries in the region, El Salvador and Guatemala. It offered them new markets for industrial output, new investment opportunities in neighboring countries, and, for El Salvador, new outlets to relieve the troublesome problem of a population at once too large and also too poor to purchase its domestically produced output.

U.S. companies also were attracted to the scheme, but not under the conditions proposed by ECLA. In the 1960s they were bursting to invest abroad and saw Central America, with its cheap and abundant supply of labor—and a potentially unified market—as an ideal location. Local business interests in Central America were eager to unite their fortunes with foreign capital and succeeded in pushing the common market plans toward a more free market approach. By the time the Central American Common Market was founded in 1961, it bore little resemblance to ECLA's original plans for balanced and autonomous development.[16]

Forty-four multinationals opened shop in El Salvador during the 1960s, raising the book value of direct U.S. investment from $19.4 million in 1950 to $45 million by 1967.[17] The oligarchy couldn't have been more content: they were partners—in joint ventures—with the likes of ESSO, Westinghouse, Proctor & Gamble, Kimberly Clark and many more.

The benefits of regional integration were immediate and dramatic: trade among the common market countries rose at an annual rate of 32 percent between 1961 and 1968, with a notable shift in composition from agricultural to manufactured goods.[18] El Salvador was in a privileged position to capture a major share of this trade: it had industrialized earlier than its neighbors; the labor movement was still divided between more radical and moderate approaches, but the more docile, pro-government federation now had twice the membership of the independent unions; and most important of all—El Salvador had no guerrillas. The 1960s were years of electoral battles—of democracy in action.

By the mid-sixties, even workers were buying television sets. Industry was producing textiles, chemicals, petroleum derivatives, paper and processed foods for the region as a whole. And the oligarchy was spreading its investments into neighboring countries. El Salvador's dream of becoming the Belgium of Central America was coming true, or so it seemed.

Seeds of Future Struggle

But for every statistic that spelled success in the 1960s, there was another spelling trouble for the modernizers' plans. Between 1961 and 1971 El Salvador's manufacturing sector grew by an impressive 24 percent. But the number of people employed in that sector grew by a meager 6 percent—or 2,500 workers.[19] Industrialization was based on labor-saving technology, introduced by U.S. firms. It forced small artisan producers out of business, without providing enough new jobs to offset the decline. And it disappointed the hopes of thousands who streamed in from the countryside expecting a better life. They lived in slums called *tugurios* that swelled San Salvador's population to 350,000 by 1969. They had no running water, no electricity, no sanitation—and they found no jobs.

Modernization in El Salvador was like a skyscraper built on a crumbling foundation, but no one dared call the structure unsteady. Not the oligarchs, who kept one foot in their agrarian past and one in the industrial present; not the military, who ruled only at the behest of the "Fourteen Families"; and not the United States, which was willing to settle for a semblance of change, so long as anticommunism remained the shared philosophy of both governments.

Agriculture was still the cornerstone of the economy—and the countryside would get harder for everyone to ignore. A decade of modernization had led to crop diversification and more efficient production methods. But without land reform, and with a birth rate of 3 percent a year, conditions in the countryside had only grown worse for the peasantry and landless laborers. Crop diversification meant pushing more peasants off the land to make way for cotton and sugar plantations. Mechanization on the coffee estates raised unemployment to a permanent level of 30 percent throughout the 1960s. *El campo* was sinking into despair, even as the rest of the country rode high on the sense of economic boom and unlimited possibilities.

But the oligarchs, and particularly the agro-front, remained blind to the dangers ahead; they boycotted any initiative to tamper with their domain. When in 1965 President Rivera decreed a raise in the minimum wage for fieldhands—to 90 cents a day—the uproar was immediate and decisive. Landowners retaliated by refusing to let workers farm the small plots they had previously used on the estates to grow subsistence crops; they stopped serving the traditional lunchtime meal of one tortilla and a handful of beans. "The situation of the *campesinos*," writes historian Thomas Anderson, "who were by law forbidden to organize for their own protection, was worse after the 1965 law than before."[20]

There were incipient efforts to organize the peasantry in the 1960s, despite the official ban on rural unions. The first initiatives were taken by urban, Church-related groups, such as the National Union of Christian Workers and the Christian Democratic Party. The archbishop of San Salvador, Monseñor Chávez y González, organized the Cooperative Support Foundation in 1963, to stimulate a cooperative movement among small peasant producers. And in 1965 isolated peasant leagues came together to form the Christian Peasants Federation (FECCAS)—an organization concerned with land distribution, wages and living conditions in the countryside. All such associations were prohibited by law, but FECCAS survived as a small seed of future struggles.

Foresight from Washington

In 1962, at the height of hysteria over the Cuban revolution, John F. Kennedy, George Meany of the AFL-CIO and business leader J. Peter Grace announced the beginning of a "new consensus" among labor, government and business at the founding ceremony of the American Institute for Free Labor Development (AIFLD) in Washington, D.C. The new institute defined its role as supporting "free trade unionism" in Latin America, by running training seminars for union leaders, setting up housing programs and the like. More explicitly, AIFLD vowed to combat communist influence in the hemisphere. In the mid-sixties its leadership claimed credit for the overthrow of two presidents (Cheddi Jagan in Guyana and Goulart in Brazil), and channeled monies from the CIA to trusted labor allies.[21]

Although AIFLD generally concerned itself with the urban workers' movement in Latin America, U.S. officials were more concerned with the countryside in El Salvador. They would never forget that the poor peasants of the Sierra Maestra had sustained Castro's revolution. And with the oligarchy's united resistance to agrarian reform, it took no great foresight to see guerrilla "focos" in El Salvador not ten miles from the capital.

In 1965 AIFLD signed a contract with the Rivera government to organize training seminars for "apt" peasants—mainly tenants and sharecroppers. Three years later, a network of AIFLD-trained leaders set up the Salvadorean Communal Union (UCS)—a cooperative that pledged to better the life of the peasantry through self-help projects often funded and designed by AIFLD.[22] Formally, the UCS was illegal. But it was tolerated, even supported by the government, on the advice of embassy officials who argued that it could provide El Salvador's military governments with the mass base they so sorely lacked. At a more subtle level, U.S. officials also hoped the UCS could be used as a lever against the hardline agro-front, to pry loose some reforms.[23]

Throughout the 1960s bridges, schools and roads were built at AIFLD's expense, enticing more and more peasants to join the Communal Union. But the UCS style was manipulative, and charges of corruption soiled its reputation. Rumors of CIA influence limited its growth. Still, it was a semi-official recognition that something had to be done in the *campo* besides sending in the National Guard.

The Electoral Opposition

By the late 1960s U.S. Green Berets were fighting in Guatemala, helping the army crush a guerrilla threat in the countryside and comparing the scenery to Vietnam. But El Salvador was still a showcase. There was no guerrilla threat. The labor movement was flexing its muscle and opposition parties were campaigning throughout the country. Every inch of the democratic space encouraged by the Alliance for Progress, and confidently espoused by President Rivera, was being used. But there were cracks in the showcase and soon the opposition's success would threaten its very existence.

The Christian Democratic Party was by far the largest of three opposition parties that challenged the legitimacy of military rule in the late 1960s. Founded in 1961, its leaders called it El Salvador's first ideological party, calling for widespread reforms and a "third way" between capitalism and Marxism. Christian Democracy soon found a natural base among intellectuals, small business sectors and small landowners. And it prospered under the European tutelage of German and Italian parties, eager to promote a Christian Democratic presence in Latin America.[24]

From the beginning, there were two tendencies within El Salvador's Christian Democratic Party: one, intellectually serious, ideological, struggling with the meaning of Christianity and politics and later influenced by a Marxist intellectual tradition. The other tendency was pragmatic, organizational, anti-ideological and *caudillista*, in the tradition of machine politics. If Roberto Lara Velado and Rubén Zamora were of the former tendency, José Napoleón Duarte and Julio Rey Prendes were eminently of the latter.

When asked to describe Napoleón Duarte, a man who has known him for the last twenty years said, "An engineer, that is the word that sums him up best. And an anticommunist." Duarte, the consummate fixer, the pragmatist for whom there is always a solution. Combining pragmatism with charisma, Napoleón Duarte soon became the shining star of Christian Democracy in El Salvador. He ran for mayor of the capital in 1964 and won by a sizeable margin. He made the most of that highly visible post by running an activist and populist administration.

Street lighting was introduced for the first time in San Salvador. New markets were built in the downtown area. Garbage pickup was modernized to please the middle class. And in the working class barrios and *tugurios,* Duarte organized a community development program to build sewage systems, schools—and a substantial political base for his party. He was reelected to a second term as mayor, and then a third in 1968.

To the left of the Christian Democrats were two smaller parties: the National Revolutionary Movement (MNR) and the Party of Renovation (PAR). The first, despite the militant tone to its name, was a rather tame group of middle-class professionals, known more for their intellectual acumen than for their ability to attract a significant mass base. The MNR espoused social democratic politics and pushed for reforms, but it abjured the anticommunism of the Christian Democrats, and Duarte in particular. By 1969 its leader was Guillermo Manuel Ungo, a law professor and businessman.

More threatening to the established order was the Party of Renovation, a progressive, nationalist party of workers and intellectuals in which the Communist Party had a certain influence. From the mid-sixties until it was outlawed soon after the presidential elections of 1967, the PAR brought the hard issues of Salvadorean reality to the ordinary worker and campesino: agrarian reform, the distribution of wealth, repression. In the 1967 election, its standard bearer, the dean of the medical school, Fabio Castillo, took his campaign to villages and hamlets where previously only the official word had ever been heard. Castillo's campaign was a first awakening.

The 1967 elections led to a smooth succession from one modernizer to the next. Colonel Julio Rivera was replaced by Colonel Fidel Sánchez Hernández, a career officer and candidate of the Party of National Conciliation (PCN). But the Christian Democratic candidate, Abraham Rodríguez, placed a very respectable second in the race. That success, and the party's clear ambition to unseat the colonels by the next round in 1972, contributed to a new hope in the land. The fear that had pervaded every sector of society for so many years had receded into bad memories. The latent discontent, so long repressed, seemed diverted by the prospect of political change.

In the cities, and especially the capital, the contrived labor peace of the early sixties was coming to an end. A drop in the world price of agro-exports caused the economy to falter, and workers were no longer willing to pay the price. Intense competition for jobs and the strict limits on strike activity, codified by Rivera in 1965, had kept wages at the low level that had attracted investors in the first place. As the grand hopes for a better life failed to materialize for the working class, the pro-government unions in the CGS began to lose control over the rank and file. The more radical unions, grouped in a new federation called the FUSS, gained in strength. And in 1967, after a wave of separate and illegal strikes, the two federations called a general strike joined by 35,000 workers.

Even the emerging middle class wanted more from modernization. Inspired by the new possibilities of peaceful change, the recently formed teachers' union, ANDES, went out on strike for better pay and working conditions in 1968. They camped out in front of the Ministry of Education, attracting national attention to their cause. But the government's response, while selective, had a chilling effect. Thirty ANDES leaders were arrested during the strike. Strike supporters Gilberto Martínez and Saúl Santiago Contreras were active in the radical FUSS. They "disappeared" after their arrest by National Guardsmen on January 30, 1968. Three days later, their mutilated bodies washed ashore on the Pacific beaches of La Libertad. The middle class was profoundly shocked.

Still, people believed in the prospects of political change. The opposition parties scored remarkable gains in the legislative and municipal elections of 1968: the Christian Democrats won the mayoralties of three major cities, including Duarte's reelection in San Salvador, and eighty smaller towns. The party also won twenty-two seats in the National Assembly, while the social democrats (MNR) captured three more. The opposition was a stone's throw from control of the legislature. All eyes were cast toward the elections in 1970 and the presidential race in 1972. Napoleón Duarte dreamed of becoming Latin America's second Christian Democratic president, next to Chile's Eduardo Frei.

But events would drastically change the prospects of the opposition before the next elections could roll around. There is nothing like a war to make people forget, for a time, that they have no job, or prospects for finding one; that the land no longer yields enough to sustain a family; and that the rich are unwilling to share their enormous wealth. A war brings national unity—for a while.

The "Futbol War"

Tegucigalpa, May 25, 1969 (AP). In a speech on the effects of economic integration in Central America, the Minister of Foreign Affairs of Honduras linked Colgate toothpaste, made in El Salvador, to the increased incidence of cavities among Honduran children.

San Salvador, May 26, 1969 (UPI). El Salvador's under-secretary for Economic Integration ... countered accusations made by the Honduran foreign minister concerning the alleged poor quality of certain imported Salvadorean goods. He argued that Glostora, a hair cream manufactured in Honduras, causes dandruff.

Tourist information: El Salvador has'an area of 21,393 square kilometers and a population of 3.75 million. Honduras has a territory of 141,521 square kilometers and a population of 2.25 million ... The President of Honduras is General Oswaldo López

Arellano, educated in North American military academies. The President of El Salvador is General Fidel Sánchez Hernández, educated in North American military academies, a UN observer in the Korean conflict and a past president of the Inter-American Defense Board.

San Salvador, June 15, 1969 (AFP). Sources in Honduras indicate that paramilitary groups, among them an ultra-rightist band called "La Mancha Brava," are forcibly evicting hundreds of Salvadorean peasants from lands in Honduras they have farmed for many years. There are many reports of atrocities. Hundreds of Salvadorean families have begun crossing the border into El Salvador, in what appears to be the beginning of a massive exodus that could involve the entire Salvadorean population resident in Honduras.

San Salvador, June 17, 1969 (AFP). The local press here is unanimous in demanding that the Sánchez government "take drastic measures against Honduras."

San Salvador, June 23, 1969 (UPI). The Salvadorean national soccer team defeated the Honduran selection two goals to one, evening the semi-final series for the World Cup. . . . The night before, groups of Salvadoreans, led by General José Alberto Medrano, Chief of the Intelligence Services, Director of the National Guard and frequently identified by opponents to the regime as the CIA's man in the country, created disturbances in front of the hotel where the Honduran players were staying. Two were killed and seven persons were injured by the police during the attempt to disturb the sleep of the Honduran team. . . . The deciding game will be played in a neutral court, presumably in Guatemala or Mexico.

San Salvador, June 25, 1969 (AP). El Salvador broke diplomatic relations with Honduras. In a newspaper

editorial, *El Mundo* said that El Salvador should civilize Honduras by force. . . .

An old Salvadorean writer, a liberal-democratic op-
positionist well known for his sarcasm commented:
"Now we're told that El Salvador has been chosen
by God to civilize Central America by hook or by
crook. It's said that we are the Israelis of the Isthmus
and the Hondurans the Arabs. General Fidel Sánchez
is our Moshe Dayan. He's not one-eyed, but he is
sort of a midget. At least that's something."

> —*Historias Prohibidas del*
> *Pulgarcito*, Roque Dalton

The Deeper Conflict

The tensions that led to war between El Salvador and
Honduras in July 1969 had many causes—the least of which
was the soccer madness that led the foreign press to ridicule
the conflict as a "Futbol War" between hot-blooded Latins.

By 1969 the Central American Common Market was
coming apart at the seams. The advantages of the scheme
were not equally shared among its members, and the inequalities were nowhere more apparent than in the relations
between El Salvador and Honduras. Lower import duties
had allowed El Salvador to replace the United States as Honduras' main supplier of manufactured goods, despite the
poorer quality and higher production costs of Salvadorean
products. But Honduras, far less industrialized than its
neighbors, had little to offer in return. Its fruits and minerals
were shipped to traditional markets in the United States. Its
cattle and cotton duplicated El Salvador's own production.
Honduras faced not only a serious balance-of-payments def-
icit with its neighbor, but aggressive Salvadorean businessmen had been investing in Honduran industries. Many
Hondurans, and especially the press, described their country
as the colony of an "imperialist" neighbor.

Problems between the two countries pre-dated the Common Market. Their common border had been in dispute for
decades, provoking repeated clashes along the northern rim

of El Salvador's Chalatenango and Morazán provinces. But more fundamental was the traffic across that border—a one-way flow of Salvadorean peasants unable to find an idle plot of land at home to the spacious and unsettled lands of Honduras.

In the early 1900s the Honduran government had encouraged this flow, offering free land to immigrants willing to farm in remote parts of the country. Thousands of Salvadorean peasants fled the terror of 1932 by migrating to Honduras to farm or work the plantations and mines. But as conditions inside Honduras changed, and Salvadoreans competed for jobs and land with equally destitute natives, the attitude of the Honduran government changed as well.

Both governments tried to regulate the problem with treaties in 1962 and 1965. But Honduras was a convenient and even necessary escape valve for what was called El Salvador's "surplus population" by successive governments bent on avoiding reforms. The terms of the treaties were systematically ignored, and when the second treaty came to an end in 1969, the Honduran government refused to extend it.

There were 350,000 Salvadoreans settled in Honduras by that time, many of them squatting on public lands. Although Honduras had much more land than El Salvador, relative to its population, the same pattern of concentrated land ownership was evident. The modernization of the banana plantations, owned by United Fruit, reduced the demand for labor in the 1960s. And the heightened influx of Salvadoreans, fleeing a faltering economy, drove land rents and prices to exorbitant heights. Salvadorean peasants soon became a convenient scapegoat for a military government, headed by General López Arellano, faced with tremendous labor unrest, land seizures and strong opposition parties. The elite in Honduras, alongside United Fruit, pressured the government to do something to combat the increasing violence.

Many Salvadoreans had lived in Honduras for decades; they were married to Hondurans and had only a vague remembrance of their native villages. But when the López Arellano government invoked a section of the agrarian reform law, passed in 1962 but largely unenforced, the key clause read "Honduran by birth." All those not included were given thirty days to leave the land.

The tales of forced evictions and atrocities against Salvadorean peasants were given first-page spreads in the Salvadorean press, provoking calls for immediate retaliation. Honduran newspapers carried banner headlines: "Salvadoreans Cleansed from Ten Towns in Yoro," as tens of thousands of refugees crossed the border to El Salvador, pushing oxcarts or carrying all of their meager possessions on foot.[25]

They returned to a country where 20 percent of the workforce was unemployed in 1969 and another 40 percent was underemployed, working no more than 120 days a year.[26] The government of Sánchez Hernández had enough problems with labor strikes and Christian Democrats threatening to capture the legislature by the next elections in 1970.

The 100 Hours War

On July 14, 1969, Salvadorean air force planes bombed the airport at Tegucigalpa, the Honduran capital. It was the beginning of a five-day war fought with guns and bullets and planes provided to both sides by the U.S. government. Two thousand people died and four thousand more were wounded before the Organization of American States (OAS) sent a peace-keeping force to monitor an unsteady truce. Honduras closed its market to Salvadorean goods, and the Common Market was in shambles. Refugees were herded into camps.

But there was a silver lining for the Sánchez Hernández government. The army returned from the front to cheering crowds; the president was a war hero; the ruling party had never been more popular; and the opposition parties were demoralized. The legislative elections of 1970 reversed the opposition parties' electoral gains of the 1960s, leaving the Party of National Conciliation (PCN) in full control.

Blinded by this temporary respite, the oligarchy went back to business as usual. The PCN began searching for a suitable successor to Sánchez Hernández, another colonel to carry on the modernizing tradition. And the opposition began to rethink its strategy, undo its divisions. It was only a matter of time before the euphoria of war would fade, and the problems that caused it would come to the fore once again.

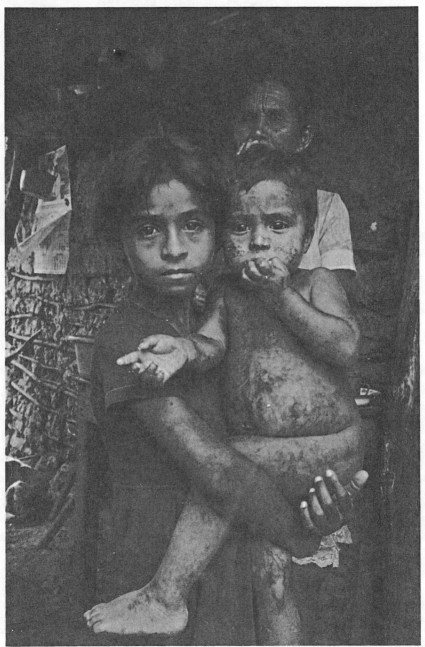

I.K. Silverman

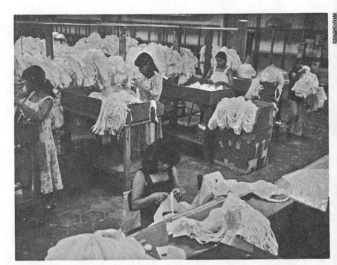

Right: a bra factory in San Bartolo, the free trade zone outside the capital.

Facing page: a campesino family in Chalatenango province.

Meiselas

CHAPTER III

The Writing on the Wall

A revolution happens because what we know as society can no longer manage itself. Those who run that society are in doubt about what should be done and fight among themselves. The suffering and want of the rest—of those who are ruled and oppressed—have become more acute than ever before. And because of those conditions, ordinary people who never before saw themselves as subjects in history, as those who act upon events, take tiny and then bigger steps to decide their future for themselves.

For forty years, since the failed rebellion of 1932, there were many efforts to reach that goal in El Salvador: elections, general strikes, peasant unions, armed struggle. And there were as many efforts to keep it from happening: death squads, exile, electoral fraud, repression and massacre.

The history of the 1970s brings together all these things; for in that decade, El Salvador's revolution took shape. The year 1972 was a turning point. After that moment, as after 1932, things would never be the same.

For the electoral opposition, 1972 was the long-awaited

moment, the crucial chance to test elections as a means of achieving change. The electoral battles of the 1960s had been fought—and lost—separately, despite considerable gains. But by 1970 it was clear that the opposition's only hope lay in unity.

The Communist Party, after years of debate over strategy, had decided to embark on an electoral course and in 1969 formed an electoral front called the Nationalist Democratic Union (UDN). Seeing in this the chance for a united opposition, the social democrats, led by Guillermo Ungo of the MNR, mediated between the UDN and the Christian Democrats, generally leary of any alliances with the left. By the 1972 elections they were ready: all three parties formed an electoral coalition—the National Opposition Union (UNO, meaning one). Its candidate for president was José Napoleón Duarte, and for vice president Guillermo Ungo.

Napoleón Duarte left his job as San Salvador's mayor in 1970 to prepare for the presidential race. His popularity was at an all-time high. In the huts of campesinos and in urban shacks, pictures of the Pope, John Kennedy and "Napo" were the only decoration. All those years of building sewers and water mains, dedicating schools, pushing the party's call for reforms, had to pay off in 1972. With Ungo as his running mate, Duarte campaigned energetically throughout the country. His Indian features, his easy manner, the *chispa* (spark) of his banter and oratorical style made him a formidable challenge to the official PCN candidate—a lackluster career officer named Colonel Arturo Molina.

Molina had been handpicked by the incumbent president, Fidel Sánchez Hernández. But by 1972, large sectors of the oligarchy, primarily the ultra-conservative agro-front, distrusted Sánchez Hernández and the PCN. He was thought to be "soft" on subversion and dangerously inclined toward reforms as a means of releasing political pressures. The agro-front searched for their own candidate in 1972, and found what they wanted in General "Chele" Medrano, founder of the right-wing paramilitary group, ORDEN, and former head of the National Guard. Medrano had established his own party a year before, called the Independent Democratic

United Front (FUDI).[1] He was a war hero; a man in the Martínez mold.

While the PCN worried that Medrano's candidacy might drain support from its ranks, there was little doubt that the real contest in 1972 lay between the PCN and the UNO coalition. The situation called for drastic measures: shortly before the elections, Napoleón Duarte's car was ambushed after a campaign stop in Morazán; his driver was killed. President Sánchez Hernández reportedly then made a deal with Guatemala's president, General Arana Osorio, to join an invasion of neighboring Belize, which Guatemala claimed as part of its territory. The quid pro quo for the deal was permission to ship El Salvador's "surplus population" to Belize, but England sent troops and a naval squadron to protect its colony and the plot was foiled.[2]

These activities reflected what both sides knew: the opposition's prospects for victory in 1972 were very real. The illusion of an economic miracle had been shattered by the war with Honduras. The nationalist euphoria fed by the war was decidedly over, and the discontent that never had died found new forms of expression by the early 1970s.

Ideologically, the first rumblings were heard within the Catholic Church about a new theology based on a commitment to the poor. Priests were challenging the fatalism of the peasantry; leaving their churches to organize the poor. One of these, José Inocencio Alas, was arrested in the town of Suchitoto, drugged, tortured and left naked in the mountains. Alas survived, but shortly before the elections another priest, Nicolas Rodríguez, was arrested by the National Guard. His body was found days later, completely dismembered.

In the cities, a second teachers' strike by the National Association of Salvadorean Educators (ANDES) again brought thousands into the streets, and new sectors of the population started organizing for the first time. Shantytown dwellers in San Salvador invaded municipal lands to set up squatter communities. And, in an entirely new development, small guerrilla groups made their first appearance. In 1970 Ernesto Regalado Dueñas, the scion of one of the wealthiest oligarchic families, was kidnapped. He died under obscure circumstances while still in captivity.

A Lost Victory

Throughout the campaign, the UNO coalition faced continual harassment, red-baiting and intimidation, and on election day, February 20, it braced itself for the final round. In it, the PCN went all out: in one province, La Unión, PCN governor Enrique Velásquez expelled all opposition candidates from the election district. In the capital, several ballot boxes contained not a single vote for the opposition, raising suspicions that the ballots had been pre-marked for the voters. Maneuvers were less subtle in the countryside, where UNO backers were roughed up by National Guardsmen and members of ORDEN.[3]

On February 22, 1972, the Central Election Board announced a slim but adequate victory for the PCN: 314,000 to the UNO's 292,000. Fireworks went off at PCN headquarters, while the UNO supporters sat glumly. Then, in the afternoon of that same day, the Election Board of San Salvador province issued a statement: the Central Election Board had made a mistake about the returns from the capital. Recalculating the national results, the new vote total was the UNO 321,000 votes; the PCN, 315,000. The undreamed-of had happened.

Then a news blackout was imposed. Wednesday, no word. Thursday, nothing. On Friday, February 25, the Election Board published still another set of figures handing victory to Colonel Molina of the PCN. Subsequent scrutiny of the results showed that vote totals in the rural provinces of La Unión, Chalatenango and Sonsonate had been doctored to achieve the desired result.[4]

UNO's militants refused to accept the outright fraud without a fight. They demanded that Duarte call a general strike, remembering the strike in 1944 that led to Martínez' downfall. But Duarte feared that a failed attempt to reclaim victory would destroy his carefully crafted image as a moderate. At the crucial moment he vacillated, and the UNO leadership saw no choice but to swallow defeat.

But one month later, a new chapter was added to the saga. Opposite the Casa Presidencial sits Fort Zapote, commanded in 1972 by Colonel Benjamin Mejía, a maverick and intellectual of sorts who read poetry to his troops. Mejía belonged to that tradition of military officers who led the initial rebellion against Martínez in 1944. On March 25, he and other officers of his command crossed the street and arrested President Sánchez Hernández on charges of violating El Salvador's constitution.

It was six o'clock in the morning when Mejía went on radio to announce the coup d'état. His followers had taken control of the country's communications network and enlisted the support of several key garrisons. Even Duarte joined the coup belatedly, although press reports would call him the ringleader; he went on the radio at noon to urge people to build barricades and put tacks on the road leading from the Sonsonate garrison to the capital, where troops were expected to defend the Sánchez Hernández government.

But few civilians heeded the call; they had no means to defend themselves and armed columns were converging on the capital from garrisons in Sonsonate and San Miguel. The National Guard and most air force units had remained loyal to Sánchez Hernández. Unmarked planes unloaded their bombs on Fort Zapote—a gift from General Somoza in Nicaragua and Arana Osorio ("the Jackal") of Guatemala, operating under the convenient umbrella of the Central American Defense Council (CONDECA). Many saw the hand of the United States behind the scenes, calling on its allies in the region to save the Sánchez Hernández government.

By late afternoon on March 26, 1972, the uprising was over. It left a toll of two hundred dead in the fighting and bombing, but many more were to die in the ensuing weeks and months of retaliation. Napoleón Duarte found asylum in the Venezuelan embassy, but government soldiers ignored the tradition of diplomatic immunity, entered the building and arrested him. They broke his cheek bones with rifle butts and cut off the tips of three fingers as souvenirs.[5] Eventually,

Duarte was put on a plane to Guatemala, hardly a haven for would-be reformers, and from there fled to safety in Venezuela.

The easy way to electoral legitimacy was over for the army by 1972. Fraud had always been a part of the electoral process, but in the 1960s it was subtle and small-scale; just enough to maintain a certain distance between the PCN and the opposition, but not really essential to the triumph of one colonel after another. After 1972, fraud and intimidation were both pervasive. No longer restricted to the campaign or the polling date, repression became a fact of everyday life, stretching from one election to the next. And there was no time to lose after 1972; the military had to prevent the opposition from growing steadily stronger.

On July 19, 1972, two weeks after the inauguration of El Salvador's new president, Colonel Arturo Molina, the National University was attacked by tanks, planes and artillery. Eight hundred people were arrested that day; fifteen more, including the university's president, Rafael Menjívar, and the dean of the medical school, Fabio Castillo, were chained together and flown to enforced exile in Somoza's Nicaragua. The university stayed closed for two years, as Molina tried to eliminate the "brains" behind the opposition and the center of student unrest.

The opposition parties that had worked for so many years, only to win, then lose, the election, were scattered and broken. Some members turned to cynicism, leaving politics aside to make their modest fortunes as middle-class professionals. Others preferred to pretend that 1972 never happened. They doggedly set out to rebuild their parties and prepare for the next electoral round, hoping that some outside force would compel the military to respect its outcome. And still others chose to find a new way. For them, 1972 marked the abandonment of all hope for electoral change.

The Revolutionary Alternative

"I belong to two countries.
Cuba
And my own."

The words are Roque Dalton's, El Salvador's revolutionary poet; the feelings are those of all who have fought for substantive change in Latin America. The revolution in Cuba was an awakening of hope, and has remained so despite twenty years of U.S. propaganda. But in the early days of fighting in Cuba's Sierra Maestra, many on the left, and particularly the communist parties of Latin America, regarded Castro and his rag-tag band as adventurers and nothing more. In El Salvador as elsewhere, the Communist Party had opted for the electoral route to power—however distant that power seemed. It remained in the UNO coalition through the Nationalist Democratic Union (UDN), and stayed wedded to that coalition well after the stolen victory of 1972.

But throughout Latin America, the success of Cuba's revolution caused great debate within the left. In Venezuela, Bolivia, Colombia and Guatemala, guerrilla "focos" attempted to duplicate that success in the 1960s, and became the target of Green Beret search parties and the new counterinsurgency techniques that were the underside of the schools and clinics paid for by the Alliance for Progress. Even as it was failing in Vietnam, counterinsurgency worked well against these nascent, still isolated guerrilla bands. Che Guevara was captured in Bolivia and killed. But the sympathy he evoked, the struggle he came to symbolize throughout the continent, kept the debates alive and fostered new attempts to catalyze revolution through armed struggle.

The experience of Cuba, of Che, of the Tupamaros in Uruguay and the Vietnamese, held a powerful attraction for many in El Salvador by the early 1970s. The challenge led to intense debate within the Communist Party—the party that led the insurrection in 1932, experimented briefly with armed struggle in the early 1960s, and then embraced electoral politics as the only route to structural change. The debate was initiated by Salvador Cayetano Carpio, a baker by trade, who became the party's secretary general in the late 1960s.

Carpio argued against the party's reliance on electoral means, to the near exclusion of all else. He accused party moderates—led by Shafik Jorge Handal—of trying to put a brake on militant trade union actions, of foresaking revolution for evolutionary change, when even that was prohibited by the oligarchy's adamant resistance to reform. But Carpio's was a minority position. He remained in the party, arguing his views, until 1969—when the Communist Party's endorsement of El Salvador's "patriotic war" with Honduras produced a final break. Carpio could not go along with the party's support for the Sánchez Hernández government, or a war fought on both sides by workers and peasants, in the interest of their oppressors. Years later Carpio recalled that "it was impossible to get the party to understand the need for a political-military strategy, that is, an overall revolutionary strategy, and that this had to be demonstrated to our people in practice. . . ."[6]

At age fifty, Carpio left the party. In the wilderness outside, he and the small group of men and women that followed his lead had no clear plan of action, other than to study the lessons of Latin America's guerrilla movements and learn from their failures. "From the start," Carpio later maintained, "we ruled out the guerrilla foco theory," which prevailed in the 1960s and led to the establishment of rural guerrilla bases in several Latin American countries. These "focos" were crushed with relative ease in the late 1960s, by local militaries assisted by counterinsurgency experts from the United States. Carpio based his rejection of this theory of revolution "on the experience of some guerrilla movements in Latin America and in other countries that were removed from the people, that failed to reach out to them to organize them and that succumbed to militaristic designs. . . ."[7]

But in those first few years, Carpio's group engaged mainly in minor military actions. In 1972 the group took a name: the Popular Liberation Forces—Farabundo Martí (FPL), restoring to history in its name the hero of 1932. They began to build FPL support groups in the countryside and cities.

Other armed groups emerged in this same period, formed by left-wing Christian Democrats, disenchanted by the party's stubborn, and in their eyes, futile pursuit of victory at the polls; by people moved to action out of deeply religious backgrounds; and members of the independent left.

In 1971 they formed the People's Revolutionary Army (ERP)—a "chaotic organization," in the words of one of its founders, Joaquín Villalobos, "composed of different groups with different approaches to strategy, but sharing the desire to promote armed struggle in El Salvador."[8]

The ERP's audacity in carrying out a series of kidnappings in the early 1970s earned it a greater reputation than the FPL. But both groups were gnats compared to the Salvadorean army. Many people even doubted their existence, except in the minds of a military bent on persecution. Others were too busy to notice what was happening, obsessed with the prospects of an economic boom by the mid-seventies. Foreign capital had set its sights on El Salvador and liked what it saw.

A National Transformation

The depression that followed the war with Honduras was short-lived in El Salvador, thanks to new injections of capital and higher coffee prices on the world market. Luxury hotels were being built for the thriving tourist trade; high-rise office buildings to house the oligarchy's new foreign partners; and four-lane highways to ease congestion in the capital. Amidst the glitter of preparations for a Miss Universe pageant in 1975 no one seemed to have time to ponder the effects of frustrated hopes for electoral change.

To be sure, the slum communities circling the capital were expanding, but so were the new industrial zones that now housed modern factories shrouded by landscaped gardens. Between 1970 and 1975, foreign investment in El Salvador climbed from $66.6 million to $104.5 million, with U.S. investment in the lead.[9]

The attraction was clear: a government eager to please, and an almost inexhaustible supply of labor, paid at the hard-to-beat rate of four U.S. dollars a day. Maidenform, Texas Instruments and other U.S. companies made El Salvador their home in the 1970s. But gone were the days of import substitution, the motto of the sixties. El Salvador's market was now the world. Maidenform bras were produced for reexport to the United States. Computer chips for Texas Instruments were sent back to Texas for final assembly and reshipment to markets around the globe. Salvadoreans were not supposed to consume the products of their labor. How could they at four dollars a day?

President Molina called it a "National Transformation" that would turn El Salvador into another Taiwan. He bent over backwards to cater to his foreign guests. Roads, ports and airports were modernized at state expense. Tax and exchange laws allowed foreign companies to increase and repatriate profits. State institutions, like INSAFI (created originally to encourage the development of local industry and crafts), gave out long-term loans at low interest.

And as if all this were not enough, a new free trade zone was established in San Bartolo, just outside the capital, where strikes were outlawed and foreign companies could operate tax-free. It became a haven for runaway shops escaping unions and higher wages in New York City and New England. As a U.S. towel and robe manufacturer told *Women's Wear Daily,* "The Salvadorean is pleased to work; it is a national trait."[10]

What this new form of modernization required above all else was political stability and a cooperative working class. The Salvadorean Industrial Association, headed by Joaquín Christ, decried "the negative influence of labor strikes on the industrial development of the country," and counseled that "a climate of security and stability must be created in order to restore confidence to investors and businessmen."[11] Toward this end, key leaders of the labor movement and opposition parties were exiled in the early 1970s. And there was no pretense of fair play in the legislative elections of March 1974: the UNO ran a full slate of candidates, but the Central Election Board simply proclaimed the PCN candidates the winners, posting no results.

Organizing Discontent

The 1974 elections thus marked another small step along the road to revolution. In the town of San Francisco Chin-

amequita, where UNO candidates claimed an impressive victory, the official results showed a landslide for the PCN and
the National Guard was called in to quell the spontaneous
outrage of the townspeople. They had erected barricades of
rock and occupied the city hall, imprisoning the outgoing
mayor inside.

But when the Guard arrived, machetes were no match
for their machine guns. Many died and many more "disappeared" in the weeks that followed, as local members of
the paramilitary squads accompanied the police, pointing out
house by house those who opposed the government, those
who voted for the UNO slate.[12]

In this climate of frustration and despair, different currents of the opposition began to experiment with new political forms. The two guerrilla organizations, the Popular
Liberation Forces (FPL) and the People's Revolutionary
Army (ERP), were grappling with questions of strategy, de-
bating ways to organize the discontent of El Salvador's poor
and ways to link their armed struggle for revolution with
everyday struggles for bread and land. The FPL in particular
was developing a strategy to build a worker-peasant alliance—a way to unite the two most significant sectors of El
Salvador's working poor; to address their most immediate
economic demands and lead that struggle toward political
ends: the overthrow of the oligarchy and the army. The ERP
stayed closer to *foquismo* and military actions; but both groups
stressed the ultimate goal of creating a socialist society.

In this period, the Christian Peasants Federation (FEC-
CAS) already was expanding its presence in the northern
and central parts of the country, while a similar organization,
the Farmworkers' Union (UTC), began organizing in the
province of San Vicente. Urban-based organizations, such as
the teachers' union (ANDES), industrial unions and the student movement, were becoming more active. Conditions
were ripening for breaking down the barriers between city
and countryside; for breaking through the insularity of specific sectors, each with its own set of needs and demands, and
building coalitions of the oppressed. But there were still
many obstacles, as the FAPU experience of 1974 would demonstrate.

The Fapu Experiment

By the mid-seventies, the bustle of "national transformation" in the capital was having its impact on the countryside as well. In May 1974, President Molina announced plans to build a giant dam at Cerron Grande, the country's largest lake, to provide electricity to the cities. The construction project would necessitate the flooding of surrounding lands. Some 15,000 peasants faced immediate eviction.

Peasant opposition to the project, organized by FECCAS, became a rallying cry for the student movement, labor unions, church groups and teachers. Together they formed a new organization called the United People's Action Front (FAPU), and encouraged other organizations to join them.

But FAPU's unity did not last long. Contention grew over who would control it, and debates went on over its role within the larger context of the opposition. Many groups, influenced in part by the guerrilla organizations and in part by their own experience with elections, saw FAPU as a new form of organizing; a means of breaking with the pattern of channeling discontent into elections, only to cry "fraud!" in their wake. The Communist Party, however, saw things differently. It insisted on pursuing its electoral course in alliance with the Christian Democrats and the social democrats in the National Revolutionary Movement (MNR). FAPU fell apart in less than six months.

Roque Dalton—The Death of Revolutionary Innocence

Less than a decade later, FAPU's short existence can be seen as an important precedent for coordinated efforts between peasants and urban groups, between guerrilla activists and grassroots organizations, and between conflicting strategies for revolution. But at the time it seemed these differences would forever turn the opposition against itself. Within the left, the FAPU experience sharpened debate over the relative importance of military actions and grassroots organizing among the poor. The People's Revolutionary Army

(ERP) in particular was torn apart by this debate and nearly destroyed. The story is one of the darkest chapters of the Salvadorean left.

By the early 1970s, the ERP had a sophisticated strategy of military actions. Its kidnappings of prominent business-men and oligarchs were meticulously planned and carried out. But the experience of mass work within FAPU, and a characterization of the Molina regime as increasingly fascist, led one faction within the organization to conclude that the hour of insurrection was near; that military preparations had to take precedence over all else. Out of the same experience, another faction reached a different conclusion: the need to build solid political organizations, along the lines of FAPU, as a necessary complement to military means. One man who argued for that second view was Roque Dalton, El Salvador's greatest living poet and popular historian.

Roque Dalton's life was the stuff of legend in El Salvador. In 1960 he was arrested by the Lemus government and sen-tenced to be shot. But the government fell only days before the scheduled execution. He was arrested again, but this time an earthquake split the prison walls and Dalton escaped—to Mexico, Europe, Havana, then Prague. "The dictatorships of El Salvador," wrote Eduardo Galeano, a friend, "the little country which was his land and which he carried tattooed all over his body, could never handle him."[13]

In 1973, after thirteen years of exile, Roque Dalton re-turned to El Salvador and joined the ERP. He was not an important leader of the organization. His work was essen-tially analytical, preparing studies of Salvadorean society that also would inspire the poetry he sent up from the under-ground. But in 1975, the infighting between factions made him a target of bizarre accusations, including the handy CIA label applied to political enemies. On May 10, the leadership of the ERP murdered Roque Dalton and another man who shared his views.

"We all meet death in a way that resembles us," wrote Galeano. "I always thought Roque would meet death roaring with laughter. I wonder if he could have. Wouldn't the sor-row of being murdered by those who had been your com-rades have been stronger?"

Years later, the ERP would acknowledge that "pragmatism, nearsightedness, the thirst for power and individual control—and excessive militarism," had led to "tragic consequences" for the organization.[14] They paid dearly for the execution of Roque Dalton, remaining isolated from the Salvadorean left for many years and undergoing a series of bitter splits. The largest, shortly after Dalton's death, led to the formation of a new organization called the National Resistance (RN). Advocating closer ties to the popular movement, the RN tried to avoid the errors of the past by creating a separate and subordinate guerrilla branch, known as the Armed Forces of National Resistance (FARN).

Reflections

A revolution is a rush of life through a crack in the appearance of things. It roars forward; it staggers; it ambles. It is no one's careful plan or, if so, only in retrospect.

In this century, there are those who have declared themselves revolutionaries. The best of them are scientists. They are humble before the phenomenon which they study and of which they are a part. They are men and women who see a more equitable, more just society as possible on this planet. And they struggle to make that vision real, trying not to destroy it in the agony and fight to win.

They make mistakes, sometimes so terrible that forgiveness may be impossible and self-criticism hollow. In such moments, those who share their hope feel the deep pain, the sadness and despair of being without hope, of being no better than the world is today, of being no more able to heal the pain than those who inflict it.

Revolutionaries talk about objectives, strategies, timing and tactics. They often disagree until events prove one or the other right or wrong. And when it is once again possible to agree, those differences, those unwanted legacies of distrust often interfere.

But a revolution is not made by revolutionaries. The revolutionary only guides it, explains it, leads it, tries to channel it toward clear and rational ends. In the end, it is the people who make a revolution.

In the mid-seventies in El Salvador, the people were taking their first steps toward making revolution. Shedding the stoic resignation that had accompanied their suffering for so long, they were starting to build their own organizations to fight for their own set of demands.

For these people, the decision to become politically involved was not an intellectual act. It was an act of self-preservation, a fight for sheer survival against the terrible odds of seeing one's child die of malnutrition, one's sister raped by the National Guard. And in the aftermath of 1972 and 1974, political involvement no longer meant voting. It meant joining the new popular organizations and lending a new meaning to democracy in action; it meant civil disobedience; and it meant facing the most brutal repression that El Salvador had known since 1932.

Fighting Back

On July 30, 1975, students at San Salvador's National University staged a protest march against the army's invasion of a branch campus in the western city of Santa Ana. The protest march would become a milestone in the history of the popular movement. It was El Salvador's Kent State.

Just south of the U.S. embassy, a bridge crosses a highway that speeds cars to the east and west of the capital city. As the demonstrators proceeded along 25th Avenue, on to the bridge, armed soldiers took up positions at the other end. The students turned to retrace their steps, not wanting to risk a confrontation. But that end had been blocked as well. The troops opened fire. The students spread themselves on the ground; some jumped from the bridge in desperation. The firing continued and then stopped, leaving twenty bodies on the bridge.

In a clean-up operation as efficient as the killings, military ambulances arrived to gather the bodies, some still alive, their moans piercing the professional calm of the soldiers. And behind the ambulances came the lumbering street clean-

H.E. Mattison

Meiselas

Above: left to right, junta members Colonel Jaime Abdul Gutierrez and Napoleon Duarte, and Minister of Defense Guillermo Garcia.

Left: mothers of the disappeared awaiting news of their children from the first junta, October 1979.

Facing page: chaos inside the cathedral following the funeral of Monsenor Romero.

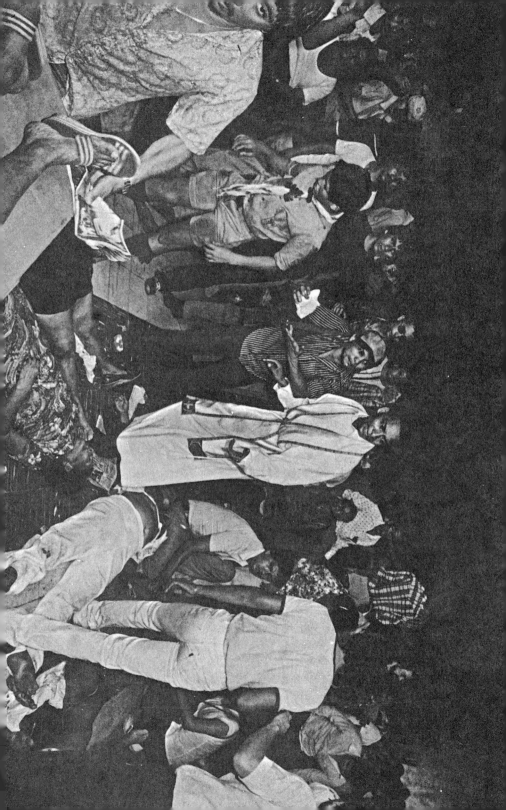

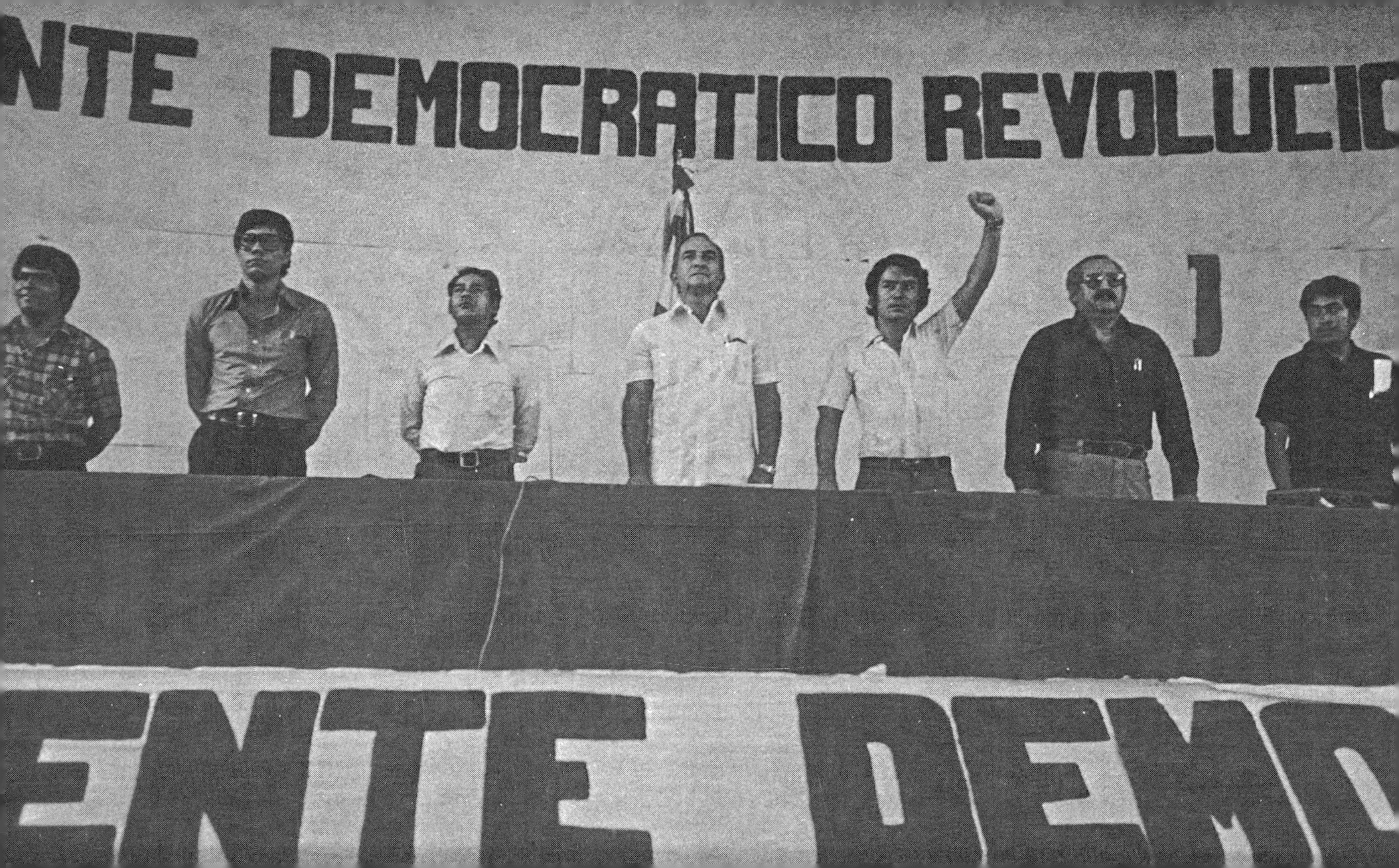
NTE DEMOCRATICO REVOLUCIO
ENTE DEMO

Left: Guillermo Ungo, Enrique Alvarez and Ruben Zamora at the United Nations, July 1980, as part of the FDR's diplomatic offensive.

Facing page: formation of the Democratic Revolutionary Front, April 1980. From left to right: Juan Chacon (BPR), Juan Jose Martel (MPSC), Leoncio Pichinte (LP-28), Enrique Alvarez (Pres.), Manuel Franco (UDN), Luis Buitrago (MNR) and Saul Villalta (FAPU).

Right: Juan Chacon, secretary general of the People's Revolutionary Bloc, kidnapped and murdered with four other FDR leaders on November 27, 1980.

ers, washing the blood away. At least twenty people were gathered up by the ambulances, but none were seen again.

The Engineering and Architectural Students Association put an ad in the capital's largest daily: "We are certain that [Reynaldo Enrique Hasbun—an engineering student] was wounded and arrested while still alive, and taken in an ambulance with destination unknown, although we have inquired about him in all of the hospitals of San Salvador and nowhere have received any information."[15]

José Domingo Aldaña, 20, a second-year economics student, whose mother was a teacher at Sacred Heart College, was among the dead. So was Guillermo Aparicio, 20, a law student; and Sergio Antonio Cabrera, 21, a third-year student of medicine.

Witnesses had seen María Evelia Miranda, 20, crushed by an armored car after being wounded by gunfire. A writ of habeas corpus was entered by her family, but there was no response.

News spread through San Salvador, to Santa Tecla and Santa Ana, that students had been massacred in broad daylight, on one of the capital's busiest streets. And in a reaction that was in part spontaneous, and in part reflected years of organizing, hundreds of people converged on the Metropolitan Cathedral and said they would stay to protest the massacre.

No one had ever occupied a church before. Few people had heard of the organizations whose names appeared on crude, hand-painted placards: the Union of Shantytown Dwellers (UPT), the High School Students Movement (MERS), the Revolutionary University Students (UR-19), and more. ANDES, the teachers' union, was there in force along with FECCAS, the Christian Peasants Federation. Amassed inside the cathedral, these diverse groups gave themselves a new, collective name: the People's Revolutionary Bloc (BPR)—known simply as *el Bloque*.

The Popular Organizations

The *Bloque* was the first of a new kind of organization that quite literally would revolutionize the concept of politics and political participation in Salvadorean life. Formation of the BPR was followed closely by the reorganization of FAPU, and then by the creation of the People's Leagues (LP-28) some two years later. All of these popular organizations shared certain basic characteristics: they were profoundly democratic, allowing workers and peasants, students, clergy and professionals to participate, many for the first time, in political discussions and decisions. They meant an alternative to vanguard or reformist parties, to electoral coalitions and parliamentary blocs. They channeled the cynicism generated by decades of electoral fraud into acts of civil disobedience, into massive rallies and protest demonstrations. Concretely, in their everyday practice, they showed people that in unity there is strength.

The popular organizations gave a voice to people like Leoncio Pichinte, who finished the sixth grade in Tenancingo, and left to find work in the capital as a dishwasher, bartender, and then construction worker. There he joined a union and later, in 1977, joined the People's Leagues. They gave a voice to Facundo Guardado, born in the town of Arcatao, Chalatenango province, in 1954. A fieldworker, he began to work with the Farmworkers' Union (UTC) in 1972, and later became secretary general of the People's Revolutionary Bloc.

The popular organizations were internally diverse, both with respect to the sectors they organized and the political goals of their members. Some people joined to fight for electricity in the *tugurios,* or higher wages, or lower rents on the land. Others, with a longer trajectory in the trade union movement, or with ties to the guerrilla organizations, clearly posited socialism as their goal. But all were united by one common denominator: hatred of the army and the oligarchy, and determination to end their rule.

In the mid-seventies, the popular organizations were strongest in the countryside, where the need for their existence was most tangible, most desperate. The timebomb of suffering and despair that is *el campo* would have exploded no matter what happened, because the life of the poor campesino had reached the point where, as so many say today, "It is better to die quickly fighting than to die slowly starving."

El Campo

President Molina's vision of "national transformation" barely touched the countryside, where conditions always got worse instead of getting better. In 1961, 11.8 percent of rural families had no land; by 1975, 41 percent were landless.[16] According to the Ministry of Agriculture, a typical family of six required $533 a year in 1975 for the basic food necessary to survive. Sixty percent of the population earned less than that amount.[17] Agricultural experts estimated that a typical family must have seven hectares, or seventeen acres, of good land to produce sufficient food and income to feed itself. Yet in 1975, 96.3 percent of the rural population had five hectares or less.[18]

There was no escape valve for the rural poor, despite the hopes raised by industrialization in the cities. The creation of jobs could never keep up with the birth rate, or with the displacement of workers by new technology. More often than not, those who migrated to the cities ended up as shoeshine boys, or petty thieves, or prostitutes. Or they traveled on to neighboring countries in search of land or work. Most of the rural poor stayed in *el campo,* no longer expecting things to change.

Chavela and Lencho were typical. They lived with four children on a lot 100 feet wide by 30 feet deep, in the province of La Libertad. The house was set among a clump of trees with a small patio beside it for the chickens to wander. There was no room to grow anything on that parcel. During the harvest season, Lencho picked cotton on the nearby plantation, but the rest of the time he wandered daily up and down the coast, looking for work. He told us there was a chance to pick coconuts that day at a *finca* by the ocean; the past week he had worked as a mason's helper on a construction site in La Libertad. Next week he would do what he could find.

Chavela was feeling weak but shrugged at the suggestion of going to a clinic. San Salvador was too far; there were too many children to care for; but there was nothing closer by.

It was so common a scene: the husband running daily to find work; the wife anxious for her family, herself, her children; the youngest child wandering naked, his bloated belly the telltale sign of malnutrition; and the eldest soon to join his father in the constant search for work.

Order in the Countryside

People in the countryside had grown used to the suffering; it was part of life. But hopes of change need a vision of something possible, and in the mid-seventies hunger was not all that stalked the villages. The National Guard had its own little gestapo in every village, organized as the Democratic Nationalist Organization—but more commonly referred to as ORDEN, its Spanish acronym meaning order.

ORDEN was founded in the late 1960s by General "Chele" Medrano, then head of the National Guard. He described its purpose as that of "[integrating] the campesino population into national politics; [organizing] the peasantry in order to indoctrinate them to carry out an ideological campaign on behalf of representative democracy and the free world against the dictatorial communist world. . . ."[19]

These were weighty notions for a peasantry that knew only the bounds of the nearest market town. But ORDEN recruited its members not through ideological persuasion, but by dispensing small favors that meant an escape from the lowest rungs of rural poverty. Small peasants who joined the organization were granted favorable credit terms; seasonal workers could hope for permanent employment on the large estates; the unemployed would be hired for public works projects in the rural districts. And in return, they became "the body and bones of the army in the countryside," according to the boasts of General Medrano.[20] By the mid-seventies, it was estimated that ORDEN's membership ranged in the tens of thousands.

That the popular organizations could exist, survive, even flourish in such conditions reflected the development of a new consciousness, one that enabled people to look beyond the hopelessness and confront the dangers of being denounced by an ORDEN spy. This consciousness was nurtured by an institution itself undergoing profound change and questioning: El Salvador's Catholic Church.

"If Your Child Dies of Hunger, He Will Go to Heaven"

The Church's "role in the world," so long unquestioned by a tradition of obedience and acceptance of God's will, became the central question among its members during the 1960s. Particularly after Vatican Council II in 1964–65, and its document called *The Church in the World*, intense debates, doubts and discussions put new energy into an institution that had little wealth in El Salvador, and less dynamism, especially when it came to challenging the existing order. Similar questioning was going on within the Church elsewhere in Latin America: Brazilian priests, like Dom Helder Camara, harsh critics of that government's repression, were one example; the guerrilla priest in Colombia, Camilo Torres, was another. In 1968 the bishops of Latin America gathered in Medellín, Colombia, and ratified the growing demand of a new breed of priests and nuns to engage the world and change it. Their final statement read:

> [The Christian] believes in the value of peace for the achievement of justice, he also believes that justice is a necessary condition for peace. And he is not unaware that in many places in Latin America there is a situation of injustice that must be recognized as institutionalized violence, because the existing structures violate people's basic rights: a situation which calls for far-reaching, daring, urgent and profoundly innovating change.[21]

In El Salvador these words legitimated the ideas of a new generation of religious people committed to their work among the poor and to change rather than acceptance. They pushed others to rethink their work and that of the Church. But none of this had really crystallized; the questions were rarely spoken aloud, and never preached.

Then Father José Inocencio Alas started to speak out from his pulpit in Suchitoto: "There is a pyramid of oppression at whose base are the hungry, sick and naked campesinos, intimidated by tendentious phrases like 'You'll be accused of Communism! We'll call the National Guard. Seek Eternal Salvation! Give thanks to God if your child dies of hunger—he will go to heaven!' There are too many Christians who go to Communion but avoid community organizations; who are afraid to join the peasant leagues or the workers' movement. To live Christianity dreaming of heaven is to forget this earth, which is also of God."[22]

The National Guard surrounded Suchitoto in 1969, demanding that Father Alas leave town. But his parishioners said no. They believed in his words, as did the new priests at the Jesuit Seminary in San Salvador, St. Joseph's.

One of their teachers was Father Rutilio Grande, a Salvadorean-born Jesuit from the village of El Paisnal, some twenty-five miles to the north of San Salvador. Although profoundly orthodox in his theology, Grande had developed a reputation as a critic of the Church's work and an advocate of a greater commitment to the poor. His outspokenness cost him a position at the seminary; and he asked to be sent to the parish church near his birthplace, in the town of Aguilares.

Aguilares is a town of 10,000 people, with 20,000 more in the outlying villages belonging to the parish. There, all the contradictions and injustices of El Salvador are united in a single place. Four sugar mills and their adjacent plantations dominate the fertile Aguilares valley. Their owners visit from time to time, but live their lives in the capital, attending to their banks and factories. The campesinos of Aguilares rent left-over, rocky parcels of land. Sometimes they have to dig holes between the rocks to plant each grain of corn, since plowing or spading is impossible. And unable to subsist on these small plots, they work when they can on the large sugar estates for a wage of $1.75 a day.[23]

Rutilio Grande wanted to awaken the campesinos to their worth as human beings. Influenced by his studies at the Latin American Pastoral Institute in Ecuador, he decided to form a team of four priests to work in Aguilares. Following a growing practice throughout Latin America, they went to live in the villages and hamlets of the parish. They listened to the campesinos and they talked to them of the meaning of being a Christian. At the heart of their work was a new understanding of the relationship of the campesinos and their concept of God. For many of them, God was like the *patrón*, or like the comandante of the National Guard, who expected servility. That servility restrained a much deeper rage, one which burst out during drunken brawls when machete blades flashed on Saturday nights against family members or friends.

In each village, the priests held nightly meetings at which a passage of scripture was read and discussed. They did not try to explain the meaning of the passage in terms of their years of study, but to help the campesinos explain what *they* thought the scripture meant in terms of their daily lives. In the 1970s the ratio of parishioners to priests in El Salvador was ten thousand to one. The Jesuits in Aguilares could stay in each village for only two short weeks, and then move on. So they encouraged the campesinos to continue this process of discovery on their own, by electing Delegates of the Word (lay preachers) to continue the reading of the Bible and its discussion. Slowly, the impersonal distant church of Sunday mornings became a church of equals and a community.

The weekly meetings of the base communities were part religious service, part town hall, political forum and fiesta. A chapel was little more than the ubiquitous corrugated tin roof on four posts. The scene inside, on any particular night, might have looked like this:

The Delegate of the Word stands before the congregation, his white shirt newly pressed. Before him the community sits on hand-made benches: the men, their straw "cowboy" hats in their hands; the women, shawls covering their shoulders and the occasional suckling infant breaking the attentive silence.

The story is from the Gospel according to Saint Mark: the tale of the rich man.

"How hard it will be for those who have riches," the Delegate reads, "to enter the Kingdom of God. It is easier for a camel to go through the eye of a needle than for a rich man to enter the Kingdom of God."

It is time for discussion. What does the story mean?

A toothless old man, one eye closed in a long-forgotten fight, says slowly: "God does not believe the rich to be part of his kingdom. God prefers the poor. A camel—I once saw a picture—is larger than a horse. A needle—its eye is very small. There is no fit."

A dark-eyed girl wearing her best white dress shyly raises her hand:

"That to be loved by God, you must—no, we must—share what we have with our sisters and brothers."

This commitment to the poor was a profound change from the good deeds that the Church had been doing for the poor, acts of old-fashioned charity. It meant arming the poor with their greatest weapons: their own self-worth, their intellectual capacity, their own courage. When a landowner spoke disrespectfully to a campesino, that person could recall that he was the beloved of God, of special concern and equal to the *patrón*. His liberation was the fulfillment of God's plan. "God is not somewhere up in the clouds, lying in a hammock. God is here with us," Rutilio Grande would say, "building a kingdom here on earth."

Building such a kingdom on earth would require many changes, and the acceptance of a new responsibility. The Delegates, the believers, "by virtue of their conversion and growth in faith," said Father Rutilio, "they naturally are becoming agents of change—as the very Gospel asked them to be."

Even the Bible Is Subversive

In Aguilares, the outlawed Christian Peasants Federation (FECCAS), founded in 1964, had struggled for years with minimal support. By 1973 it was becoming a vehicle for the exercise of that new responsibility. Some 1600 workers at Cabañas sugar mill stopped work, demanding that the owner pay what had been promised verbally. Some FECCAS members were also Delegates of the Word. Eight months after the Jesuits arrived, the landowners of the area called them "communists"; the base communities, "cells."

Many in the Church warned Grande to slow down. In a Christmas homily in 1975, after FECCAS had joined the People's Revolutionary Bloc (BPR), he said, "We can't unite with political groups of any kind, but we cannot remain indifferent before politics which point to the common good of the great majority, the people. We cannot be disinterested in the here and now."[24]

The message and practice of Rutilio Grande and his colleagues in Aguilares was taken up by clergy throughout El Salvador. Nuns were sharing in the new experience—the Liberation of the Word—and laying a basis for their own liberation within the hierarchy of the Church. Priests in San Vicente, Chalatenango and Morazán worked with base communities in their regions. The oligarchy muttered that "bad priests" were the real brains behind FECCAS and the Farmworkers' Union (UTC) active near San Vicente. These priests were sowing hatred, they said, and behind them were the Jesuits.

But the work continued. In his most famous sermon, Father Grande spoke these words:

> The enslaved masses of our people, those by the side of our road, live in a feudal system six centuries old. They own neither their land nor their own lives. They have to climb up into trees, and even the trees don't belong to them. Mouths are full of the word 'Democracy,' but let us not fool ourselves. There is no democracy when the power of the people is the power of a wealthy minority, not of the people. You are Cains, and you crucify the Lord in the person of Manuel, of Luis, of Chavela, of the humble campesino.
>
> I am quite certain that very soon the Bible and the Gospel won't be allowed to cross our borders. We'll get only the bindings, because all the pages are subversive. And I think that if Jesus himself came across the border at Chalatenango, they wouldn't let him in. They would accuse the Man-God, the prototype of man, of being a rabble-rouser, a foreign Jew, one who confused the people with

exotic and foreign ideas, ideas against democracy—
that is, against the wealthy minority, that clan of
Cains! Brothers and sisters, without any doubt, they
would crucify him again.[25]

While the oligarchy tried to convince the Molina government to eliminate the communist menace in priestly disguise, and crush rebellion in the countryside, some in the
government, including Molina, feared things had gone too
far. Repression, yes. But with a touch of reform. Perhaps
"national transformation" *could* be extended to the countryside.

Forbidden Words

In 1976, the government of Colonel Arturo Molina proposed a modest, even meek, program of "agrarian transformation." ("We don't use the term agrarian reform," Molina
explained, "because that's Marxist terminology.") A pilot area
was chosen in the eastern cotton-producing lowlands, in the
provinces of San Miguel and Usulután. There, according to
the government's own figures, five families—0.14 percent of
the farmers—owned 21.5 percent of the land; while 70.5
percent of the farmers owned only 6.2 percent of the land.[26]
The average wage in the area was $1.20 a day. Unemploy-
ment was 55 percent. If things didn't change soon, Molina
argued, the troubles in San Vicente and Aguilares would
spread to this area as well. He hoped to prove that small
changes could make a difference.

The pilot project called for expropriating 120,000 acres,
purchased at full market price, and distributing small plots
(no less than 7.4 acres) to 12,000 peasant families. It was
hoped that these new owners would finally enter the market
economy, expanding the internal market for consumer
goods; while new investments would flow into industry from
payments for expropriated lands.

Molina's "agrarian transformation" marked the first attempt in the country's 155 years of independence to reverse
the pattern of land ownership and heed the signs of social

unrest. The colonel tried to sell the plan to the oligarchy by calling it their life insurance policy. But the premium was too high for a group accustomed to unfettered power and convinced that their way of life could endure forever.

Only a small minority supported the reform—some of the same modernizers that argued for industrialization in the 1950s and 1960s. The U.S. embassy was staunchly in favor of the plan. And the Jesuit-run university, UCA, praised it as a step toward more extensive reforms.

On the other side, however, were the largest landowning dynasties and the most powerful organizations of El Salvador's elite. The National Private Enterprise Association (ANEP) described the controversy as "whether El Salvador will go on being a nation in which free enterprise is respected, or whether, on the contrary, it will change itself into a directed state."[27] The landowners from the pilot region formed a new organization, FARO, to fight the reform, and right-wing death squads proliferated as the initials of the White Warriors Union were carved on the homes of suspected peasant organizers, and the Falange sent death threats to proponents of reform.

In the style which has characterized them for fifty years, the oligarchy mounted a vitriolic campaign in the press, calling Molina a communist in military disguise. Molina rallied, parried, but finally succumbed. He scratched the pilot project, rather than be ousted by a rumored coup, and served out his presidential term in the traditional style: repression, in ever larger doses, to kill the contagion that was spreading in the countryside.

Would Molina's life insurance policy have done any good? At most, it might have bought some time, convinced a few that sooner or later, the oligarchy would see the light and resign itself to some measure of reform. But by the end of the 1970s, El Salvador's popular movement wanted, and demanded, more than a touch of reform. And the presidential elections of 1977 convinced more than a few that the oligarchy, and its military allies, would never budge.

CHAPTER IV

A Madness Seized the Land

Listening on a CB-radio on election day, February 20, 1977, one could hear frequent and cryptic messages:

"The level is low. There is too much sugar."
"Buy some tamales and get the little birds out of there."

The "level" was the vote count. The "sugar" was votes for the UNO candidates. "Buying tamales" was adding fake ballots for the PCN. And the "little birds" were the opposition poll watchers. This time the PCN was taking no chances. There would be no embarrassing victories for the united opposition.[1]

For the UNO, the decision to participate in the 1977 elections was a calculated but necessary risk. They had withdrawn from the legislative and municipal elections of 1976, when their candidates faced more than the usual harassment. Now they tried to reach beyond their traditional base to gain support from less vulnerable sectors. In particular, they sought support from progressive elements in the army by running a retired cavalry officer for president, Colonel Ernesto Claramount. For vice-president the UNO ran José Antonio Morales Ehrlich, a lawyer and leading Christian Democrat.

Among the oligarchy, however, the unyielding Martínez mentality was more pervasive than ever. The PCN presidential candidate reflected their rage at Molina's dangerous flirtation with agrarian reform and their nervous fear of rebellion in the countryside. The agro-front wanted an iron hand to crush the popular organizations, and they found the man to wield it in General Carlos Humberto Romero—minister of defense in the Molina government, with direct responsibility for ORDEN.

Romero's nomination as the official candidate of the PCN marked a significant power shift within the party, and within the oligarchy as a whole. The modernizers—Presidents Rivera, Sánchez Hernández and Molina—had enjoyed more than fifteen years of uninterrupted rule. They had tried to temper repression with a dose of reform, but by 1977 the oligarchy had no patience for experiments. They wanted someone who spoke the same language as Chile's Pinochet and Argentina's Videla; they wanted National Security instead of National Transformation. The agro-front, allied with extreme rightists in the military, had eclipsed the technocratic notions of the modernizers.

The months preceding the presidential election were marked by extraordinary tensions, even for a country by then so accustomed to violence. Two events in particular provoked fury—and fear—within powerful circles.

One again centered on the dam construction project near the town of Aguilares. The Orellana family, one of the original Fourteen, owned a large plantation that was flooded to make way for the dam. They were amply compensated by the Molina government, but the families who lived on the hacienda as peons and tenant farmers received nothing. Many of them had lived there for more than fifty years. They were members of the Christian Peasants Federation (FECCAS), aligned with the People's Revolutionary Bloc.

On December 5, 1976, 250 campesinos stood in the yard in front of the big house, demanding that the Orellanas assist them in resettlement. Periodically, one could hear the chant: "Blo-que, Blo-que, Blo-que," as the Orellana brothers, Francisco and Eduardo, stood on the veranda overlooking the demonstrators. Francisco had a gun.

Suddenly shots rang out. Where they came from nobody knew. But Eduardo Orellana lay dead and Francisco blamed the demonstrators. The campesinos said that Francisco had panicked and started shooting wildly, fatally wounding his brother.

Within days, the newspapers were filled with paid ads from the largest landowners' and business associations. They charged the FECCAS "hordes" with Orellana's death, and accused the "communist priests" of fomenting rebellion. "Among them the parish priests of Aguilares stand out," said an ad in the morning *Prensa Gráfica*. It mentioned Rutilio Grande by name.

Then on January 27, 1977, a month before the elections, another oligarch was felled. The People's Revolutionary Army (ERP) kidnapped Roberto Poma, president of the National Tourism Institute, a strong promoter of modernization and a close associate of the president. Responding to family pleas, Colonel Molina agreed to the kidnappers' demands. Two guerrillas were freed and a large ransom was paid. But Poma had been wounded during the kidnapping in an exchange of fire between the ERP and his bodyguards. He died while still in the kidnappers' hands.

The Monday Massacre

The enraged oligarchs counted on the elections to settle accounts, since the outcome was never in doubt. But the final tally was so implausible—three to one for the PCN—and the popular reaction to the fraud so strong, that the reign of terror signaled by Romero's election began well before he took office.

For five consecutive days after the election results were posted, nearly 50,000 people crowded into a square called Plaza Libertad in downtown San Salvador. They camped out under the covered arcades that surround the plaza, and under the statue of Liberty, a graceful woman holding wreaths in both hands as if to bestow them on some lucky person in the square below. The crowds listened as the UNO candidate, Colonel Ernesto Claramount, denounced the rigged elections and demanded a new vote. The night of February 27, 1977, UNO supporters erected barricades at the four entrances to the plaza where young men stood guard armed with sticks, keeping watch for the police. Earlier that evening, Father Alfonso Navarro had celebrated mass with those assembled in the square, now diminished to three or four thousand.

At 1:00 a.m. on Monday, February 28, trucks bearing members of the army, the National Guard, National Police, Customs Police and the Treasury Police arrived. They sealed off all but one entrance to the square and turned on the high-powered hoses. The crowd huddled under the statue and sang the national anthem to give themselves strength:

> "We salute you, we proudly
> call ourselves your children."

When the soldiers opened fire, two young men standing near the statue fell immediately to the ground. The crowd panicked and swarmed into El Rosario church, which soon filled with tear gas. The rest fled up the single street which the security forces had left open.

It was a trap. Each side street was blocked and soon the breathless and terrified crowd were herded into a concrete canyon formed by the abutments of a railroad bridge. They were separated into groups of five and made to run a gauntlet of forty soldiers, who took particular pleasure in beating them with rifle butts. For some, the end of the gauntlet was a bullet.

By 4 a.m., Plaza Libertad was empty. An American journalist who was there said, "I was kept out of the plaza, so I could hear only the screaming and the shooting. Then, when it was over, I got in and found it literally covered with blood, although the bodies had been removed. But perhaps the most horrible thing was when I returned again an hour after *that* to find they had hosed down the plaza and there was a chill as though nothing had happened at all."[2]

But something had happened. Along with the UNO's

failed hopes and defeated efforts, after the massacre and the declaration of a state of siege, came the growing conviction that the oligarchy would never surrender its power to the popular will. Every day, more and more people joined those who said the struggle must take a different form.

Another popular organization took its place beside FAPU and the People's Revolutionary Bloc. Its name commemorated the massacre—the People's Leagues of February 28th (LP-28).

And in Washington, a new president had taken office with respect for human rights as part of his platform. The fraud in El Salvador had been so blatant that a Congressional committee heard testimony to examine the propriety of sending U.S. military aid to the new regime.[3]

"For the Sake of National Dignity"

When historians write the history of the Salvadorean revolution, the year 1977 may well be deemed the most important. Although General Romero had won the elections he would not take office for another six months. During the lame-duck presidency of Colonel Arturo Molina, El Salvador suddenly gained international notoriety.

Between the February elections and Romero's inauguration in July, a kind of madness seized the land, one that revealed all of the contradictions, all of the anomalies, all of what was absurd about the oligarchy that had ruled El Salvador for a hundred years. Perhaps they sensed that time was running out. But certainly they never believed that their way of life would end.

Typical of the oligarchy's blindness and rank stupidity was their vicious attack on the Church, that sector of society most capable of bringing international support to its defense. Perhaps it is the peculiar provincialism of the Fourteen Families and their military servants that explains why they seriously thought that they could intimidate and kill Catholic priests without provoking an international storm of protest.

Since the result of the election was never in doubt, the campaign against the Church started early. Just before the

February election, a priest in the parish of Tecoluca, where the farm workers union, FECCAS-UTC, had been active, was arrested by the National Guard. For nine hours electric shocks were applied to his feet and hands, while his jailors periodically threw ice water on his naked body to heighten the pain. Finally, through the intervention of his bishop, Father Rafael Barahona was freed.

Less than a month later, on March 11, 1977, Father Barahona left Tecoluca in his car in the morning. Unable to return that evening, he gave his brother the car to get back. As his brother approached a turn, gunshots bounced the car to a halt. Barahona's brother was killed, mistaken for a priest.[4]

The following day, March 12, 1977, another man was murdered. His death was to change the course of history in El Salvador, in unforeseeable ways.

It was 5:55 in the afternoon on a very dusty road near Aguilares. Father Rutilio Grande rode with a young boy and an old man toward the village of El Paisnal, where Rutilio was to say evening mass. A truck behind their Land Rover came closer, the dust putting a blanket over the bright green stalks of cane along the roadside. Several men stood beside another truck just ahead, their arms holding something at their sides. One of them, a policeman from Aguilares, dropped the cigarette he was smoking: a signal.

As Rutilio's jeep passed the men, they raised what they were holding and opened fire. The bullets pierced his throat, his ear, his skull. The old man who had come along to protect Rutilio grabbed his throat to stop the blood, until a second blast killed the old man. Then from the rear, the sound of still another automatic rifle cut through the priest's back and splintered his pelvis.[5]

Word swept through El Paisnal, Aguilares and San Salvador: "They killed Rutilio." Soon it was on the wires and by morning, human rights and church organizations around the world knew that a new martyr had been added to their lists.

Meanwhile, the U.S. Congress was holding hearings on human rights violations in El Salvador. Molina protested, calling this undue interference in his country's internal affairs. A few days after Rutilio's murder, on March 17, 1977, President Molina announced that El Salvador would accept no further military aid or training from the United States, "for the sake of national dignity."[6]

"The Hour of Resurrection"

Midnight in Aguilares, the night of Rutilio's murder, Archbishop Oscar Arnulfo Romero stood silently in a small white room, barren except for a few treasured books. This had been Rutilio's home. The archbishop had been a good friend of Rutilio Grande. Both were known as orthodox clerics, but while Rutilio worked among the poor in Aguilares, the archbishop had emphasized the spiritual side of the Church in his own work.

Archbishop Romero had been named by the Vatican on February 3, 1977, just weeks before the elections that brought General Romero to power. He was considered the more conservative of two candidates for the position, and his appointment caused deep consternation among the progressive clergy. They saw it as a step backward from his aging predecessor, Monseñor Chávez y González, who stopped work on San Salvador's cavernous cathedral saying "we must stop building cathedrals and start building the Church." Would the new archbishop try to put a brake on building this new church among the poor? Archbishop Romero later confided that, indeed, he had been named to put the radical priests in their place: "My job was to finish you off."[7]

But the murder in Aguilares changed all that. Rutilio's death was a moment of personal crisis and conversion for the shy, scholarly archbishop. Despite the state of siege still in effect after the election, he called for demonstrations to mourn the slain priest and his two companions. He sent a letter to President Molina demanding an investigation and declaring that he, as archbishop, would attend no official functions until the murders were solved. He declared that all Catholic schools were to be closed for three days and students sent home with a discussion guide on the persecution of the Church. And he ordered that only one mass be celebrated on Sunday, the ninth day remembrance of Rutilio Grande's death.

The oligarchy yelled "sacrilege!" and conservative bishops charged that the new archbishop was breaking canon law. But the 100,000 people who gathered inside and outside the cathedral that day applauded the archbishop's new resolve. To them, he became simply "Monseñor," a man who always had time to listen and always a new idea to strengthen the work of the Church. He set up a permanent office in the chancery to investigate violations of human rights; he wrote a column for *Orientación*, the weekly newspaper of the archdiocese; and he met regularly with the young clergy and nuns and members of the base communities.

Most important of all, perhaps, were the archbishop's weekly sermons that brought hope—and information about national events—to those who filled the cathedral to overflowing week after week, and to those who listened to his sermons over the Catholic radio station, YSAX. His sermons became the most popular program in the country; and the transistor radio became a weapon in the struggle for consciousness and dignity.

In April 1977 Romero wrote his first pastoral letter, an Easter message to his people. It said: "If I were looking for an adjective to describe this time of change in the archdiocese, I would not hesitate to call it the hour of resurrection."[8]

"Be a Patriot—Kill a Priest"

Between February and July 1977, seven priests were refused reentry to El Salvador; eight were expelled; two were killed; two tortured; one beaten; two imprisoned and four threatened with death. A friend, a Salvadorean priest, wrote of the fear: "My house has been surrounded by police and National Guardsmen since February 15 (night and day). They take the license numbers of every car that arrives . . . Those of us who live here have spent the past few weeks sleeping in a different place every night."

Kidnappings, land invasions, protest marches—all were laid at the door of the Church, perhaps because the oligarchy refused to believe that an illiterate people could think for themselves. There had to be some powerful force behind it—Cuba, Moscow, the Church. . . . In April 1977, when the Popular Liberation Forces (FPL) kidnapped the foreign minister, Mauricio Borgonovo, and carried out their threat to kill him when the government refused to exchange political prisoners, a new leaflet appeared in the capital. Entitled "The Church and the Kidnappers," it pictured a bishop, his robe imprinted with the slogans of the various guerrilla organizations. Soon after, another priest was killed, Father Alfonso Navarro, machine-gunned in his house with weapons available only to the security forces of the government.

But killing priests was not enough for the oligarchy. The peasantry was already contaminated by their ideas. They needed to be taught a lesson, and what better place than Aguilares—where the strength of the popular organizations confirmed the oligarchy's version of events: the "communist priests" were to blame for the spirit of rebellion enveloping the land.

On May 17, 1977, the Salvadorean army moved into place. The long-promised reckoning with the people of Aguilares was a well-planned operation which, with macabre humor, they dubbed "Operation Rutilio." The ostensible reason for the attack was a land occupation on an estate near El Paisnal, led by the People's Revolutionary Bloc. The year before, the owner of the land had rented it out; this year, she hadn't. The campesinos knew they would starve without the land; so they occupied it. Their crops were about to come up when the operation began.

When the army arrived at El Paisnal, they found that the squatters had already fled. One peasant described what happened next: "When they didn't find us at the occupation, they went on to search all the nearby *cantones*. They set many houses on fire after searching them and took loads of children and women prisoners, throwing them onto trucks. Nothing more is known of them . . ."[9]

From El Paisnal, the soldiers marched on to Aguilares with tanks and armored cars. One witness told about it: "On Thursday, at five in the morning, the town of Aguilares was completely full of *guardias*, national police and soldiers. At

this time they machine-gunned the parish church of Aguilares where the priests were, three of them, the one from
Guazapa and two from Aguilares. At the parish church there
were also campesinos who had gone there to sleep that day.
The sacristan and other campesinos, when they noticed that
soldiers were machine-gunning the church, went up into the
bell tower. So the *guardias* from below with a G-3 and machine
guns shot at the bell tower, killing the sacristan and another
campesino." The witness added, "They spent all day Thursday searching the town, house to house, and beating and
carrying off all the people who had Rutilio Grande's picture.
Then on Saturday, the *guardias* had the nerve to go out with
their loudspeakers telling the people not to be afraid . . ."[10]

How many died is uncertain. The army buried the bodies
and did not allow families to go to the burials. According to
one peasant: "At around 2:30 in the afternoon, you could
see that one army squadron was just digging graves and
another was just bringing in the bodies and burying them."
People in Aguilares said that fifty people had been killed and
the whereabouts of hundreds was unknown. Three hundred
villagers huddled in the jails while Aguilares was occupied
for a month.

That summer, a flyer circulated through the plush
neighborhoods of the capital, San Benito and Escalón: "Be
a Patriot. Kill a Priest." Then in July, a threat was delivered
to the entire Jesuit community in El Salvador—thirty-three
men in all. Signed by the White Warriors Union, the message
read as follows:

> All Jesuits without exception must leave the country
> forever within thirty days. . . . If your order is not
> obeyed within the indicated time, the immediate and
> systematic execution of those Jesuits who remain in
> the country will proceed until we have finished with
> all of them.[11]

From Washington, a Mixed Message

At the Jesuit residence house in San Salvador on July
22, the clock ticked the deadline day away. Outside, the Na-

tional Police sat on their motorcycles, their Uzi sub-machine guns at the ready. The National Police had left behind their Mr. Hyde personalities and now their alter-egos sat guarding the Jesuits. The sunlight bounced from the mirrored surface of their glasses. Watching the scene, one smiled ruefully. The White Warriors Union would not attack. Impossible. For they were sitting there in the sunlight, on motorcycles, in uniform.

General Carlos Humberto Romero had already concluded, barely three weeks into his term, that killing priests had its price. The international outcry from church and human rights organizations around the world was deafening. Archbishop Romero, breaking with tradition, had refused to attend the inaugural ceremonies. And Washington—El Salvador's steadfast ally of eighty years—was exerting new pressures.

Jimmy Carter came to the White House intent on burying the memory of Watergate and Vietnam. His campaign promises to bring morality into the field of foreign affairs drew sincere young reformers to State Department posts. There they tilted against traditional diplomats whose whole professional experience taught them that human rights and its moral imperatives had nothing to do with diplomacy and even less with power politics.

But in 1977, El Salvador was still among the safe places to grandstand about human rights. Few people knew where it was; few people cared. It had no strategic raw materials, no oil, no U.S. bases. The amount of U.S. investment was negligible compared to other countries in the hemisphere. Its new president was no favorite in Washington, having come to power over the crushed bones of the agrarian reform supported by the United States. So for a time, the State Department moralists won out.

Jimmy Carter conveyed the new U.S. attitude on human rights to General Romero by delaying the naming of a new ambassador, and by sending Patricia Derian, head of the human rights division at the State Department, to investigate the situation first hand. Since Molina had refused U.S. military assistance, however, the administration's trump card was economic aid. In July 1977 Washington withheld its approval of a $90 million Inter-American Development Bank loan for a major dam project in El Salvador, pending improvement in the country's record on human rights.

The oligarchy, meanwhile, was adamantly demanding stronger measures against popular unrest. "Whenever the peasants make the least demand," a conservative lawyer told the *New York Times,* "people begin talking about 1932 again. So the reaction is always to put down the peasants before they get out of control. The discussion among the rich families now is whether 20,000 or 50,000 or 100,000 peasants should be killed to restore peace."[12]

General Romero was caught in the middle. Worried about the state of the economy, and the potential impact of a U.S. decision to hold back on loans, he opted first for a conciliatory approach. He announced that political exiles could return; that the status of political prisoners (for the first time not denying their existence) would be studied. And he called for a "dialogue with different sectors that make up our society," a reference to U.S. pleas to make peace with the moderate opposition, and the Christian Democrats in particular.

Even as Romero talked about the need for dialogue, however, the killings in the countryside continued. In August, Felipe de Jesús Chacón was arrested by the National Guard in the northern province of Chalatenango. "Don Chus" was a Delegate of the Word, an organizer of the base communities in Chalatenango. His son, Juancito, was a member of the People's Revolutionary Bloc—later to be its secretary general. On August 27, 1977, Don Chus' body was found, drawn and quartered, being eaten by dogs. "They cut the scalp from his head and stripped the flesh from his face," said eyewitnesses at the scene.[13]

Archbishop Oscar Romero traveled to the northern village to say mass in the chapel where Don Chus had led so many meetings of the local base community. "These days," the archbishop said, "I have to walk the roads gathering up dead friends, listening to widows and orphans and trying to spread hope."[14]

But hope was dimmed when Washington began to ease its pressures on the Romero government. It was clear that the repression and terror that wracked the country prior to

Romero's inauguration had not subsided. The state of siege declared after the Monday massacre was still in effect and the repression simply had receded deep into the countryside where General Romero hoped it would escape world attention. But it was equally clear to Washington that the popular organizations were growing; that the guerrillas were continuing their reprisals against members of the government, the oligarchy and the National Guard. Debates in the State Department grew heated over how hard to push the new regime toward "a democratic opening"; and how to respond to the general's small concessions. Perhaps human rights were a luxury that El Salvador could not afford.

When General Romero lifted the eight-month state of siege in October 1977, the Carter administration responded immediately by approving the stalled $90 million loan and by naming a new ambassador, Frank J. Devine, with little to recommend him as a strong advocate of reform. Patricia Derian, head of the State Department's human rights division, voiced strong objections to these moves.[15] But Washington and El Salvador were closing ranks.

Legalizing Repression

His relations with Washington now on the mend, General Romero could turn his attention to the demands of the right. The popular organizations would have to be crushed—but world opinion was still an obstacle, and it would have to be done within the framework of the law.

In November 1977 El Salvador's Legislative Assembly, firmly controlled by the governing party, passed the Law for the Defense and Guarantee of Public Order (*Ley de Orden*). It was a classic sedition law, outlawing all criticism of the government and placing severe restrictions on free association, communication and the exchange of information. Not only those who advocated but those who admitted the existence of so-called social disorder were subject to criminal prosecution.

One particular focus of the law was to stop the increasing flow of information to human rights critics abroad. Since the attack on Aguilares, little packets of news clippings had been arriving in the offices of church and human rights activists around the world. Usually they were mailed from outside El Salvador, dumped by travelers into the first mailbox off the plane. The *Ley de Orden* contained special provisions, making it a crime to "spread at home or send abroad, by word of mouth, writing, or by any other means, false or tendentious news or information destined to disturb the constitutional legal order, the tranquility and security of the country, the economic or monetary system or the stability of its value or public effects." Those who fed such information to the mass media were singled out for special punishment.

The law was so draconian in its dismissal of basic human and civil rights that once again El Salvador became the focus of international protests. But the law's implications were somehow lost on the Carter administration. One day after the law was approved, the new ambassador, Frank J. Devine, addressed the American Chamber of Commerce: "We believe that any government has the full right and obligation to use all legal means at its disposal to combat terrorism."[16]

The Real Targets

Terrorism has a broad definition in El Salvador, and the *Ley de Orden* affected all sectors of the opposition from moderate to guerrilla. But the main focus of its attack were the popular organizations which by November 1977 had extended their base from the despairing countryside into the capital itself.

In 1977 the average *daily* wage in the urban manufacturing and service sector was $2.80. And despite constitutional guarantees, only three legal strikes had been tolerated since 1945.

Since its reemergence in 1976, the United People's Action Front (FAPU) had gained considerable influence within urban unions once controlled by the government, and even among those which traditionally had strong ties with the Communist Party. In the new industrial zone of San Bartolo, the People's Revolutionary Bloc (BPR) had started organizing new unions in the runaway garment and electrical plants, as well as in the sweat shops that dotted the capital.

In contrast to the Communist Party, which cautiously had tried to work within the limits of the official Labor Code, the strategy of FAPU and the BPR was to ignore the cumbersome procedures designed to smother the unions in red tape. They opted for direct action and called illegal strikes.

In November 1977, shortly before the *Ley de Orden* was decreed, workers from two striking factories, joined by campesinos from the FECCAS-UTC, occupied the Ministry of Labor, sitting down at the desks of the bureaucrats and blocking the exit of its employees. It was the first time in anyone's memory that people had dared to occupy a government office in order to press their demands. Negotiations with the striking workers were reopened as a result, but it was to be the last time. The *Ley de Orden*, enacted later that month, gave the government sufficient "legal" cover to dismiss even the most minimal demands and crush all protest. Not surprisingly, a profound radicalization of the urban workforce accompanied the escalating repression.

On February 23, 1978, FECCAS-UTC—the peasant union affiliated with the People's Revolutionary Bloc—presented a proposal to the government's Agricultural Development Bank. It called for lower interest on loans, lower prices on fertilizers and insecticides, and lower rents on the land. It noted that the cost of renting made any kind of return so minimal that it was impossible for the campesino to survive. The bank's president agreed to discuss the proposal with the union's delegates, but on the appointed date, March 17, he refused to meet with them.

Four hundred farmworkers and peasants staged an impromptu march through the capital that day. The police opened fire, killing at least four persons and wounding over thirty. One group of peasants, who managed to flee the capital aboard a bus, was followed by an army helicopter. Again the police opened fire, and the peasants returned it. Five campesinos and one policeman died.[17]

All this was sanctioned by the Law for the Defense and Guarantee of Public Order. The peasants had failed to get a permit for their march through the streets.

"Socialism Will Take Away Your Cows"

Before the base communities, before the peasant union FECCAS, before ORDEN, there was everyday life and history. The López family will not talk to the Mejía family because many years ago—when, no one can say for sure—a Mejía got drunk and cut off the hand of a López. And then, there is Don Paco, the chief of the community—at least according to him and his followers. When he walks along the roadway one can see the handle of the automatic pistol protruding from his belt. Don Chepe, his rival, thinks Don Paco is a thief.

Now this history—and the poverty and rage it reveals—has taken a new expression. Don Chepe is a member of FECCAS; Don Paco, a member of ORDEN since he retired from the National Guard. Both are peasants. Both are poor. And one could say that it is only by accident that they followed different paths.

"I don't know anything about communism," one peasant union member said to a reporter. "I do know I am always hungry. I know my children cannot go to school because they have no clothes.

"When there are jobs in the harvest season we work from dawn to dusk for one and a half *colones* (60 cents) a day. I have no land of my own. I can't afford to rent any." When asked why he joined the base community in his parish and from there, the Christian Peasants Federation (FECCAS), his answer is typical of so many others: "Because we hope we can make the government listen."[18]

A member of ORDEN described his attempts to rise out of the humiliation born of poverty:

"I'll be frank that they didn't ask me or many of the other members if we wanted to belong to ORDEN. I don't know how they found my name, but the truth is that one day the departmental governor brought me the registration list and a membership card.

"We are well organized. I'm in charge of one of the bases. Each base has six members. In this region there are many bases. We have six sub-officers, and each sub-officer commands six bases. The sub-officers are in direct contact with the colonels and in indirect contact through them with the governor. In this department I calculate that we have 5,000 members, without exaggerating. . . .

"Even though you might not believe it, this card makes me a member. We can arrest anyone we want to, anyone who goes around putting strange ideas in the people's heads. Here in my *cantón* I feel like a little Romero. Here I am the Law."[19]

Some act as *orejas*, the ears, and keep track of who did what, with and to whom. Others are the *dedos*, the fingers, and pick out the government's "enemies." And whichever they are, they have a message: that socialism, communism and revolution are evil.

> "Socialism will take away your lands, your cows and your hens."
> "Under socialism, the government takes children away from their parents."
> "Under socialism, they kill old people once they get to the age of 60 and they burn the bodies; they don't bury them in the ground."
> "Under socialism work is slavery and there is no freedom."
> "The revolutionaries and the communists sell out the fatherland; they aren't true nationalists."[20]

Under General Carlos Humberto Romero, ORDEN was used more effectively and more frequently than ever before. It grew to a force estimated at between 50,000 and 100,000, providing a mass base for the ruling PCN and a cover for the killings in the countryside. General Romero consistently defended ORDEN as a "civic association" created to defend El Salvador's democratic institutions.

On Easter week, March 1978, FECCAS and ORDEN came to blows in the town of San Pedro Perulapan, a BPR stronghold twenty-five miles from the capital. Armed men surrounded the chapel where a meeting of the base community was being held. Tránsito Vásquez, a member of FECCAS, was taken away. He was found the next morning, his head hanging from the branch of a tree. It appeared to be looking toward its body, which lay on the ground below.

Skirmishes continued for the next few days between members of FECCAS and ORDEN, peasants from the same village. Then the army joined the attack, launching a "search and destroy" mission in all areas where FECCAS was active. Thousands fled, whether to safety or death no one knew.

On April 11 Amnesty International sent General Romero a letter "expressing concern" at the reports of detentions, killings and torture during the military operation at San Pedro Perulapan, while the BPR denounced the regime's genocide. Yet the Carter administration remained silent. It was still on record as saying that conditions had improved in El Salvador, still sending $10 million worth of economic aid. Ambassador Frank Devine defensively praised "quiet diplomacy," a term not generally associated with the Carter years but nonetheless apt for describing its policies in the spring of 1978.[21] "I feel greatly disappointed," said the archbishop of San Salvador, "because we had hoped that U.S. policy on human rights would be more sincere."[22]

Terrorism or Revolutionary Violence?

The National Palace in Managua, Nicaragua is about 350 miles from El Salvador's capital. On August 22, 1978, this overbearing, becolumned building was occupied by the Sandinista National Liberation Front (FSLN), with scores of officials and legislators held hostage inside. The daring occupation lasted two days. At the end, red and black bandanas covering their faces, the Sandinista men and women were driven in a bus to the airport and flown to Panama, their demands for the liberation of hundreds of political prisoners and a sizeable ransom met.

In September, the FSLN took several towns: Estelí, León, Chinandega and Masaya. Somoza responded to what by then was a popular insurrection by sending in the air force and leveling much of Estelí. His National Guard killed all who were remotely suspicious—especially teenaged boys and girls. The insurrection was temporarily quelled, but the pillars of repression in Central America had begun to crack.

To take up arms, to use violence—these are difficult,

painful decisions for those who hope to end oppression and create a more just society. To die and to kill are ultimate questions.

Yet societies do exist so repressive, so exploitative, so unjust that the right to life itself is at stake, and the defense of one's life and the life of the community justifies the use of violence to end violence.

In El Salvador, Archbishop Romero consistently condemned all violence, no matter what its origin. But he made a clear distinction between the original violence—the "institutionalized violence" of the state, the economic system, the National Guard and ORDEN—and the responsive violence of the left. As Jon Sobrino, a Jesuit priest and close friend of the archbishop explained, "He did not judge sin from a hypothetical center, but from the point of view of the oppressed . . . . He avoided denouncing everything and everyone equally, such that no one would feel under attack . . . . He denounced the kidnappings and assassinations of innocent people. But he made clear that a massacre, or the bombing of a civilian population is not the same as burning buses; profaning a church is not the same as occupying a church."[23]

The right to "alter and abolish" an oppressive government is a fundamental right of the modern era, born with the nation state and affirmed in the blood of the English, French and American revolutions. The critical question is when is a government so oppressive that the resort to violence is morally justified and politically sound.

In the early seventies, debate within the Salvadorean left focused on the merits of the electoral way over armed struggle. But as elections grew more fraudulent, the armed struggle seemed to many both necessary and justifiable. Still, recent history in Latin America, most notably the death of Che Guevara, brought the lesson that taking up arms could isolate the left from the people at large. For those whose liberation was at stake, the guerrillas could become, at best, a nuisance or, at worst, a lightning rod to attract indiscriminate repression. Essential to the armed struggle, strategists said, was the bond between the guerrillas and the people.

In 1980 Salvador Cayetano Carpio of the Popular Liberation Forces (FPL) reflected on El Salvador's guerrilla movement of the early 1970s: "If we had to begin with guerrilla warfare, it was a passing stage, part of an overall plan that conceived the people as mastering all means and forms of struggle"—from the struggle for immediate, basic demands to military combat. "That conception," he continued, "took us far away from the idea that the guerrilla force on its own can make a revolution, that the guerrilla force isolated from the people replaces the people in their prime task of carrying out their own transformation."[24]

Beginning in 1975, the popular organizations gave ordinary campesinos, workers, students and church people the unusual chance to participate in changing their lives and a new experience of community. The thousands who shared this novel adventure in democracy, however, were protected by the many fewer with guns who were prepared to teach the oligarchy and the armed forces that repression had a price.

The slaying of hated ORDEN members in the countryside, attacks on a National Guardsman who intimidated a FECCAS member and the kidnapping of oligarchs and foreign businessmen were a response to the repression of the popular organizations and its members. Some called it terrorism; others feared that it would bring more repression. Others saw these acts as justified revenge for the massacres of unarmed workers and peasants—a form of both retribution and deterrence.

By 1978 kidnappings were commonplace in San Salvador. The most sensational were the work of the Armed Forces of National Resistance (FARN), which kidnapped several foreign businessmen in succession, raising cash by ransom for the political struggle and weapons, and explaining their demands through paid ads in Central American newspapers and even the *New York Times*. The kidnappings would continue, said the FARN, until the government restored democratic rights. Government officials and local oligarchs began packing their families off to Miami and hiring bodyguards for personal protection, as they too became kidnapping targets of the guerrillas.

To the factory worker and hungry campesino, the businessman in the wealthy suburb of San Benito was, in the best of times, an abstraction. Occasionally as his Mercedes passed through the factory gates or disappeared in a cloud of dust on the dirt road to his *finca,* he was real. As real as the National Guardsman whose inquiry on a lonely road could lead to a jail cell or worse. Each was a symbol of authority, sustaining his rule through an image of invincibility, acts of charity and guns. The armed struggle scratched at the veil of invincibility; the repression neutralized their charity. And they were left with their guns.

What did it matter if businessmen and soldiers were kidnapped and killed? What had they ever done for us?

In November 1978 the dilemma of revolutionary violence struck the Church. A young priest, Ernesto ("Neto") Barrera, was killed in a shoot-out with the National Guard. "Neto" had been active in the slum communities of San Salvador. Later he was assigned to St. Sebastian's church in Ciudad Delgado, a working class barrio in the capital. After the shoot-out the government claimed that Barrera was "an important guerrilla leader," a member of the FPL.

The lives and deaths of Rutilio Grande, Father Navarro and other priests already had caused deep divisions within the Church as to its proper role in society and politics. What if Ernesto Barrera *were* a guerrilla? A reaction from Archbishop Romero was expected in his sermon the Sunday after Barrera's death.

"When we think of terror and terrorism we also think of the terrorism of those who wear this country's army uniform," the archbishop began to the applause of three thousand parishioners. "This terrorism is also horrific and murderous." Then the archbishop went on to question the veracity of the government's claim. "We have no knowledge," he said, "that [Ernesto Barrera] participated in illegal political activities."[25]

But questioning the charges was not a way out. Unexpectedly, the archbishop received a long letter from the Popular Liberation Forces (FPL). It spoke of Christian participation in the armed struggle and told of Barrera's membership in their organization, his example, and the respect that the FPL had for his Christian faith. Father Barrera was a member of the FPL.

From the base communities of the Church where Barrera had worked came other responses:

"Whatever Neto's political choice was, we believe in him and are proud that he is a brother in faith. We consider his witness of the Gospel as exemplary. Moved by faith, hope and love, he gave his life in God's name, for the people. He announced the Good News to the poor.

"We are involved in a violent situation; the only question is which side are you on?"[26]

1979: The Beginning of the End

As more people began to make choices, the lines of struggle became sharper and the two Romeros, the general and the archbishop, came to represent two poles of the conflict. Appropriately, both Romeros traveled to Mexico in January 1979, a month that set the pace for the year to come.

General Carlos Humberto Romero went to Mexico to secure a contract for Mexican oil and, more importantly, to erase the image of his government as an international outlaw. The trip was a disaster on both counts: the oil agreement was tentative at best, and his hosts were less than effusive in receiving the tarnished dictator as their guest. But the damning blow came when a report on human rights in El Salvador was leaked to the press.

The report—which contained the results of an investigation by the Human Rights Commission of the Organization of American States—had been one year in the making. The OAS Commission had visited El Salvador in January 1978, at the invitation of an overly confident president. General Romero took great care to camouflage his apparatus of repression, hiding the evidence of years of torture as best he could. But the commission managed a peek beneath the veil of secrecy and was shocked by what it saw.

Commission members met with families of the disappeared and victims of the repression. Others had done that before, only to have these testimonies dismissed by the government as biased lies. But one night—their last night in the capital—the Commission members received word that they could meet with someone who had been in one of the oft-mentioned, but never proven, clandestine jails at the National Guard headquarters. The ex-prisoner told them how to find the secret cells.

On the pretense of not having completed their investigations, the group returned to *Guardia* headquarters unannounced. As they were led through the winding corridors of that bleak, gray building, one of them turned suddenly, following the instructions of their secret informant. "Where does this door lead to?" he asked as he entered and the others followed.

There they found the room which had been described by their informant as the interrogation chamber. On a table was a variety of electrical apparatus, which, as their report would later state, "could have been used to apply electric shocks." There was a two-way mirror in the rear. Then they walked down a passageway where, witnesses told them, victims of torture were tied to bedsprings. There were the bedsprings. They were stacked up against a door. And behind the door were the secret cells, exactly as described. One of them was one meter wide, one meter high and one meter deep. The walls were covered with cockroaches. Using a flashlight they read, as they were told they would, the names of people who had inhabited that dismal place: *Lil Milagro Ramírez. Aquí estuvo Carlos Madriz*—here lived Carlos Madriz.[27]

General Romero was bombarded at a press conference in Mexico City with questions about the report. In addition to revealing the secret cells, it condemned ORDEN and the security forces, and reserved its harshest words for the Law of Public Order. Romero would repeal the law one month later, but the damage to his image abroad, and to his relations with Washington in particular, was irreparable.

That same month of January, Archbishop Romero joined the bishops of Latin America at Puebla, Mexico, convened to take stock and chart a direction for the future work of the Church. The new pope's presence underlined the importance of the meeting for a Church that had been deeply divided by the radicalized course set in Medellín three years before.

The Salvadorean Church was no exception. Bishop Aparicio, president of El Salvador's National Conference of Bishops, railed against "the malicious or misinterpreted theology of liberation which has become the theology of violence."[28] He and other conservatives within the Church managed to prevent the archbishop from leading the Salvadorean delegation to Puebla. But Archbishop Romero decided to attend nonetheless. On the eve of his departure, another priest and friend, Octaviano Ortiz, was killed by security forces. The archbishop left for Puebla saddened and stunned.

At Puebla, Archbishop Romero received the recognition and support he needed to strengthen his position within the Salvadorean Church and against a government intent on silencing his voice. Forty bishops signed a letter of solidarity with the archbishop, praising his faithfulness to the Gospel. And at a special gathering in his honor, one young man stepped forward from the crowd: "I was a Catholic and I am a Salvadorean. I left the Church years ago. You have made me proud to have been born a Catholic. To be a Salvadorean."[29]

Human Rights: A Lost Cause

In February 1979, one month after the devastating OAS report released in Mexico, the U.S. State Department presented its own human rights report to Congress. It ranked Nicaragua and El Salvador as "the most serious violators of individual freedoms in Latin America and the Caribbean."[30]

The fates of those two countries would be tightly linked in the year ahead, as the crisis in Central America forced Jimmy Carter to refine his commitment to human rights. It was an election year. The Shah of Iran had just fallen from his throne. And the loss of this trusted U.S. ally was being blamed on an overemphasis of human rights in Washington—at the expense of national defense. Jimmy Carter, critics charged, had "destabilized" Iran and abandoned the Shah in his hour of need.

Ironically, the administration's attitude toward human rights abuses in Iran had been noticeably lenient: to wit, Carter's embarrassing New Year's toast to the Shah as a pillar of stability and the subject of his people's undivided love. "Crucial allies"—including Iran, the Philippines and South Korea—were spared the administration's wrath and coaxed through quiet channels, while the dictatorships of Latin America were publicly and persistently rebuked. Now even that would change.

By the time the Sandinistas launched their final offensive in the spring of 1979, Jimmy Carter—up for reelection—had broadened his definition of "national security" and, implicitly, tightened the conditions for taking a strong stand on human rights. Only if the alternative to a tyrant was politically acceptable to the United States would Washington risk withdrawing its support from a trusted ally. And if that alternative were to the left of acceptable in the eyes of the United States, then it was better to stay with the tyrant until a better alternative could be found or forged.

Nicaragua, then, was the first country to call Carter's bluff on human rights. No one in the administration tried to defend Somoza's desperate acts of barbarism during the popular insurrection of 1979. But the FSLN was not acceptable to Washington and the foremost objective of U.S. policy in that period was to prevent a Sandinista victory— even as Somoza's bombs continued to devastate the country.

Washington wanted a solution to the Nicaraguan conflict that would keep the structure of U.S. influence in place— that structure being Somoza's brutal National Guard. But Carter was not prepared to order a unilateral U.S. intervention in Nicaragua, and his hands were tied when the OAS refused to back his proposal for a multilateral "peace-keeping force." The OAS called it multilateral intervention, and called instead for Somoza's unconditional resignation.

Finally, in July 1979, Carter began to negotiate with a provisional junta established by the Sandinistas in Costa Rica. They struck a deal: Somoza would resign and Francisco Urcuyo, president of Nicaragua's Chamber of Deputies, would serve as a transition figure until a new government, including Sandinistas and "moderates," could be formed. The agreement also called for preservation of the National Guard, and its eventual merger with elements of the guerrilla army.

It had all the elements of a graceful defeat of Carter's original goals. But Urcuyo, in an unexpected trick of history, decided to renege on the agreement and stay on as president. The deal fell apart. And the Sandinistas marched triumphantly into Managua on July 19, 1979, with no strings attached.

Again, the accusations against Carter flew fast and furiously. The adminstration had "lost" another country. El Salvador would pay the price.

CHAPTER V

In Search of a Center

"We're next and we know it," said a Salvadorean businessman over drinks at the Sheraton Hotel. The pool is the largest in Central America, surrounded by lush bougainvillaea and lavender orchids; the tennis courts stretch endlessly; but the breathtaking view of El Salvador's volcanoes, imposing but said to be unthreatening, reminded him of something. The afternoon papers had carried pictures of triumphant rebel columns entering Managua, and Sandinista soldiers still in uniform, bathing irreverently in Somoza's marble tub.

Nicaragua had endured forty-five years of rule by one Somoza or another. El Salvador had no single tyrant, just seventeen military governments since 1932.

Unlike Nicaragua, where Somoza's greed had driven even the wealthy into the arms of the opposition, El Salvador's elite were still united in their resistance to change. But by the summer of 1979, foreign investors, always the first to jump ship, were closing their factories and moving elsewhere. Local businessmen and landowners were packing their families off to Miami or Guatemala City, while they dug in for a last-ditch stand against "communist aggression."

To the rest of the world, everything that had been happening in El Salvador over the past ten years had appeared, if at all, as one-paragraph column-fillers in the daily press: Priest Killed in El Salvador. Executive Kidnapped. Twenty Demonstrators Killed. But all that had changed in May 1979, when El Salvador made headlines on prime-time television.

Television is an extraordinary medium. For thirty seconds, a tiny country pops onto the screen and acquires an identity, however compressed and incomplete. On May 9, 1979, a CBS cameraman stood with his equipment in front of the Metropolitan Cathedral in San Salvador. He watched as 300 protestors sang songs on the cathedral steps decked with red and yellow flowers, the colors of the People's Revolutionary Bloc. The protestors carried signs demanding the release of five BPR leaders, "disappeared" that week by the Romero government.

The protest became a story when two olive green trucks appeared in the square, depositing helmeted police armed with automatic rifles. They were joined by National Guardsmen. Seconds after their boots touched the pavement, they began firing and the television cameras rolled. Protestors near the top of the cathedral steps tried to crawl over one another to get inside. A body convulsed as a bullet hit. A young man rolled dying down the steps. And as the camera panned across the street, sharpshooters behind cars in the parking lot picked off protestors one by one.

It played as the lead story on Walter Cronkite: El Salvador, the place where they shoot peaceful demonstrators on church steps. Twenty-three people are dead.

The incident provoked the worst crisis yet for the Romero government. When the BPR leaders first disappeared, its members occupied the French and Costa Rican embassies to attract international attention. After the cathedral massacre, ten *Bloque* (BPR) members sat in at the Venezuelan embassy. Churches all over the country were occupied; FAPU called a rally of support; and a Committee of Mothers of the Disappeared announced another protest.

The government released two of the BPR leaders, Facundo Guardado and José Ricardo Mena, but nothing was heard of the other three. Most believed that the security forces had already killed them.

The occupations continued. At the Venezuelan embassy, a military cordon stood perpetual guard, while electricity, food and water were cut off to those inside. Late in the afternoon of May 23, BPR members organized a supply march to take food and drink to the occupiers. Led by women and children, they marched toward the embassy. Again the security forces opened fire. Fourteen people died.

Revenge came quickly for the thirty-seven killed in those two weeks. The Popular Liberation Forces (FPL) killed Romero's minister of education, Carlos Herrera Rebollo, in an ambush. The government declared a thirty-day state of siege and called for a "national dialogue," inviting none of the opposition parties or popular organizations to participate.

El Salvador had left the back pages: by summer it was the "next Nicaragua" on the evening news and journalists compared the situation to the Sandinista insurrection of September 1978. Alan Riding, Central American correspondent for the *New York Times,* warned that "increasingly, the Carter administration faces a problem similar to that posed by Nicaragua last year; it either awaits the outcome of the approaching confrontation of the extreme left and right, or it intervenes more openly in an effort to force a centrist solution."[1]

The common wisdom among liberals in Washington was that Jimmy Carter had intervened too late in Nicaragua, hanging on too long to Somoza, trying to wrest reforms, and losing the opportunity to negotiate with moderates and preempt a Sandinista triumph. Now the State Department was abuzz with plans to avoid "another Nicaragua" by saving El Salvador. William Bowdler, a negotiator and architect of plans ranging from the capture of Che in Bolivia to negotiations with the Sandinistas, flew to El Salvador as special envoy to see what could be done. Viron P. Vaky, assistant secretary of state for inter-American affairs, went to talk some sense into General Romero.

Romero, whose election in 1977 had prompted two congressional investigations, now had to listen to more American complaints. There were "*problemitas*" with his rule, Vaky told him. The Law of Public Order had become a rallying cry against his government, while doing little to crush the opposition. His moves against the unions had backfired into a rising wave of strikes; the security forces had proved incapable of containing the flourishing guerrilla groups; and the hundreds of students and peasants, young lawyers and teachers, union leaders and activists who had "disappeared" in the course of his rule were ghosts coming back to haunt him. In short, his presidency was a disaster. Could the president, the envoy delicately asked, consider moving forward the date of the next presidential elections from 1982 to next year? No, General Romero replied with some fervor, he could not.

In early September, Vaky appeared before Congress to lay out a new doctrine about what kind of governments the United States would encourage in Central America.[2] They were governments respectful of human rights, committed to economic and social reform and not a threat to U.S. interests. Vaky's words were clearly an ultimatum to General Romero and, implicitly, guidelines for anyone interested in replacing him.

The Vaky doctrine had a certain realism about it. It acknowledged that the upheavals in El Salvador and Central America were the product of domestic inequalities and the abuse of elementary human rights. There were no foreign masters pulling the strings. But Washington's realism went only as far as the options it was prepared to contemplate, and these were very limited by the fall of 1979. In El Salvador, years of fraud and exile and growing cynicism had sapped the opposition parties of their dynamism and popular base. The vacuum had been filled by the audacious tactics of the popular organizations. By all accounts, they were the most powerful force in opposition to Romero's rule, but Washington refused to contemplate a role for them. The popular organizations talked openly of socialism; they were led by ordinary workers and campesinos, market women and teachers. All of Washington's efforts were directed toward heading them off and finding a more suitable successor to military rule. But time was running out.

In September 1979 every inch of every wall in downtown San Salvador was covered with graffiti proclaiming 1980 as the year of El Salvador's liberation. Demonstrations against Romero took place almost daily: *Si Nicaragua venció, El Salvador vencerá,* was the demonstrators' chant. If Nicaragua triumphed, El Salvador will triumph too. The People's Leagues occupied the labor ministry demanding the release of 500 political prisoners; FAPU led wildcat strikes and work stoppages in factories across the country; the BPR held its national congress in a movie theater in downtown San Salvador. And guerrillas attacked the National Palace in the most daring action yet.

In September, General Romero told Alan Riding: "Of course everything is possible, but I definitely believe that the armed forces have the capacity to contain a general insurrection in the country."[3] But he was taking no chances. His brother had been killed in a guerrilla ambush the week before. On September 11, Romero flew to Guatemala to meet with the Guatemalan and Honduran presidents to solicit support and, just in case, to make arrangements for a hasty getaway. His preparations were not premature.

The Conspirators

Young military officers, members of what was becoming known as the *juventud militar,* had been meeting secretly for several months, never more than a handful at a time. In September they came to seek the advice of Monseñor Romero, archbishop of San Salvador. Romero, while sympathetic to the left, was still seeking ways to avoid the loss of human life. So he listened to the young officers' plans for a coup, promising not to judge them beforehand.

The officers, mostly lieutenants, captains and colonels, were scared and worried and troubled. Scared of a revolutionary tide in which they felt they could drown; worried about the lack of alternatives open to them as career officers; troubled by their consciences which revolted against the bloody rule of a corrupt military apparatus at the service of a wealthy few. They wanted reforms, but not the kind of revolutionary upheaval they sensed in the streets. They believed, naively, that Monseñor Romero could use his rumored contacts with the left to convince them to give the coup a chance.

The young officers were not the only ones talking about the need for immediate change. For months, another group had been meeting, composed of progressive businessmen, moderate opposition parties, intellectuals from the Catholic University, centrist and leftist union leaders, and progressive Church members. The group had coalesced into something called the Popular Forum, and began the work of building a broad coalition to pressure for reform. As the impossibility of obtaining any concessions became apparent, this group also considered the possibility of a coup, and began seeking contacts with like-minded elements in the army.

In its efforts to "intervene more openly to force a centrist solution" to the crisis, the State Department was also an active force. Ambassador Frank J. Devine kept in close touch with the young military and the Popular Forum, as well as other representatives of El Salvador's moderate opposition. But U.S. officials did not feel entirely comfortable with any of these options. They thought the young military men were too young, too inexperienced in politics to walk the fine line between advocating reforms and abetting revolution. The Popular Forum had close ties with the popular organizations and could not be counted on to keep them at bay.

But another, more promising coup was also in the works, masterminded by mainstream army colonels who agreed that General Romero had gone too far. These officers were aware of the young officers' plans. And they waited.

The October Coup

The coup came quietly when it came, and as no surprise to anyone. The first announcement was broadcast to the world by the BBC on October 14, 1979, at 8 p.m. local time. "In the tiny Central American republic of El Salvador, it is reported that the country's president, General Carlos Humberto Romero, has been overthrown in a coup d'état by members of the Salvadorean armed forces." No further news or confirmation came out of El Salvador until the next day, when sporadic shooting at noon told the capital that a barracks rebellion was underway.

According to what can be pieced together from confused and often conflicting versions in both the media and private interviews, the young officers acted first and were joined in the uprising by one barracks after another. By 5:30 p.m. on October 15, General Romero and his top officers were on a plane to Guatemala, provided by that country's president. Power in El Salvador was up for grabs.

Militarily, the young officers had been clear and effective in their strategy to oust a dictator. But politically, they had only a vague notion of what should follow. They detested the oligarchy's greed and the corruption of the army high command. They saw clearly the need for reforms, but they feared the power of the popular organizations. And they wanted, above all, to refurbish and preserve the integrity of the military institution.

So when the older army colonels, who had lagged behind in preparations for a coup, demanded a place in the new order of things, the young officers saw no need for a confrontation with their elders. They perceived no conflict of interest or purpose: their elders spoke as they did of the need for reforms and a cleansing of the national conscience. And besides, the young officers' ingrained respect for hierarchy remained intact, even as they ousted their commanding general.

Negotiations between the two groups led to an agreement to eliminate those officers close to the ousted dictator and to a joint proclamation, read over the radio on October 15, by Colonels Majano and Gutiérrez, chosen by their respective factions to form the core of a new revolutionary junta.

The first proclamation of the "15th of October Movement" was a curiously grim statement:

In light of the anarchic situation [created] by the activities of extremist elements, which the [Romero] government proved incapable to control . . . the

armed forces will direct the country's destinies for
a prudent length of time in order to: first, lay the
bases and create the appropriate environment for
a true and dynamic democracy; and second, conduct
free elections which reflect the will of all Salvadoreans.

We call on the extremist forces of both the left
and right to abandon violence and participate peacefully in the country's democratic process, respecting
the will of the majority which, we repeat, the army
will enforce.[4]

Reform or Revolution?

The two new leaders of the junta were as different as
the factions they were there to represent. Colonel Adolfo
Majano was 41 years old at the time of the coup but looked
much younger—an inquisitive mestizo face behind wide
glasses, a soft-spoken demeanor that at first seemed to indicate judicious reserve and later revealed itself as near-fatal
indecisiveness. He had received his military training in Mexico and was at different times close to that establishment and
to the effusive populist leader of Panama, Omar Torrijos.
His political sympathies lay closest to the moderate social
democrats, but he was no politician. By his own admission,
Majano did not emerge as a leader of the young officers'
faction until the coup was underway. He was judged a more
acceptable nominee to the new junta than some of the more
radical colonels, whose presence might alarm the U.S. embassy.

Colonel Jaime Abdul Gutiérrez suffers from a bleeding
ulcer, which perhaps explains his often dour disposition. Or
perhaps it is his bureaucratic past as an army administrator
that gives his speech its flatness, its lack of commanding tone.
Gutiérrez came to the junta as a compromise candidate of
the older colonels, since their other nominees had raised
eyebrows among the military youth: Colonels Guillermo
García and Vides Casanova were late-coming critics of Romero's rule, and they were known to hold conservative views

on social reform. Colonel Gutiérrez, at least, had the merit of being bland.[5]

These were the first signs of tensions between the young officers and their elders, but the uneasy allies went on to negotiate appointments to three civilian slots on the new junta—a necessary cosmetic to cover the tarnished image of the military establishment that had served the oligarchy so dutifully for nearly fifty years. Ambassador Frank Devine could not have been more pleased. Struggling for an air of detached objectivity, he said, "[the new junta] creates a much more acceptable international symbol *for us,* and to the extent [that] it offers some hope of easing the country's problems, I wish it well."[6] Devine added that if the new junta improved the human rights record and requested economic and military assistance, the request would be considered favorably.

Many people in El Salvador were dubious that an entrenched oligarchy and its military allies could be peacefully deposed at the flick of a proclamation. The new Revolutionary Junta promised land reform. Governments had promised that before, only to be toppled or brought to their senses before suffering that fate. Would the oligarchy now take the long view, put forth by Ambassador Devine in countless meetings with the Chamber of Commerce? Would they buy the line that reforms had to be swallowed now to avoid revolution later?

And how would the popular organizations, second only to the military as the country's largest and most organized force, react to the junta's promises? They had tasted their own collective power in the streets of September. They knew that credit for Romero's ouster belonged to their "disappeared" sons and daughters, to husbands and wives gunned down in demonstrations and priests slain on the way to mass. Would they now wait and see whether the new junta delivered on its promises, or would they try to wrest power for themselves?

Another unknown: How would the guerrillas—the political-military organizations of the left—react to this moment? They were primed for revolution, with underground rifle ranges in the center of the capital and a war chest estimated at between $70 and $150 million from ransom demands. Joaquín Villalobos, commander-in-chief of the People's Revolutionary Army (ERP), conveyed their skepticism: "Our history is full of military coups led by people who at first adopt the platform of the people before allowing things to go back to the way they have always been."[7]

The coup had not taken any of the militant opposition groups by surprise, but for several days they vacillated in working out their own positions and characterizations of the coup. Some argued that the new junta should be given a chance to prove itself; others that it was a maneuver inspired by the United States to disorient the popular forces with talk of reform, while preparing the repression. Events would soon unify their views.

Weeks before the coup, members of the People's Revolutionary Bloc had occupied five factories in the capital to press their wage demands in absence of the right to strike. Such actions, under Romero's rule, typically resulted in beatings, arrests, and later, the disappearance of those presumed to be the ringleaders. But the October coup was supposed to change all that.

It didn't. On the morning of October 16, one day after Romero's hasty departure, combined security forces and army troops stormed the factories. They detained seventy-eight people, some of whom were tortured—eighteen were killed.[8] Adolfo Majano, the colonel with a conscience, went around to police headquarters and ordered the release of those detained. Majano's conscience would bother him a lot in the days and months to come as he tried to undo the dirty work of his fellow officers. But he could never bring the corpses back to life.

At 6 a.m. the following day, the army attacked a populous suburb of the capital, held by the People's Revolutionary Army, encircled it with tanks, strafed it from helicopters, and according to a hospital check done that afternoon, left behind twenty-four dead.

Amnesty International issued a report on the incidents: "Security forces acted with the same brutality as those under Romero. . . . Within a week, the new government was held responsible for more than 100 killings of demonstrators and

striking workers who had been occupying farms and factories."[9] It was an inauspicious beginning for the new regime.

The Thinking Man's Coup

The next day, October 18, Colonels Majano and Gutiérrez presented the civilian members of the five-man junta
to the nation at a well-attended press conference in the Casa
Presidencial. Román Mayorga Quiróz, the 37-year old rector
of the Jesuit-run university, and Guillermo Ungo, 48, the
soft-spoken intellectual who headed El Salvador's social democratic party (MNR), would constitute a strong progressive
presence on the junta. Mario Andino, 43, an engineer and
manager of the Phelps-Dodge subsidiary, was brought in as
a representative of the private sector, and at the insistence
of the United States.

The press conference went well enough: the new junta
promised to strengthen ties with revolutionary Nicaragua
and reestablish relations with Cuba. It pledged to try the
members of the Romero regime for corruption and brutality
and to hold free elections in February 1981. Mayorga promised that "we will not allow the military insurrection to become just another coup d'etat"[10].... And Ungo, in an
interview many months later, would recall that day, and his
decision to join the new junta, as "a risk that had to be taken.
It was the last possibility for peaceful change."[11]

The cabinet was named next. It was an impressive group,
worthy of what one wit called "the thinking man's coup."
Salvador Samayoa, a 29-year old philosophy professor, was
minister of education; Héctor Dada, an economist and member of the Christian Democratic Party, headed the Foreign
Ministry; Rubén Zamora, also a Christian Democrat and former political prisoner, handled the Ministry of the Presidency; and Mario, his brother, was attorney general.

Enrique Alvarez Córdova, a millionaire dairy farmer,
had served as minister of agriculture to presidents Rivera
and Molina, only to resign in frustration at their failure to
enact reforms. Now he agreed to assume that post once again,

in a cabinet committed to land reform as a top priority; he was denounced by the oligarchy as a traitor to his class.

Alone on the left, the Communist Party decided to support the new government, "because we believe it is going to comply with its promises and open the possibility of democratizing the country."[12] The party contributed Dr. Gabriel Gallegos to the cabinet as minister of labor.

Seated beside these men of impeccable democratic credentials was Colonel José Guillermo García, neatly pressed and neatly shaven—the new minister of defense. García, 46 years old, was a soldier by training and a schemer by instinct. He had aspired to the presidency in 1977, only to lose the PCN nomination to General Romero. More recently, his nomination to a seat on the new junta had been blocked by the military youth. But García was not disheartened. The powerful Defense portfolio gave him jurisdiction over all security forces and the army. Colonel Gutiérrez admired him as a mentor.

García would show remarkable staying power in the months to come as the junta and cabinet went through several permutations. But he was a man accustomed to power. As General Romero's chief of communications at ANTEL (the National Telecommunications Agency), he was nominally in charge of running telephones and telegraphs, telex and radio and television circuits. In practice this post had always been headquarters for the clandestine intelligence services. Local speculation was that García's enormous power and survival capacity came, like J. Edgar Hoover's, from the fact that he had the goods on *everyone*.

Together with García came three significant new appointments that did little to reassure skeptics that the old functions of the security forces would change with the new regime. Colonel Reynaldo López Nuila, a man with a murderer's fame and a face to match, was named to head the National Police; and Eugenio Vides Casanova, "old green eyes," took command of the National Guard. Colonel Francisco Moran headed the Treasury Police, an archaic corps whose initial functions had been to supervise rural taxation, but which gradually had evolved into the most notorious of the country's torture squads, custodians of the "disappeared."

With the junta and cabinet now in place, it was not long before the popular organizations began to test the government's commitment to change. In late October, the United People's Action Front (FAPU), the People's Revolutionary Bloc (BPR) and the People's Leagues (LP-28) occupied the Metropolitan Cathedral, the labor and education ministries, forty radio stations and several coffee *fincas*. They demanded higher wages, lower prices for consumer goods, land reform, public trials of Romero's officers and an answer to the whereabouts of the "disappeared."

Archbishop Romero, who castigated the left for its intransigence, nevertheless expressed the doubts of many: "We recognize the junta's good will," he said. "But this government can only deserve the confidence and collaboration of the people when it shows that its beautiful promises are not dead letters, but rather real hope that a new era has begun for our country."[13]

But this unsteady alliance of progressives and hardliners did not deliver on its promises. The government's credibility dropped when a FAPU demonstration was fired upon by the army and police. It plummeted when security forces opened fire on a march staged by the People's Leagues, killing at least eighty-six. And it would continue to fall in the eyes of broad sectors of the population, including the Church, as they demanded answers to the "mystery" of the disappeared.

The Clandestine Jails

It was a national nightmare under Romero and those before him, the practice of disappearing suspected opponents of every political persuasion into filthy, night-black cells where the victims were held naked and shackled, fed a daily ration of two tortillas and moldy beans, and systematically tortured.

Lil Milagro Ramírez was a teacher and former member of the Christian Democratic youth movement, an enthusiastic and driving young woman with a pixie's smile. She was also a member of the national leadership of the National Resistance (RN). On November 26, 1976, she was "disappeared" by the security forces and held captive together with five other guerrilla activists. She shared a cell with Ana Guadalupe Martínez, a member of the rival People's Revolutionary Army, who later described the nightmare of their imprisonment in a book called *El Salvador's Clandestine Jails*.[14]

On January 27, 1977, the ERP kidnapped a wealthy industrialist and rancher, and in exchange for his release demanded the liberation of Ana Guadalupe and another ERP guerrilla held in an adjoining cell. Ana Guadalupe recalled that on the day of her release a guard came to take her away, without explaining why. "Lend me your shoes," she asked Lil Milagro, who still had a pair, and Lil Milagro did. They never saw each other again.

Someone else, who subsequently escaped from the clandestine cells, saw Lil Milagro some time before the coup. Her hair had grown down to her heels, her face was a skull, her health had been broken by starvation, beatings, repeated rape and a brutal abortion. She was unbent in her political convictions. According to the whispered gossip and rumor that sometimes make their way out of the military barracks, Lil Milagro and other survivors of the years of torture in the secret jails were assassinated the day after the coup by their jailors, to prevent any word of the obscene reality of those dungeons leaking to the outside world.

On October 19 the brand new junta held a public meeting with the Committee of Mothers of the Disappeared. It was a pathetic scene, not so much because of the suffering engraved in the faces of those poorly dressed women allowed entry for the first time into the Casa Presidencial, but because of the embarrassing demonstration of impotence on the part of the country's nominal leaders. Five days had passed since a decree ordering the release of all political prisoners had been issued. No prisoners had appeared.

After the mothers indignantly refused to look for their children personally in the government dungeons ("We know we won't find them there," said one. "It's up to the government to explain where they are.") Roman Mayorga, the former university rector, spoke: "I'm overwhelmed by the problem. I have no idea where your children are. I pray they are still alive. I just don't know."[15] He buried his face in his hands.

The Erosion of Power

December 1979 was an extraordinary month. Every day brought another demonstration by the popular organizations, swollen in size by the sense that finally, with or without the junta, things were about to change. Lottery vendors, men and women who never before had marched, much less addressed a crowd, held a rally in the capital to demand benches and toilets in the National Lottery Office. Three thousand workers occupied a cotton mill demanding higher wages and the takeovers spread throughout the countryside, as the oligarchs watched with growing alarm and made their own preparations.

The junta took steps to placate the demands of the popular organizations. They ordered a 30 percent increase in the minimum wage for fieldworkers to $4.50 a day, and began discussing plans for an agrarian reform. But each step provoked an outcry from the right. "Ominous unconstitutional agrarian reform decrees are being prepared by the Communist infiltrators," read an unsigned newspaper ad. "The threat of plunder envelops us. Don't await the Communist yoke passively. Unite farmers, so that together we will triumph."[16] The oligarchy hadn't changed. They still saw reforms as tantamount to revolution.

But there was also growing evidence that resistance to reform came from within the government itself, as each long-awaited move to halt the brutalities of the past seemed to stop half way and hang there in limbo. A Special Commission of Inquiry was created by the junta to investigate the whereabouts of the disappeared. Several weeks later it announced that all the names on a list of 276 persons should be presumed to have died in the custody of security forces. No legal steps were taken against those responsible for the torture and murder.[17]

Back in November the junta had issued a decree outlawing ORDEN and revealed documents that proved it had been run by a special staff of forty within the Casa Presidencial. But by December it was obvious that ORDEN had been reborn as the Broad National Front. It continued to operate hand-in-glove with the security forces and the army, and no arms were confiscated from the tens of thousands of ORDEN members who continued to terrorize the *campo*.

Ungo, Mayorga and other progressives in the government were despondent as "the last chance for peaceful change" vanished before their eyes. The military were backing away from their commitment to reform; the power of Colonels García, Gutiérrez and Vides Casanova had eclipsed the civilians' presence on the junta. And Ungo and Mayorga realized that the only counterweight to the power of the oligarchy and the army were the popular organizations. Yet they were powerless to implement reforms, or to stop the repression that was driving their only potential allies down the road to insurrection.

Even the young military officers who initiated the October coup were now far removed from power, Majano's seat on the junta notwithstanding. They had been too trusting, too naive in letting their military elders insert themselves into key positions.[18] In November they tried to set up an advisory board that would serve as an intermediary between the junta and the military hierarchy. Like a cat toying with a mouse, Colonel Gutiérrez played with their demands: "There are jealousies among some of the younger officers. [They] feel they gave a boost to this government and it is natural they should want to continue developing it. They want an advisory board, which is fine. But we will have to negotiate its powers. A board would be acceptable only insofar as its powers are limited to military affairs."[19]

By all accounts, the U.S. embassy played an intermediary role in this power struggle between the progressive and hardline factions in the government, leaning heavily toward its older, more familiar allies in the army. In November 1979, when President Carter sent a Defense Survey Team to El Salvador to assess the situation, neither the embassy nor the military thought to inform Ungo or Mayorga of the delegation's visit.[20] Washington resumed military aid to El Salvador that same month and dispatched a Mobile Training Team to teach "riot control" to Salvadorean troops. The rationale, in the face of persistent reports of human rights abuses under the new regime, was that new equipment would go exclusively to the army, which was more "professional" than the security forces and less prone to excess. A special training course for Salvadorean troops at the U.S. School of the Americas in Panama included a three-week course called "The Human Rights Aspects of Internal Defense and Development."[21]

Looking Ahead

By the time of the Defense Survey Team's visit, the United States had concluded that a confrontation between the junta's civilians and the armed forces was inevitable. Once enchanted by Ungo and Mayorga's contribution to the junta's reformist image, U.S. officials began to deride them as "idealists" with little knowledge of or patience for the practicalities of power. The search for substitutes was already underway.

In November 1979 the embassy initiated a round of talks with Napoleón Duarte, the leader of the Christian Democrats, back from seven years in exile. Several of the party's younger members were already in the cabinet, but wheeler-dealer politicians of the old school, like Duarte and Julio Rey Prendes, San Salvador's mayor, had been left out of the October conspiracy. Now they sensed that the wind was changing in their direction.

When the emissaries from the State Department said it was going badly for the junta, that its members didn't seem to have what it takes to rule a country, that the party's help was needed, the Christian Democrats were ready with a set of conditions: they wanted the army to publicly commit itself to an agrarian reform and nationalization of the banks and export trade; and they demanded that the private sector be kept out of the junta.

Convincing the military to embrace the Christian Democrats was no easy task. They were not eager to share power with anyone, much less the party they had robbed of victory in 1972. But the United States held the purse strings that could save an ailing economy and finance the army's war against the left. García, Gutiérrez and the other colonels now fully in control of the government acknowledged the worth of civilian participation to soften the criticism of foreign governments and woo the U.S. Congress.

Still, the bargaining process was complex and lengthy. If the Christian Democrats came in, García, Vides Casanova and the sinister Nicolás Carranza, then vice-minister of defense, would have to stay. If the civilians got their agrarian reform, the military would have to be given free rein to crush the left as it best saw fit. Finally, in late December 1979, an arrangement was worked out.

Meanwhile, the left was developing its own response to unfolding events. Another series of talks were taking place among three revolutionary organizations. Their leaders, whose names meant nothing to the American public, were legends to most Salvadoreans. Salvador Cayetano Carpio, leader of the Popular Liberation Forces (FPL), and "Ernesto Jovel" of the Armed Forces of National Resistance (FARN), were founders of the armed opposition. They were also long-time rivals, who saw that the growth of the revolutionary movement now dictated the need for greater coordination.

They were joined at these meetings by Shafik Handal, secretary general of the Communist Party. The party had followed an electoral course since the mid-sixties, allied with the Christian Democrats and the MNR, and estranged from much of the left. After the electoral fraud of February 1977, the party began to contemplate the need for armed struggle, but Handal later explained that few concrete steps were taken: "Eleven years of legal struggle and electoral participation had left their mark. . . . Over 87 percent of the CPS membership in February 1977 had joined the party during that period and had been educated in that form of struggle."[22] Only in April 1979, at the party's Seventh Congress, did the Communist Party move toward forming an armed guerrilla force: "Our decision was a bit late," said Handal, "but still in time."

Of the major guerrilla organizations of the left, only the

People's Revolutionary Army (ERP) was absent from these meetings. The group had formed a separate party in 1976—the Party of the Salvadorean Revolution (PRS)—to counter the excessive "militarism" of its past. But there was great bitterness within the left over the ERP's execution of Roque Dalton in 1975. The wounds had still not healed.

Forced To Take Sides

On December 18, 1979, hundreds of Salvadorean army troops, supported by helicopter fire and armored tanks, attacked two haciendas and a slaughterhouse where members of the popular organizations were on strike. At least thirty-five people were killed and dozens more wounded.

The fresh wave of killings hastened discussions that were already underway among the leadership of the popular organizations. The nuances of line and ideological definition that sometimes threatened to paralyze the talks among the guerrilla groups seemed irrelevant to the members of these mass fronts, who were quick to sense how much stronger they would be if they could act in unison. The repression only furthered the trend toward consolidation and resolved the disagreements that once divided the popular organizations over what hopes to place on the junta. By late December, the battle lines were clearly drawn.

The government itself was not immune to the effects of the repression. On December 28 the justices of the Supreme Court, the heads of state agencies and eleven of the twelve cabinet ministers wrote a letter to the Permanent Council of the Armed Forces (COPEFA), a group set up to monitor the junta's program. The message was simply stated and focused on the role of Colonel Guillermo García: "The minister of defense and some of the regional commanders are exercising power against the postulates of the military youth movement."[23] It asked that a dialogue be opened between the government and COPEFA on the one hand and the popular organizations on the other.

On December 29 five government officials, including Salvador Samayoa, minister of education, and Enrique Alvarez Córdova, minister of agriculture, submitted their resignations. Their statement read in part: "We see now that this political project was, from the very beginning, a maneuver against the people. But we do not regret having participated in this government, having put all our efforts and skills toward a different outcome. But now that everything is clear, we would regret for the rest of our lives any further collaboration."[24]

The next move belonged to Guillermo Ungo and Román Mayorga. They presented their colleagues on the junta with an ultimatum: either García goes or we go. García stayed, and the two civilians resigned on January 3, 1980, along with nine more cabinet ministers and thirty-seven other high-ranking officials. The center had collapsed.

But in a matter of hours, the Christian Democrats, ready in the wings, announced that they were prepared to save the junta from itself. Rubén Zamora, a respected member of the party's left wing, had refused to add his resignation to the stack. As minister of the presidency, he spoke on the radio on January 4—explaining that the crisis was normal, that after so many years of misgovernment and cruelty, things could not change overnight. He read from the platform of the Christian Democratic Party, and announced that the army had agreed to work with them toward reforms. The illusion of a centrist junta, besieged by two extremes, was preserved. But Rubén Zamora would swallow the bitter pill of reality before long.

The Second Junta

Héctor Dada, small and unmistakably intellectual in appearance, until five days previously foreign minister of the Salvadorean government, sat in a smoke-filled room at the Christian Democratic Party headquarters and did his best to look like a Tammany Hall politician. Slapping his knee, he vigorously told reporters: "I'm no fool, I'm accepting a post on this junta because I know I'll have real power. We've talked this out with the military, they know if we walk out on them they're lost. They can't do without us, they'll have to keep their promises." Three days later, on January 9, 1980, he and another soft-spoken Christian Democrat, José Antonio Morales Ehrlich, and a nominal independent, Ramón Avalos Navarrete, took their oaths of office at the Casa Presidencial, smiling nervously for the television cameras. Colonels Majano and Gutiérrez were all that remained of the first junta, but their presence allowed the U.S. government to downplay the event as a "cabinet crisis," easily resolved.

No television crews were invited to cover another press conference earlier that morning. In a small dark room, with blaring radio music as background, a huddle of journalists sat in front of a table covered with red and black flags and a small assortment of weapons: hand grenades and Uzi submachine guns, M-16s and a couple of pistols. On the other side of this display sat some of the most wanted people in El Salvador, their faces prudently covered with improvised hoods.

In their amazement at such a gathering, the newspaper journalists initially found it hard to concentrate on what was being said: there was Salvador Cayetano Carpio behind his hood and the code name "Marcial," the legendary union organizer and former head of the Salvadorean Communist Party who broke with the party in 1970 to form the Popular Liberation Forces (FPL). There, amazingly, was "Ernesto Jovel," at age 24 the master planner of a spectacular series of kidnappings in 1978, formerly an organizer in a furniture factory and now leader of the Armed Forces of National Resistance (FARN). There was Shafik Handal, of the Communist Party, survivor of twenty-five years of persecution and frequent clandestinity, a man even his rivals recognized as "brilliant." "Fermán Cienfuegos" of the FARN was there as well. In those days he still was known under another name in San Salvador, as a dapper businessman with a nice family. But perhaps most surprisingly, there was "Ana María," the FPL's second in command, an elderly woman with a slight stoop and vigorous opinions.

The reason for the press conference was immediately stated: the leadership of the FPL, the FARN and the CPS wished to announce their unification into a coordinated command structure—the *Coordinadora Político-Militar*. It was an announcement of momentous significance, ending years of factionalist strife. Shafik Handal compared it to the unity agreement among the three currents of Nicaragua's Sandinista Front, "which led to the victory of the Nicaraguan revolution."[25] El Salvador's ERP still remained outside the unified command, but unity talks with that group would proceed as well.

After the formal press conference was over, the guerrilla leaders chatted with small clusters of dazed journalists, blithely unaware of the dangers the reporters thought imminent: a sudden storming of the house by government troops, an ambush outside the door. "Marcial," a courtly gentleman, took "Ana María's" elbow and led her to a comfortable chair. "Ana María" effusively thanked the press for the risks it was taking to be with them. "Fermán" answered questions in his deliberate, almost academic style. Handal's smile was detectable even behind his hood when a journalist asked if it were possible to interview "Don Miguelito" Mármol, the legendary survivor of the 1932 uprising, and arranged the meeting immediately. Several hours after it had begun, the gathering broke up gradually, the journalists torn between their curiousity to ask more and their eagerness to get out. They had met what the U.S. embassy had labeled the "Pol Pot left," and the label didn't seem to fit.

The Popular Organizations Become One

Three days later, on January 11, a stocky young man with a stunning smile walked toward the stage of the law school auditorium at the National University. As he took his seat on the platform, his intense eyes looked out beneath the thick dark eyebrows that drew a line clear across his face and studied the hundreds who sat there anxiously awaiting the historic announcement.

For Juan Chacón, it had begun in 1975, when he left the fields of Chalatenango to become a factory worker in the capital. There he joined the People's Revolutionary Bloc in 1976. One year later, his father, "Don Chus," who stayed behind in Chalatenango to continue his work as a Delegate of the Word, was killed and dismembered by the National Guard.

Juan Chacón never forgot. He mastered the politics of the *Bloque,* its analysis, its methods of work. He had a striking capacity for organization and an indefatigable energy. In September 1979, he stood on the stage of a movie house in downtown San Salvador to accept the applause of other *Bloque* members after he was elected their secretary general. He was 23 years old.

Now Chacón shared the stage in the law school auditorium with the leaders of the other popular organizations. Leoncio Pichinte, 28, was there for the People's Leagues (LP-28); Mario Aguinada Carranza, an accountant, and the old man of the group at 33, was there as secretary general of the Nationalist Democratic Union (UDN). His brother, a railroad worker, had been a deputy in the National Assembly until his mysterious assassination in 1976. There too was Alberto Ramos, 28, secretary general and founding member of the United People's Action Front (FAPU), a student leader since 1972.

They were there to announce the unification of their organizations under the *Coordinadora Revolucionaria de Masas,* and to announce its plans for a future "democratic and revolutionary government." They called for the overthrow of the existing regime and an end to the oligarchy's power. They pledged land reform, the creation of a new people's army to replace the old, a national health-care system, and a literacy campaign to ensure full participation of the people in the new order of things.

In that small auditorium literally packed to the rafters, the crowd cheered and stomped and clapped and then observed an awesome minute of silence for "the fallen martyrs and heroes of the struggle." "Because the color of blood is not forgotten," they chanted, "the massacred will be avenged."

To celebrate the unification of the revolutionary forces, a mass demonstration was called for January 22—the forty-eighth anniversary of the *matanza* that took 30,000 lives in 1932.

The Unity March

A lemon-yellow sun, peering over the hills on a cloudless January 22, greeted the first few gathering thousands of demonstrators setting up the front line columns at the intersection of Avenida Roosevelt and Avenida Gustavo Guerrero. The crossroads is the divide between the raucous, graceless, treeless downtown area, crowded with department stores and shops of every kind, and the sloping hills and curving avenues of the residential neighborhoods, with houses walled off from the outside world and turned dreamily inward toward their luxuriant gardens.

At the center of the residential district is a small oval park surrounded by fancy boutiques, pharmacies, a supermarket and a busy McDonalds. Here stands the statue of El Salvador del Mundo.

At the opposite end of the Avenida Roosevelt axis, in the hub of the downtown area, sits the Metropolitan Cathedral. A small, dusty plaza faces its gray concrete steps, so many times the site of bloodshed, and to the church's right the National Palace, a two-story gray building one block wide. On its upper story, olive-green clad National Guardsmen paced nervously, sweating in their black helmets and black Prussian boots.

As the soldiers paced, the demonstrators' columns swelled up the Avenida like swarming bees. Thousands and yet again thousands of shabbily dressed Salvadoreans surged toward the crossroads and quickly, as if this had all been rehearsed many times before, took their places behind the standard bearers of the different popular organizations. The demonstrators were not yet quite aware of just how large, how historically important, their numbers were when a crop-duster plane suddenly appeared overhead and sprayed the crowd with insecticide. The few journalists present at that early hour, trying to cough the poisonous stuff out of their lungs, were scandalized. For many of the demonstrators, rural fieldworkers just in from the cotton plantations, there was nothing new or disturbing about the plane: their bosses regularly carried out spraying missions over the fieldworkers' heads. Why shouldn't they now try to exterminate rebellion as if it were merely a larger breed of pest?

At 11:00 a.m., the demonstration stretched as far back as the El Salvador del Mundo statue, twenty blocks from the crossroads and out to the nearest hill slopes on either side of the Avenida Guerrero. There were columns of state employees, organized slum dwellers, factory workers, electricians, teachers and, endlessly, the farmworkers and peasants who had slipped through the roadblocks to enter the capital before dawn.

Every individual was there as an organized member of a movement whose methods and goals he or she approved of and shared. Each person had a task and a voice. Unlike Nicaragua, where the Sandinistas were initially a small vanguard who relied on the people's spontaneity to work out their own ways of participating in the struggle, the Salvadorean movement was already immensely coordinated, and could plan activities quite meticulously from one week to the next. Conversely, those sizable sectors of the urban and rural population not organically part of the popular organizations would remain somewhat baffled as to how to participate later on.

At 11:10 a.m. the march started moving toward Cathedral Square, a great chanting defiant avalanche. At 12:50 p.m. the first column entered the square and moved on toward nearby El Rosario church. At 1:00 p.m. the first shots rang out, the thudding booms characteristic of the military's regulation G-3 machine gun, a combat weapon thoroughly inappropriate for routine urban police needs, yet carried by all the security forces as well as the army. The first bodies slumped to the ground in front of the cathedral, and as the now terrified crowd broke ranks and scattered down the side streets and into nearby buildings, a cluster of youths, members of the popular organizations' "self-defense brigades" took up combat positions along the avenue. But the Guardsmen who had fired from the National Palace were not interested in a fight. The shots already had accomplished their purpose, sowing the seeds of terror and breaking the demonstration. It is not recorded whether the military high command thought thus to halt the revolution.

The Salvadorean Human Rights Commission estimated the January 22 death toll at 67 dead and 250 wounded.[26] It was a high price to pay for keeping the mass movement alive and aware of its strength, and visible to the rest of the world. And in the months that followed, the price rose to intolerable levels and the popular organizations gradually were forced into clandestinity. More and more homes in the poorest and most middle-class neighborhoods were willing to store bandages and ammunition, antibiotics and black gunpowder; more and more peasants requested arms from the guerrillas. But the popular organizations still persisted in their belief that an unarmed mass movement of the people—perhaps modeled on Iran—could bring down the government; they were unprepared to take the final step toward armed struggle, and the guerrillas, in the winter of 1980, were not yet prepared to incorporate so many into their ranks. Many more would have to die before the two main forces of the Salvadorean revolution would merge.

CHAPTER VI

Ten Bodies a Day

In mid-February 1980 Christian Democratic Party regulars went out to cities and towns to publicize a rally in the capital. Alarmed by the dramatic visibility and growing unity of the left, and determined to gain leverage over the army, the party planned a huge show of popular strength. They hired buses and trucks to bring people in from the countryside, and predicted a turnout to rival in size the protests of 1972, when they were cheated at the polls. This time their main attraction was Napoleón Duarte, the man robbed of victory in 1972, ex-mayor of the capital. How could the unity of the left possibly rival this hero of the center?

Somehow, the old magic failed to work: barely 500 people turned out to attend the Christian Democrats' smallest rally ever, and a planned pro-government march was canceled to spare the party further embarrassment.[1]

Later, the Christian Democrats offered varying explanations for their debacle. The meeting site was changed at the last minute from a plaza in the populous market area to the isolated Casa Presidencial; the security forces set up

137

checkpoints at all the access roads to the capital and turned demonstrators back; there was not enough time to prepare the meeting. These were all reasonable excuses, but they did not account for the difference between that small gathering and the tumultuous sea of people who had marched to celebrate the unity of the popular organizations, with much less time to prepare and much greater government hostility.

In addition to the noticeable lack of popular enthusiasm for the Christian Democratic cause, the rally underscored the military's overt hostility toward its new partner in the junta. As Colonel Majano and Héctor Dada watched from a balcony in the elegant Casa Presidencial, Duarte, a self-assured orator, gesticulated and mouthed his speech from the back of a pick-up truck parked in front of the Casa. Across the street, on the sports field of El Zapote barracks, a roaring helicopter repeatedly rose a few yards in the air, then circled and landed again, making sure that most of Duarte's speech was lost even to those standing next to him. It has long been standard wisdom in Salvadorean power circles that whoever controls the loyalty of El Zapote, with its access to the Casa, determines the success or failure of the next coup d'état. The circling gray buzzard did not bode well for the Christian Democrats' stay at the white, airy Casa.

The Liberals' Last Hope

It seemed that Christian Democracy's only friends were foreigners: its sister parties in Venezuela, Costa Rica and Europe and its most powerful ally in Washington. The Carter administration praised the Christian Democrats as El Salvador's "last hope" for averting civil war. But its policies did little to strengthen the party's hand in its power struggle with the army.

Washington's oft-stated desire was to eliminate the extremes of Salvadorean political life and create a center where none had been allowed to exist for fifty years. The oligarchy's agro-front had never cooperated with U.S.-supported programs, from the Alliance for Progress to Molina's pilot land reform. The Carter administration blamed the current crisis on their intransigence, and had few compunctions about pushing for reform at their expense. U.S. officials courted and cajoled the more enlightened oligarchs, trying to draw them toward the junta and isolate the right.

At the same time, the administration tried to isolate the left, advocating a blend of reform and repression to neutralize its strong support among the poor. In February 1980 news reports from Washington indicated that the Carter administration was preparing a major aid package for El Salvador: $50 million in credits to help finance reforms and another $5 million in military sales credits and training assistance for the Salvadorean army. The package included a plan, tentatively approved by the National Security Council, to send three twelve-man army mobile training teams to instruct Salvadorean soldiers in logistics, communications and intelligence techniques.[2] The State Department justified the aid proposal as an effort to curb indiscriminate repression and replace it with "clean counterinsurgency"—presumably the ability to distinguish between a mere peasant and a militant, and shoot only the latter.[3]

But from El Salvador, Archbishop Romero argued that "the United States should understand [that] the Armed Forces' position is in favor of the oligarchy; it is brutally repressive and while it does not change, the aid should not be given."[4] Romero wrote a personal letter to President Carter, pleading that aid be withheld. And he went further, calling on the Christian Democrats to resign from the junta: "Your presence is covering the repressive character of this government, especially abroad. You are an important political force. It is urgent that you question how best you can use that force in favor of the poor: as isolated and impotent members of a government controlled by the repressive military, or as one more force that incorporates itself into a broad project of popular government."[5]

Liberal opinion in the United States, however, still hoped for a Christian Democratic resurgence and opposed U.S. aid to the junta on different grounds: "If peaceful change is still possible," read a *New York Times* editorial, "the reformers will have to regain power from the military hardliners. That is why American military aid at this point would signal support for the wrong factions."[6]

Within the State Department itself, there were those who

questioned the basic premise of U.S. policy—that the junta was willing and able to push reforms—and urged the U.S. government to seek accommodation with the moderate left and the popular organizations. Military aid for the junta, they argued, would create a "quagmire effect" reminiscent of Vietnam.[7]

As the debate continued in Washington, the army's actions in El Salvador belied any notion of a "centrist government" or even-handedness in the fight against left and right. Its traditional ties to the oligarchy had not been severed—only obscured by the rhetoric of the October coup. Its begrudging tolerance of the Christian Democrats was due only to their usefulness in obtaining U.S. aid. But by late February 1980, sectors of the army believed that Washington would back them no matter what, and rumors of a right-wing coup abounded. Twice, embassy officials had to publicly warn the army high command that the United States would lend no further assistance in the event of a coup d'état.

The Center Divides

Speculation about a coup centered on a former army major, Roberto D'Aubuisson, the daring new hero of the right. D'Aubuisson had been head of intelligence for the National Guard under General Romero; an overseer of the rampant torture. But in October 1979 he resigned from the army, at age 37, to protest the new junta's call for reforms.[8]

By early 1980 D'Aubuisson led the Broad National Front, progeny of the outlawed ORDEN. He was rumored to head the death squads that continued to act with impunity, leaving corpses on busy street corners or dangling from sturdy trees. With money from exiled oligarchs in Miami he purchased television time to denounce the second junta and demand that its "closet communists," the Christian Democrats, resign.

Engaged in a silent war with its military allies, under attack from left and right, the Christian Democratic Party was beset by internal tensions as well. The party had always juggled the interests and positions of different currents. Now a significant sector argued for a dialogue with the popular organizations as the only means of stemming the junta's rightward drift and gaining leverage against the army. Mario Zamora, attorney general in the first and second juntas, was among those who favored building bridges to the left.

Zamora was giving a party when gunmen burst into his living room on the night of February 23, 1980. He willingly identified himself to the intruders to protect his guests. Then he was dragged into the bathroom and shot through the head.

Just days before, that newly discovered television star, Roberto D'Aubuisson, had gone on the air to denounce Zamora as a clandestine member of the guerrillas. The Christian Democrats, stunned by the murder, blamed the retired major and vowed to resign en masse if Zamora's killers were not brought to justice.

But no one was arrested. D'Aubuisson was never questioned. The Christian Democratic Party reneged on its threat to resign. And the party that stayed in the government was only a shell of its former self.

On March 3, 1980, Héctor Dada resigned from the junta. Deeply affected by Zamora's death and the army's unwillingness to pursue his assassins, he admitted the failure of the center: "We have not been able to stop the repression, and those committing acts of repression in defiance of the junta go unpunished . . . . The promised dialogue with the popular organizations fails to materialize; and the chances for enacting reforms with the support of the people are receding beyond reach."[9] Dada left the country, fearing for his life as another party official, Daniel Escobar, was gunned down in Morazán.

Dada was the only member of the five-man junta to resign. The second Christian Democrat, José Antonio Morales Ehrlich, elected to stay on, as did Ramón Avalos Navarrete, the nominal independent, and Colonels Majano and Gutiérrez. But the crisis was much deeper. The cabinet and the lower echelons of government were decimated by the resignations of leading Christian Democrats, including Rubén Zamora, brother of the slain attorney general. "The Christian Democratic Party should not participate in a regime which has unleashed the bloodiest repression ever experienced by the Salvadorean people," read the statement signed by cabinet officials, under-secretaries and other government employees.[10] They left the government and the party, taking 20 percent of its membership with them.

Again Washington downplayed the crisis. When the Christian Democrats met in emergency session and quickly selected a replacement for the self-exiled Héctor Dada, it gave a loud sigh of relief. Napoleón Duarte—the only man whose reputation as a victim of military tyranny in 1972 could save the junta from disgrace, and Carter from embarrassment—would now take a seat on this third version of a "centrist" government.

Duarte had international contacts; he was known as a good "communicator," in perfect English learned at Notre Dame. He was hurt by the harsh criticism of past associates—especially Rubén Zamora, a friend, almost a disciple. But he was undeterred in his belief that he could bring the army to heel. Hadn't they accepted his preconditions for joining the junta, including the immediate enactment of reforms and the army's public commitment to carrying them through? Friends said Duarte was moved by a messianic zeal, convinced that he, and he alone, could save El Salvador from left and right.

Land Reform at Last

By the time this third junta was installed, protest in El Salvador had taken on a new militancy. The popular organizations, wracked by repression, had moved closer to the guerrilla organizations. For a long time, despite the ties and overlaps between the two, they had kept very distinct forms of organization with autonomous structures. But by March 1980 the two forms were merging: workers and teachers, in growing numbers, were moving from civil disobedience in the cities to guerrilla training camps in the countryside. And El Salvador's *campo*, scene of the worst repression, was a fertile recruiting ground for the fledgling people's army.

U.S. officials insisted that land reform could go a long way toward weakening the left's support among the peasantry. Ironically, the example most cited was Vietnam. Roy Prosterman, one of the main architects of Vietnam's land reform in 1970, claimed that "Vietcong recruitment declined from 7,000 men a month to 1,000 men a month while land reform was being carried out."[11] When the junta proclaimed that this time land reform would go forward in El Salvador, Prosterman became a resident consultant, promising a program that would duplicate Vietnam's "success."

On March 6, 1980, the long-awaited Basic Law of Agrarian Reform was officially announced. Phase I of the program expropriated, and compensated, estates of 1,235 acres or more. The land was to be turned over to cooperative peasant associations under the supervision of the government's Agrarian Reform Institute, known as ISTA. Phase II, to begin at an unspecified later date, would place estates of 370 to 1,235 acres (depending on land quality) under ISTA's control. U.S. experts praised the reform as the most radical effort of its kind.

On March 7 the junta declared a state of siege to implement Phase I of the reform, sending army troops to the countryside to occupy the expropriated estates, break the good news to the workers, and handle any landlord resistance. Five hundred ISTA technicians were dispatched to organize the former fieldhands into cooperatives and assist them in electing leaders. The man in charge of ISTA was José Rodolfo Viera, also secretary general of the Salvadorean Communal Union (UCS). He in turn contracted with the AFL-CIO-sponsored AIFLD to provide technical assistance to the reform.

The agrarian reform law was reinforced by badly needed financial reforms. On March 8 the junta issued a decree that nationalized nineteen locally owned banks and imposed restrictions on five foreign banks operating inside the country.[12] The bank reform was designed to democratize the credit system, which previously lent money only to wealthy landlords, and at the same time prevent the oligarchy from sending its capital abroad.

The reforms received loud applause from Washington, the main sponsor. But to reassure skeptics that the process would continue on its course, President Carter sent a new ambassador, Robert White, to monitor the situation and report back to Congress. White was a career diplomat who had made his mark in Paraguay as an outspoken advocate of human rights. He had the respect of Congressional liberals. Indeed, his nomination had been held up for weeks by Jesse Helms, the right-wing senator from North Carolina, who opposed the land reform as a giant step toward socialism. "The nomination of Mr. White," said Jesse Helms, "is like a torch tossed in a pool of oil."[13]

Editorials in the U.S. press heralded the reforms as having saved El Salvador from civil war. New stories described the stunned reaction of teary-eyed peasants, hardly able to believe the news that at last they would reap the fruits of their labor. These were complemented by reports of landlord resistance and sabotage: oligarchs slaughtering their cattle, ripping up barbed wire fences on pasture lands, driving tractors or flying cropdusters to neighboring Guatemala. The oligarchy's desperate anger was taken as further proof that finally the junta had dealt an irreversible blow to their power and privilege.

But popularity abroad did not reflect greater support at home—for the junta or its land reform. The program had serious flaws, and it was far less radical than originally portrayed. Contrary to initial claims that Phase I had affected 60 percent of the country's choice farmland, defenders of the program soon acknowledged that the figure was closer to 17 percent of total farmland and 23 percent of total cropland.[14] Critics cited even lower figures, and charged that fully 60 percent of the Phase I lands were pasture, forests and mountains unsuited to cultivation. They claimed that coffee lands, the economic backbone of the oligarchy, had barely been touched, in part because coffee tends to be produced on smaller plots and in part because many landowners, sensing that land reform was imminent, had divided their estates among family members. These medium-sized estates were subject to the still pending Phase II expropriations.[15]

Defenders advocated patience and support for the junta's efforts—wasn't some reform better than none at all? They claimed that 62,000 families would benefit from Phase I and promised that Phase II would extend its benefits to thousands more.[16] But for many Salvadoreans, Phase I was bad enough. The technical shortcomings of the reform were nothing compared to the new repression that accompanied its fanfare.

A Cover for Repression

Just ten days after the land reform and state of siege were decreed, Amnesty International released a harsh indictment of the junta—calling into question the official rationale for troop deployment in the countryside. Amnesty also charged discrimination in the distribution of expropriated lands:

> The authorities stated that troops moved into the rural areas to occupy plantations intended for expropriation in the agrarian reform. Local sources said, however, that villages supporting opposition peasant unions, such as the Christian Federation of Salvadorean Peasants [FECCAS] and the Union of Rural Workers [UTC], were attacked by troops, and the land seized was handed over to members of government organizations, including the Salvadorean Communal Union [UCS] and ORDEN.[17]

The repression was most intense where the popular organizations were known to be strong. "In Chalatenango," the Amnesty report continued, "a circle of fire was lit around a village to prevent local people from escaping; troops then entered the village, killing some forty people and abducting many others . . . . Troops operating in open coordination with the paramilitary organization ORDEN have shot or abducted peasants, razed villages and destroyed crops in Suchitoto township and Morazán [province], as well as Cuscatlán and Chalatenango."

Refugees fled to the cities, seeking shelter in churches and telling of peasants slaughtered and villages burned. But the repression was not restricted to the countryside. Alan Riding of the *New York Times* wrote of reforms "accompanied by a stepped-up campaign against leftist labor and peasant groups by army and paramilitary units."[18] Eleven union leaders were killed in the western city of Santa Ana; eleven high school students were shot in San Miguel. Roberto Castellano, a leader of the UDN, was found alongside his Danish wife in a shallow grave near the capital. All this within weeks of the reform decrees.

The state of siege, decreed within a day of the agrarian reform, allowed police to arrest people and search premises without a warrant. Street rallies and demonstrations were prohibited, and strict press censorship was imposed. A special decree banned radio and television stations from reporting on armed clashes, "actions" by the security forces and statements by leftists. This was followed, on March 13, by a bomb attack on El Salvador's Human Rights Commission and police confiscation of its documentation. A second bombing that same day shook the offices of *El Independiente*, a newspaper that had defied the new rules of censorship.

The killings averaged ten a day. The death toll for 1980 hit 660 by March.

Many who had defended the reforms at first saw with horror how well they served as a cover for repression. On March 26, the under-secretary of agriculture, Jorge Alberto Villacorta, resigned from his post. He later explained:

> I resigned because I believed that it was useless to continue in a government not only incapable of putting an end to the violence, but a government which itself is generating the political violence through repression. . . . There exists clear evidence that during the month of March, while I served as under-secretary, recently elected directors of the agricultural enterprises were killed by gunfire. . . . Recently, in one of the large estates taken over by the agrarian reform, uniformed members of the security forces accompanied by a masked person pointed out the directors of the self-management group and then these individuals were shot in front of their co-workers.[19]

Archbishop Romero said "the agrarian reform and the nationalization of banks must be judged in the context of death and annihilation."[20] But there were those who refused to connect the reform with repression. The junta claimed credit for the former, and washed its hands of the latter. Duarte blamed "uncontrollable elements" in the army, the National Guard, the National Police and the Treasury Police, and promised they would be brought under control. And in Washington, the Carter administration began discussing plans to train a crack counterinsurgency unit within the Salvadorean army; again the idea was "clean counterinsurgency" to replace uncontrolled repression.[21]

Who were these "uncontrollable elements?" To whom did they respond and how high in the command structure of the armed forces did they reach? No one, in Washington or San Salvador, seemed able or willing to provide the answers.

"In The Name of God . . ."

It was the beginning of Holy Week in San Salvador and the cathedral was packed on Sunday, March 23, as it had been every week since the violence began in earnest. The words of Archbishop Oscar Romero were always comforting; he believed that the Church should go beyond denouncing sin to announcing hope. But his words did more than that. Since the state of siege had imposed tight controls on the media, his sermons were a source of information about events at home and abroad. They encouraged reflection rather than adherence to a particular view; and, after reflection, they urged action rather than passive resignation.

That Sunday, the archbishop's sermon was broadcast on the Church radio station, YSAX, for the first time since February 18, when the station was bombed. *Radio Noticias del Continente* in Costa Rica carried his words to Nicaragua, Venezuela, Brazil and beyond. There was a large delegation of U.S. clergy present in the cathedral—men and women who came to pay their respects to Monseñor and relay his message to their own congregations.

After reading from the scriptures, Monseñor Romero began the "events of the week" section of his sermon:

"At a mass in Aguilares, we celebrated the third anniversary of Rutilio Grande's death. The repression is having its effect, there were few people, there is fear. . . .

"At a celebration in Tejutla, I was told a terrible account: On March 7, near midnight, a truck filled with soldiers, some in civilian clothes, others in uniform, broke into a house and threw the entire family out. They raped four young girls, savagely beat their parents and warned that if they said anything, they would pay the consequences."

More news of massacres, and of four refugee centers opened by the Church to receive those fleeing from the countryside. Then news that even as far away as the United States there was sympathy for El Salvador's suffering.

"I have been informed that many Christian groups in the United States have declared themselves in solidarity with the letter we sent to the President of the United States, and supporting our opposition to military aid. . . . One testimony in solidarity with this position is signed by Mr. Murat Williams, who was ambassador to El Salvador in the time of President Rivera. He says his experience corroborates the fact that U.S. aid to El Salvador always heightens the military repression."

And then the archbishop spoke of the national strike called by the *Coordinadora,* the coordinating body of the popular organizations, on March 17, 1980.

"Its goal was to protest the repression; and last Sunday I said that its goal was legitimate: to denounce something that cannot be tolerated. But the strike also had political ends—to demonstrate that the repression, instead of intimidating the popular organizations, is strengthening them. . . .

"The state of siege and the disinformation to which we are subjected . . . make it difficult to assess the strike's impact. Foreign radio broadcasts have said it was 70 percent effective, which would certainly be a very high proportion; a considerable triumph. Even if we ignore the establishments that closed down out of fear—fear of the left's actions as well as those of the right and the government—it cannot be denied that the *Coordinadora* has demonstrated its strength in the labor sector. The *Coordinadora* is strong not only in the countryside, but in the factories and cities as well. . . .

"Of course the *Coordinadora* has its faults . . . but it will be the solution to the problem if it matures and if it is able to truly comprehend the wishes of the people."

Finally, Romero had a special closing message to the soldiers and National Guardsmen and police, whom he addressed as "peasants in uniform":

"Brothers, each one of you is one of us. We are the same people. The campesinos you kill are your own brothers and sisters.

"When you hear the words of a man telling you to kill, remember instead the words of God, 'Thou shalt not kill.' God's law must prevail. No soldier is obliged to obey an order contrary to the law of God. It is time that you come to your senses and obey your conscience rather than follow a sinful command.

"The Church, defender of the rights of God, the law of God, and the dignity of each human being, cannot remain silent in the presence of such abominations.

"We should like the government to take seriously the fact that reforms dyed by so much blood are worth nothing. . . . In the name of God, in the name of our tormented people who have suffered so much and whose laments cry out to heaven, I beseech you, I beg you"—the applause was already deafening—"I order you," and it was an explosion blocking out the words everyone knew would follow: "in the name of God, *stop the repression!*"[22]

A Deafening Silence

One day after those words were spoken, a man stood quietly in the back of a church where Monseñor Romero was saying a memorial mass. Monseñor raised his arms as he finished his sermon: "Let us pray," he said. Then he collapsed, as bullets entered his chest and face. It took a few moments before the congregation took in what had happened. The gun had a silencer; there were no startling shots; but there he lay in a pool of blood, dead instantly.

Romero had rejected the government's repeated offer to provide him with bodyguards, saying that the Salvadorean people were in greater need of protection. He had expected death, but he also said that death would not silence the cry for justice.

The junta ordered three days of national mourning and vowed to track down the killers. But the judge who was put in charge of the investigation, Atilio Ramírez Amaya, was soon himself the victim of an assassination attempt and fled the country. The killers were never named. But in the most bizarre rendition yet of the U.S. media's portrayal of the conflict, as a war between two extremes, the *Washington Post* reported on March 25: "There was no immediate indication if leftist or rightist extremists killed the Archbishop. Both factions are waging a bloody war for control of the Central American nation." And the *Miami Herald* noted two days later: "Both stood to benefit from any chaos his death might have created."

Had these newspapers ever stopped to analyze the importance of Archbishop Romero to the popular organizations?

The man who broke through news blackouts in his sermons, who gave people hope to continue the struggle and encouraged them to organize, the man who said the Church recognizes the legitimate right to insurrectional violence—he lectured and scolded the left for its errors and excesses, but clearly saw in the popular organizations his people's only hope for salvation. And still it was written that the left might trade all this for the never-defined "benefits of chaos."

The archbishop's funeral, on March 30, 1980, was an outpouring of grief and shock and, ultimately, terror. Jorge Lara-Braud, a Presbyterian minister and member of a large delegation of U.S. clergy attending the funeral, wrote the following account:

> On a radiantly brilliant day, the mass began in a bit of disarray. An altar was improvised at the top of the stairs leading to the main entrance of the old, unfinished cathedral adjacent to the National Palace, headquarters of the Government. Archbishop Romero's coffin had been placed at the foot of the stairs, protected by a six-foot metal fence. . . .
>
> The plaza was jammed with the archbishop's flock— mostly poor people on whose behalf his voice had

been so compelling. . . . Fifteen minutes after the
mass began, I saw an orderly column of some 500
enter the plaza, marching eight abreast behind ban-
ners that identified them as representatives of the
huge coalition of popular organizations called "La
Coordinadora". . . . The crowds in the plaza cheered
and made way for the marchers as they filed by and
laid a wreath at the coffin. Then, still calm and orderly, the column withdrew.[23]

Cardinal Corripio Ahumada of Mexico, representing
Pope John Paul II, was nearing the end of a eulogy when
the first bomb blast was heard. Witnesses said it came from
the far corner of the National Palace. "The crowd stampeded
away from the palace. There was the immediate sound of
some return gunfire. Like a massive wave, thousands headed
for the only possible shelter, the empty cathedral behind us.
Some trying to climb the fence were killed as others in panic
trampled over them."[24]

Inside the cathedral, more than 5,000 people were
packed together with barely room to breathe. Some died
from asphyxiation, but their bodies remained erect with no
room to fall. Outside the bombs and guns were still going
off when a group from the cathedral went out to retrieve the
coffin. It was passed over the heads of those inside, to the
sound of the familiar chant: *El pueblo unido jamás será
vencido.*

And then it was over. Fifty minutes of terror, twenty-six
dead and two hundred wounded. Duarte denied any involvement by the security forces: "We made sure that there wasn't
even a traffic cop on duty that could have acted as an in-
citement."[25] The government version was that leftists had
begun the shooting, with the intention of stealing the archbishop's coffin and holding the dignitaries hostage inside the
cathedral. This version was appropriated by the U.S. ambassador, Robert White, who had blamed the right for Romero's assassination: "First one extreme tries to create panic
by shooting one person. Then the others try to take political
advantage of his death and kill more people in the process."[26]

But the twenty-two foreign delegates to the funeral, bishops, priests and clergy from around the world, published a
different version of events: no one had attempted to snatch

the coffin; there had never been pressure from the *Coordinadora* to stay inside the cathedral.

> What we could be sure of [is that] we heard and saw the explosion of a big bomb which several witnesses saw thrown from the National Palace; that shots and volleys of fire were heard, which several priests are certain came from the second floor of the National Palace; and that we saw or can prove the presence, from the earliest hours of the morning, of the security forces in the streets of San Salvador and the access roads to the city; and we can assume that some members of the Coordinating Committee were responsible for certain actions, consisting basically of burning cars; supposedly to cover the flight of the people from the square.[27]

Shortly after the funeral, the Vatican named Bishop Rivera y Damas as acting archbishop, a temporary appointment that suggested his performance would be scrutinized before any final decisions were made. The Vatican had exerted subtle pressures on Monseñor Romero to curb his outspokenness. But it was hoped that his successor would resist them as well. Bishop Rivera y Damas was a liberal, and indeed he had been the preferred choice of the progressive church against the conservative, Oscar Romero, in 1977.

But Romero's assassination cast a shadow over the Church that could not be dispelled. They had killed an archbishop! Fear crept quietly through the offices of the archdiocese. People who had worked closely with Romero found themselves in new jobs. *Orientación,* the diocesan newspaper, no longer featured news of the repression; spiritual concerns dominated the headlines. Workers at the Legal Aid Office complained of lack of support from the acting archbishop. And in his homilies, Rivera y Damas took a position above the struggle, implicitly abandoning Romero's commitment to the poor and criticizing both sides with an even hand. Intended to be "fair," his equivocal remarks were taken and used by members and supporters of the junta to buoy their cause.

The voice of those who had no voice was gone, and

Bishop Rivera y Damas was no replacement. Two years later, the funeral can be seen as a turning point. Direct popular protest and celebration in the streets had been the central strategy of the popular organizations since the coup of October 1979. The energy it generated, the sense of belonging, of hope for change and the power to bring it about, was vital to the popular struggle. The *Coordinadora* wanted to keep that energy alive, not take it underground, beyond the reach of people still undecided about what revolution should mean. The popular organizations still believed that organized protest and civil disobedience could defeat the terror of the death squads and the security forces, but they had lost their most effective champion. And the cost in human lives was running high.

An Alternative "Center"—The FDR

One day after the archbishop's funeral, a Congressional subcommittee in Washington denied his plea to stop U.S. military aid to the junta. By a vote of six to three, the House Appropriations Subcommittee on Foreign Operations approved the reprogramming of $5.7 million for transport, communications and intelligence equipment. President Carter split hairs and called the aid "non-lethal": cargo trucks, radar, riot control gear and night vision sight and image intensifiers to track down the enemy. Washington's rationale, as always, was that a progressive, moderate junta needed aid to crush the violent extremes of right and left.

But that easy symmetry of right, left and center was challenged on April 18, 1980, when 5,000 people jammed the auditorium at the National University to witness the formation of El Salvador's Democratic Revolutionary Front (FDR). Joining the five popular organizations united in the *Coordinadora* were the most important democratic forces in El Salvador—including the men that Washington had praised as the moderate center in October 1979 and again in March 1980: Guillermo Ungo, member of the first five-man junta and Duarte's running mate in 1972, representing the social-democratic MNR; Román Mayorga, also a member of the first junta; Rubén Zamora, minister of the presidency in the second junta and leader of the dissident Christian Democrats.

El Salvador's main trade unions, representing 90 percent of the organized working class, were present in the Front, as were professional associations such as MIPTES—the Independent Professionals and Technicians Movement, representing sectors of the middle class. And presiding over this broad coalition was Enrique Alvarez Córdova, renegade member of the Fourteen Families and minister of agriculture until January 1980. Having served in three governments, he had concluded that "a change at the very center of power was necessary."[28]

The FDR brought together all the democratic and revolutionary organizations in El Salvador except the Christian Democratic Party, which still clung to the trappings of power. It brought together organizations that had fought bitterly in the past over whether to participate in elections, or the role of armed struggle, or whether the October coup was a ray of hope or a sham. But by spring 1980 they could all agree on the need to oppose the junta as one united body. The doors to peaceful change had been closed; now force was required to reopen them.

The Democratic Revolutionary Front presented a platform of government described as "anti-oligarchic and anti-imperialist." It espoused strict respect for human rights, political pluralism and popular participation in the management of government. Consistent with the composition of the new united front, the FDR pledged to preserve a mixed economy that would protect small and medium-sized businesses, while expropriating the obscene wealth of the privileged few.

Commenting on the formation of the FDR, one high-ranking U.S. official called it "an unfortunate development."[29] Certainly it threw a wrench into the State Department's efforts to portray the opposition as intransigent, a "Pol Pot left" as distinct from the "pragmatic" Sandinistas. But U.S. officials promptly adopted a different tack: men like Ungo and Mayorga were dupes of the Marxists; Enrique Alvarez was the "necktie" of the left—all were windowdressing, with no real power. Yet the fact that leading figures in electoral politics, members of past juntas and cabinets, had joined the opposition dealt a heavy blow to the government's credibility worldwide and to Washington's hopes for an end to the crisis.

Then in May, Washington's hopes that at least the guerrillas would remain forever divided were dashed. Since January, three of the five political-military organizations had coordinated their actions through a joint council, but the People's Revolutionary Army (ERP)—second only to the FPL in military strength—was not included. To coordinate a counteroffensive against the government's repression, it was essential to bring all forces together, and on May 22, 1980, that was finally accomplished. A new command structure, called the Unified Revolutionary Directorate (DRU), was formed to coordinate strategy and oversee the activities of four of five guerrilla factions.*

As the unified command structure of the armed opposition, the DRU was recognized by the Democratic Revolutionary Front as the vanguard of the Salvadorean revolution. The DRU in turn acknowledged the FDR as representing the broad forces participating in the revolution, and as the foundation of a future government. Although U.S. officials still maintained the guerrillas had the guns and therefore the power, insisting the civilians were there for show, they were clearly alarmed by this new alliance. In the coming months, the State Department would spare no effort to try to draw men like Ungo and Alvarez back toward what Washington still defined as the center.

Land to the Tenants

The merger of left and center in the FDR obliged the junta to counter its effect however best it could. The agrarian reform was still its trump card, its best hope to rally popular support in El Salvador and quiet the doubts of an increasingly skeptical public in the United States. But Phase I already had come under sharp attack as insufficient and overshadowed

---

*A fifth group, the Central American Revolutionary Workers Party (PRTC), formed in late 1979, was not a member of the DRU. It included among its leadership Fabio Castillo, a member of the progressive junta of 1960, and had close ties to a new mass organization called the Popular Liberation Movement (MLP).

by the continuing repression. So in April the junta initiated another installment jumping over Phase II and proceeding directly to a newly and hastily designed Phase III, a program called "Land to the Tenants."

Under the provisions of the new program all rented lands—amounting to 10 percent of total farmland—would be turned over to tenant farmers and sharecroppers. Each beneficiary would receive only 2.25 cropped acres—well below the 17-acre minimum deemed necessary to support the typical family of six. But the junta was banking on that age-old dream of peasants everywhere: to call a plot of land—a *pedacito de terreno*—their own.

"Friend campesino," the radio blared, "you are the owner of the land you have been renting, and no one, absolutely no one, can dispute your right of possession, and no one can evict you. From now on, the harvest is yours."[30]

It was a clever political move. By postponing Phase II of the reform (it was later canceled), the junta avoided a direct confrontation with the coffee growers on medium-sized estates. The liabilities of Phase III were few: the expropriated lands tended to be of marginal value, and many of the former owners were small peasants themselves with little political clout. The junta hoped to win support from 150,000 peasant families of former tenants and sharecroppers. Where would the left be then?

The main architect of Phase III was Roy Prosterman—the man who designed the almost identical "Land to the Tiller" program in Vietnam. There, its avowed purpose had been to politically isolate the Vietcong by giving land to peasants in targeted areas. It was one component of a larger "rural development" program that included the infamous Operation Phoenix, run by former CIA director William Colby. Over 40,000 people were murdered as a result of Colby's efforts to "pacify" the countryside.[31]

In El Salvador, there was "Operation Rake"—a massive anti-guerrilla campaign in Cabañas province. Entire villages were burned to the ground as the army moved in to clean out "pockets" of insurgent strength. The Salvadorean Red Cross put the death toll at 100 peasants and 70 guerrillas in that one campaign.[32]

Each operation had its own name and target, but the results were invariably the same: thousands of peasants fleeing that *pedacito de terreno* they had waited so long for; and many of them choosing to fight with the guerrillas to get it back. To the Salvadorean army, any peasant was suspect, even children were subversive. By May, the 1980 death toll of noncombatants passed 1,400.[33]

Roy Prosterman and others who tried to make land reform work refused to see it as part of a coordinated strategy to wipe out the opposition rather than simply neutralize its support. To charges that the government created peasant cooperatives on the one hand, and condoned search-and-destroy missions on the other, Prosterman answered that reform and repression in El Salvador are "independent, co-existing realities."[34] He lamented the fact that repression was robbing the land reform of its political and economic value, even as he continued to consult on Phase III.

The position of the Carter administration was much the same: the junta was trying its best, but right-wing elements in the army and the oligarchy were determined to sabotage the reforms. Between the extremes of right and left, the junta was still the lesser evil. In time, they insisted, the oligarchy would succumb.

Washington was accustomed to having its way in the hemisphere, and believed it could shape El Salvador's future in exchange for arms and aid to the junta. But its fatal error was to refuse to acknowledge the limits of U.S. power—and the autonomy of the protagonists of El Salvador's struggle. The army, the oligarchy, the electoral parties, the popular organizations, the guerrillas—all had a stake in the El Salvador of the future. No amount of aid could buy off the army, particularly once the colonels learned it would flow despite their flagrant abuses of human rights; no amount of pressure could create a center where none existed. And nothing could persuade the oligarchy to loosen its stubborn hold on the country's wealth.

CHAPTER VII

The War Is On

"Jimmy Carter did what the communists couldn't do," said an oligarch in sumptuous Floridian exile. "He brought socialism to El Salvador. He destroyed our free enterprise system. He said 'If you want our money, our weapons, then divide the land and damn the men who made it prosper.' It was blackmail and it worked."

By "socialism" the oligarchy meant the agrarian reform. But while bitter, they were by no means resigned to their fate. On May 2, 1980, the state-controlled radio station in San Salvador reported that a right-wing coup attempt had been foiled. The oligarchy's hero, retired major D'Abuisson, was again the focal point of the plot. He had circulated a video tape to military garrisons around the country, denouncing two members of the junta—Adolfo Majano, the liberal colonel, and José Morales Ehrlich, the Christian Democrat—as communists. Unofficial reports indicated that D'Aubuisson had significant support within the army. The coup had been stopped in the nick of time.

On May 8, D'Aubuisson was captured on an estate near

Santa Tecla, ten miles from the capital, along with twenty-three co-conspirators, including active-duty officers. The arresting troops confiscated a suitcase of documents: payment records to officers in the National Police; tallies of arms purchases; plans that implicated prominent landowners in the coup plot and, on a piece of stationery from a Miami hotel, evidence that D'Aubuisson had a hand in Romero's assassination. Troops arrived just as the major was trying desperately to swallow one of the papers.

The order for D'Aubuisson's arrest had been issued by Colonel Majano, the man selected by the military youth movement to join the junta in October 1979. To Majano, still committed to the reform process, D'Aubuisson represented everything that he abhorred as a threat to the basic integrity of the army. It was time for a showdown. But Majano had badly misjudged his own strength.

On May 9, the day after D'Aubuisson's arrest, the entire officer corps of the Salvadorean army—700 men in all—gathered for a national assembly. In a move that sent a powerful message to anyone intent on purging the right, they voted to demote Colonel Majano from his post as army commander-in-chief. In his place they named fellow junta member, Colonel Abdul Gutiérrez, the bland administrator and admirer of the hardline minister of defense, Colonel Guillermo García.

Many people still believed that Majano's demotion was a concession to those who wanted D'Aubuisson's release and that in return, D'Aubuisson would be brought to trial. But the retired major had become a *cause célèbre* for the right. High-heeled women picketed the residence of Ambassador White, who had spoken out strongly against D'Aubuisson's ties to the death squads and oligarchs in exile. They carried placards saying "White is Red," "Send White to Cuba," and "Free D'Aubuisson," until U.S. marine guards threw tear gas grenades and dispersed the demonstration.

Military units reportedly joined the chorus of demands for D'Aubuisson's release, and the army high command met in all-night session with the junta to debate what steps to take next. Only the Christian Democrats continued to demand that D'Aubuisson be brought to trial; they threatened to resign if he were not.

On May 13, D'Aubuisson and his co-conspirators were released on the orders of an army major designated as special prosecutor in the case—and after consultation with the minister of defense.[1] The announcement said there was insufficient evidence to hold D'Aubuisson beyond the seventy-two hour limit set by Salvadorean law. No charges were ever brought. Nothing more was said about the confiscated documents that D'Aubuisson had tried to eat. There was no compromise. The right wing had taken all.

The Christian Democratic Party met in emergency session the next day. After seven and a half hours of deliberation they retracted their threat to resign—in a replay of February 1980, when D'Aubuisson was implicated in the murder of Mario Zamora. And once again, D'Aubuisson achieved his purpose: while the composition of the junta remained the same, Majano and the Christian Democrats were exposed as powerless adornments at best. Indeed Majano, interviewed long after these events in May, charged that "Duarte preferred to give the impression that he was powerless, but in fact he never tried to unmask those responsible for the death squads."[2]

A Carpet of Vultures

By May, the differences between D'Aubuisson and his ilk and García's circle in the junta were matters of style only: neither was playing games for the Carter administration. "The repression has changed qualitatively," said Archbishop Romero's former secretary, Father Rafael Moreno.[3] "It's bizarre, macabre." In the *tugurios* of San Salvador, chilling tales were told: the body of a man, a member of the popular organizations, had appeared one morning—one half on one street corner, the other on the next. A young woman had been found naked leaning against a fence. Her severed head was tied to the fence by its hair.

At eight o'clock at night the streets of the capital were deserted; by nine the army's trucks were rolling into the barrios and the villages—fifty National Guardsmen per truck. Small pick-up trucks with armed men in the back sped through the streets: the death squads. The Legal Aid Office of the archdiocese of San Salvador kept records of "progressive persons and people from the popular sectors" killed by the army, the security forces and the death squads, now barely distinguishable. In April the count was 480 dead; in May close to 1,200.[4]

Repression hit hardest in the *campo*. Of those killed in May, 800 were campesinos. And that did not include the 300 who were killed that month at the Sumpul River, at the border with Honduras. A full account did not come out for almost a year, when the *Sunday Times* of London published a full-page spread, with the stories and photos of survivors, and how they were found.[5]

Father Earl Gallagher from Brooklyn, New York, was wandering over the Honduran hills near the church were he worked. He gazed down at the banks of the Sumpul River to see it covered in a black carpet, a mass of vultures gnawing on the remains of the dead. In the village of Talquinta, survivors told him the bloody story of May 14, 1980.

Early in the morning, refugees fleeing a search and destroy operation in Chalatenango reached a settlement on the banks of the river. At 10:00 a.m. they were greeted by an explosion of gunfire, the start of the first joint operation by Salvadorean and Honduran troops. It was an *"operación de limpieza,"* as the Salvadoreans call it, a "clean-up" operation. As one survivor told Gallagher: "The bullets came in fistfuls. They went through the walls of houses, people were falling and cattle were dying. The bullets were everywhere."

One survivor, Genaro Guardado, described their desperate efforts to escape: "We ran into the river in flocks. Children were drowning. The Salvadorean soldiers stood on the bank and fired at us." But on the other side, Honduran troops blocked the escape. "We pleaded with them," one refugee said, "begged them. They just pushed. They didn't fire their rifles, but they wouldn't let us through."

On the Salvadorean side of the river, the army, joined by ORDEN—distinctive in black shirts with a skull-and-cross-bones insignia—pressed their offensive. Rosabel Sibran, another survivor, told Gallagher: "I saw them throw children into the air and then slash them with long machetes. They cut their heads off and slit their bodies in two."

The Salvadorean government denied the massacre had ever taken place.

A Blow to the Heart

As the junta and the military consolidated their attack, the revolutionary forces had to decide how to meet the new, and deadly, terms. The popular organizations were still strong, but the hope that if thousands could be put on the streets the government must fall, was fading. Many in the FDR and DRU began to realize that they could not meet arms with demonstrations: armed struggle was essential. Yet that struggle too required that more people be won to the side of the revolution. And if popular protest were quieted, many argued, the junta would claim the left no longer had a base.

The experience of May Day that year gave strength to this argument. May Day is a traditional day of mass protest, but this year the junta had turned out the security forces *en masse* and put ads in the newspapers warning people not to attend the planned demonstrations. The popular organizations wavered and then, fearing another bloody confrontation, discouraged participation in the day's activities. The turnout was low and the junta crowed the left was losing support. The State Department echoed its claims.

So despite the barbarity of the repression, the *Coordinadora* tried to sustain mass participation. A general strike was planned for late June, to protest the repression and reassert their popular support. It was to be short, only a couple of days, but the country would be shut down.

The two-day general strike of June 25–26 caught the junta and the U.S. embassy off guard. It was a stunning success, recalling the days preceding the flight of General Martínez in 1944: 90 percent of all businesses were closed. Buses did not run; the streets were deserted. But still the dictatorship did not fall. It struck back. Hard. And the blow hit at the heart of the popular movement.

There is a tradition in Latin America that the national university is autonomous, neutral ground from which the government and its agents are barred. That tradition has allowed intellectual exploration unencumbered by the need to compromise with the powers that be. Facing the poverty of everyday life and the menace of repression, the university—instead of being the legitimator of the status quo—has become the refuge for many of its harshest critics.

The National University in El Salvador was such a refuge. All of the popular organizations had offices there, and the FDR had held its founding meeting within its walls. The "U" was also a place for public participation: there the *Coordinadora* announced its program for a democratic revolutionary government and there, in January, Salvador Samayoa, the young philosophy professor who served as minister of education in the first junta, announced his enlistment in the FPL. Each time hundreds of people listened and applauded.

On June 27, one day after the general strike, the junta sent tanks, armored cars and 600 armed troops into the university. Troops fired into classroom buildings. Students lay on the ground under the guns of the occupiers—sixteen of them were killed. Official government statements claimed that the campus was being used as a guerrilla training ground, provoking the invasion.

The closing of the university was a serious blow to the popular movement—but not because guerrillas were being trained there. Despite the increased repression and the state of siege initiated with the agrarian reform, the conflict between the popular organizations and the junta had been surprisingly open and public. The popular organizations—with thousands of members—could not be clandestine; there had to be a place where all of these people could find out what was going on. The university had been such a place, the center of communications and coordination for the entire movement. Its loss was almost irreplaceable.

The junta pressed the initiative, targeting communities

where members and sympathizers of the popular organizations lived and worked. The *Coordinadora* responded with a call for another general strike at the end of July. But the closing of the university made coordination difficult and the will of many had frozen in fear of repression. The *Coordinadora* postponed the strike till mid-August.

The postponement intensified debate within the left over how to preserve the mass character of the struggle without running unnecessary risks. Some argued that the hour of insurrection had come; to wait any longer would mean letting the repression take its toll, and the people could stand only so much. Recognizing that a shortage of guns was critical, they believed—and argued—that sectors of the army, especially from among the young officers who had inspired the October coup, could be depended on for support. Whole garrisons could be brought into battle.

Others in the popular movement insisted an insurrection was premature: more organizing had to be done among broad sectors of the population, including government employees, professionals and small business people. And they hesitated to rely too much on the army. How many officers would actually cross over to the rebel side? And if officers with troops at their command did join, wouldn't their presence within a fragile and woefully underarmed people's army give these military men the last word? Individual members were welcome, they argued, but not whole divisions with their command structures and systems of privilege intact.

For the *Coordinadora,* the August strike was intended to prove once again the strength of the popular movement. But it was also designed to test their readiness for an insurrection. Besides a general work stoppage, the guerrilla forces and the neighborhood militias were planning military confrontations with the army. Bishop Rivera said, somewhat naively, that if each side behaved fairly, the general strike would be a measure of the opposition's strength, a kind of plebiscite. And Duarte eagerly took up that theme, invoking the archbishop's authority to promote the competition.

But the contest was hardly fair. The government was not caught off guard, as they had been in June. Postponement of the strike had given them ample time to decide how best to neutralize its effect. A series of decrees was issued to thwart the August confrontation. Decree number 269, for example, forbade participation by the public sector unions, whose workers controlled basic services: water, electricity, the docks and hospitals. Support from these unions had been crucial to the success of the June strike; this time they knew they faced stiff penalties for violations. The criminal code was amended to make activities like the occupation of churches a "terrorist crime."

On the day of the strike, the decrees were enforced by heavily armed police. Many workers, including the top leadership of the electrical workers' union, were arrested. The bus lines were militarized and trade associations controlled by the oligarchy pressured small businesses and shopkeepers to stay open. The headquarters of the FUSS, a left union federation and member of the FDR, were raided. Police were everywhere as Duarte, behind the protection of armored cars, road through the city streets to the market area, once his strongest base of support as mayor of the capital. The cameras clicked in unison and newspapers around the world published photographs of Duarte, in his casual *guayabera*, mingling with the market women; the captions read "business as usual."

By the second and third day of the strike, economic life in the capital was back to normal. Only in the suburbs could one see into the future: armed clashes broke out between the army and neighborhood militias in Ayutuxtepeque and Mejicanos. In San Antonio Abad, an intense gun battle flashed between the army and the guerrillas, and families fled the area. With the failure of the strike, debate flared more hotly within the left: how could they confront the repression that was ravaging their attempts to maintain a public and popular presence?

The issues were the same as before the strike: the timing of the insurrection, the role of progressive sectors within the army, the scarcity of weapons and the need to strengthen the structures of popular participation, particularly in the cities where the enemy's intelligence network was most efficient.

As usual, the arguments were very public. Inevitably, so much discussion about potential support for an insurrection within the army tipped off the high command that danger lurked within the ranks. Gossip had it that the officers who might go over to the other side were close to Colonel Majano. So in September, Minister of Defense García signed a new monthly duty roster shifting several Majano supporters away from troop commands. Others were scattered to diplomatic posts around the world.

The arguments about strategy threatened the unity of the political-military organizations just when such unity was most needed. By late fall all factions within the FDR and the DRU agreed that the mass movement must go underground. The neighborhood committees would become militias; the younger members of the popular organizations would form the base of an insurgent army. The war had begun.

Coordination among the guerrilla organizations, instituted in the DRU, no longer was sufficient for conducting the war. In November, the Popular Liberation Forces (FPL), the People's Revolutionary Army (ERP), the National Resistance (RN), the Communist Party and the new Central American Revolutionary Workers Party (PRTC) decided to unite under a single command. They designed a single flag, red background with a white star in the upper left hand corner and in the center, the initials of the new organization: FMLN, the Farabundo Martí Front for National Liberation.

The Diplomatic War

A revolution is fought not only in the field but in the capitals and cities of the world. Diplomatic and public opinion must be won to the justice of the cause; allies must be found and money raised. In mid-1980, the cause seemed hopeless. The State Department line dominated perceptions throughout Latin America, Europe and of course the United States: the people of El Salvador were caught between extremists on both left and right; only the junta could bring about meaningful reforms. Little was known of the repression; still less of the collapse of two governments since October. Virtually nothing was known of the country's history and the roots of its conflict.

In May 1980, the newly formed Democratic Revolutionary Front (FDR) laid out plans for visits to Europe, Latin America and the Caribbean, and the United States. Delegates were to go from country to country, explaining what was happening in El Salvador and seeking diplomatic and political support.

The first stop on the diplomatic long march was Costa Rica, which along with Panama had been an important Central American supporter of the Nicaraguan revolution. The delegation was headed by FDR President Enrique Alvarez, the patrician reformer, and included Guillermo Ungo of the National Revolutionary Movement (MNR), Rafael Menjívar of the Movement of Independent Professionals and Technicians (MIPTES), Héctor Silva of the Popular Social Christian Movement, formed by those who left the Christian Democratic Party in March 1980, José Napoleón Rodríguez of the United People's Action Front (FAPU), and Juan Chacón, secretary general of the People's Revolutionary Bloc.

In an emotional rally in a movie theater in a suburb of San José, Costa Rica, Alvarez announced to a tumultuous crowd:

"The Salvadorean people have had to take up arms to end the conditions we have been subjected to for the last fifty years—by military governments, by the oligarchy and U.S. imperialism. The people have risen in arms to say "Enough" and to take power the only way they leave us, the way of armed struggle."

From the crowd: *El pueblo armado jamás será aplastado!* The armed people will never be crushed.

"Our people have struggled for many years to use all the peaceful means possible, but each government in turn has left us no other way. We have fought for the peaceful road, we have struggled along the electoral way. We have tried all of these roads but each has been closed to us, time and again."

The crowd: *Si Nicaragua venció*
    El Salvador vencerá!

"One of the obligations that our delegation has is to ask the nations of the world to keep hands off El Salvador and to say that the Salvadoreans have the right and the capacity to win this victory and to install their own democratic and revolutionary government.

"We also ask the solidarity of the peoples of the world to support the just struggle of the Salvadorean people. We ask for understanding of our cause and help to prevent the direct and massive intervention of U.S. imperialism."[6]

The cries, the chants and the applause went on for ten minutes.

All summer delegations set out: to Mexico, the Caribbean, Europe. Everywhere they went they met with exiled compatriots—migrants and refugees who shared with them the familiar *tamales* and *pupusas* (cheese, bean, and meat-filled tortillas). They talked in foreign capitals, to local newspapers, with opposition leaders, government officials, ambassadors. They spoke to near-empty halls and before crowds of thousands; slept in hundreds of hotels or generously given beds; made thousands of telephone calls and ran up bills for everything.

In July, Alvarez led a four-member delegation to the United States, with Ungo, Rubén Zamora, head of the Popular Social Christian Movement, and Salvador Arias of MIPTES. There as elsewhere they met with church and political activists, Salvadorean exiles, congressional aides.

One meeting was off the record. Assistant Secretary of State for Inter-American Affairs William Bowdler listened politely to the four, all of whom had served in the first junta. Then he played on the old theme, suggesting they were powerless civilians covering for the guerrillas, and asked why they did not return to the junta and build a government of the "center." The FDR leaders responded tolerantly that that had already been tried.

"The State Department contradicts its own words," said Rubén Zamora shortly after his meeting with Bowdler. "On the one hand they tell us that we are so weak that some alleged madmen on the left will eat us alive. On the other hand, they urge us to go in with the junta so that it can rely on our strength to break the oligarchy!"[7]

The delegation found a much warmer reception in Europe, among the parties affiliated with the Socialist International and several governments. The International had begun to take an active interest in Third World developments in the mid-seventies, under the leadership of West Germany's ex-chancellor, Willy Brandt. Where social democratic parties existed in Latin America, they were encouraged to join the International—and among them was El Salvador's National Revolutionary Movement (MNR), headed by Guillermo Ungo.

Social democrats in Europe reasoned that regional stability in Central America could best be served by encouraging reforms, or, if necessary, by tolerating revolution. They had provided important diplomatic and, in some cases, material support to the Sandinistas in Nicaragua. Now they were prepared to go against the advice of the United States and aid the FDR.

Ungo visited the capitals of Europe, drawing on his ties to the Socialist International. Where member parties were in power, in Germany, Austria, Sweden and elsewhere, he found the effect of party support for the FDR just a few steps short of diplomatic recognition. In other countries with strong socialist parties, such as France, England and Spain, the contacts meant resources and logistic support for the FDR's tours. The bills were piling up.

And in Latin America, Mexico was the strongest supporter. The government of López Portillo allowed the FDR to set up its main offices abroad in Mexico City. Massive street demonstrations in Mexico, and throughout Central America, expressed a generalized sympathy with the FMLN/FDR cause. FDR leaders talked with President Jaime Roldós of

Ecuador and Panama's General Omar Torrijos—hoping that the general's very active support for the Sandinistas would now be extended to their own terrain.

By October 1980, the FDR had received commitments from a variety of countries to introduce a United Nations resolution condemning human rights violations in El Salvador, and an FDR delegation traveled to New York to promote it.

But in El Salvador, the repression continued to pummel the opposition, with mutilated bodies appearing on the streets at the rate of twenty a day. The FDR grew increasingly anxious that the continued absence of its leaders might hurt the morale of the popular organizations, the trade unions and professional associations within the coalition. Two members of the Human Rights Commission were killed driving home from work. Felix Ulloa, the rector of the university, was shot in broad daylight by gunmen in a passing car. Anyone visible, anyone potentially a leader of the opposition was being picked off. The FDR decided that Juan Chacón should return; jokingly he said his suit chafed; his place was with his *compas* at home. Enrique Alvarez, meanwhile, with his quiet passion for the revolution, his oligarchic breeding, was extraordinarily effective on the diplomatic front. But he was a central force in bringing the different sectors of the opposition together, from peasants to technocrats and middle-class entrepreneurs. He, too, was needed at home.

At the end of October, a delegation of FDR leaders arrived at the Metropolitan Cathedral in San Salvador to attend the funeral of Felix Ulloa. As they entered the cathedral, the crowd turned to stare. Alvarez, of the oligarchy, walking with Chacón and the rest. He had burned his last bridges, crossing permanently to the side of Pichinte, Ramos, Ana María, Ana Guadalupe, the unknown people making El Salvador's revolution. There was hope, if these people dared to return.

Five More Martyrs

Thanksgiving Day, November 27, 1980. The telephone rang in New York at mid-day. Bill Wipfler of the National

Council of Churches told us the news he had just heard himself. Two hundred soldiers and police had surrounded the Jesuit high school in San Salvador, not three blocks from the U.S. embassy, where key leaders of the Democratic Revolutionary Front were preparing a press conference. Some twenty men, heavily armed and dressed in civilian clothes, went up the long driveway and entered the gray building, forcing everyone inside to lie face down on the floor. Then several dozen people were taken away at gunpoint and in full view of the soldiers outside. Among them were Manuel Franco, of the Nationalist Democratic Union (UDN), Enrique Barrera of the National Revolutionary Movement (MNR), Humberto Mendoza of the Popular Liberation Movement (MLP); Juan Chacón of the *Bloque* and Enrique Alvarez, president of the FDR.

For many around the world, the reality of El Salvador was suddenly brought home that day. They had met Alvarez, had listened to Chacón. In New York the telephone trees were set into motion, as one person called the next, urging everyone to send telegrams to the junta demanding freedom for the five, contacting human rights organizations, the media, anyone who had met the FDR leaders in July, anyone who cared. We did it numbly, setting hope against all we knew of El Salvador by then, against the other calls in March, the night of the archbishop's murder, or October, when two members of the Human Rights Commission disappeared.

At first, the wire services reported that the Salvadorean military had made the arrests. Then, as telegrams poured into the Casa Presidencial, the junta denied all knowledge of the incident and a newly formed death squad, calling themselves the Maximiliano Hernández Martínez Brigade, claimed credit for the kidnappings. Its earlier work had included the beheading of four young men. Their bodies had been found in the gutter of the Avenida España with a note: "Long live El Salvador! Long live the massacre of 1932!"

Then, close to midnight, another telephone call. Five bodies had been found on the shores of Lake Ilopango, seven miles from the capital. Alvarez' left arm was missing; Chacón's face had been horribly mutilated; his left fist was clenched in defiant salute above his head on the blood-covered ground. Franco, Barrera, Mendoza—all of them had been tortured; their bodies showed signs of strangulation.

We changed the wording on the telegrams. Protest brutal murders of five FDR leaders. Demand investigation.

In New York, Guillermo Ungo, his lips drawn tight, sorrow and rage coloring every word, said "the deaths are a definite confirmation that the dialogue and negotiations have ended. They are trying to liquidate those who talk of peace." Within weeks he would replace Enrique Alvarez as president of the FDR.[8]

Ambassador White called the murders "an unspeakable crime." The junta called it "a demonstration of what the extremist groups seeking power at any cost are capable of doing," absolving itself of any blame. And Colonel Majano took a "personal trip" outside the country, fearing he might be next. On November 4, a bomb had exploded near the Ministry of Defense, seconds after his car passed the spot. Only people with links to the military could have had access to the area.

The murders of the FDR leaders made the growing concern about how to wage the popular struggle desperately real. Until that night there was a strange, almost formal quality to the conflict. Despite increased terror in the countryside, there persisted a belief that it was no more dangerous to fight openly than be killed as a suspected subversive. And leaders of both sides knew who the others were. El Salvador is a small country; everyone in political life knows everyone else. Bodyguards were few. Major leaders of the popular organizations could be seen driving or walking along through the streets of the capital. But after November, the FMLN/FDR imposed rigorous security measures inside the country and agreed that top FDR leaders should continue the diplomatic battle abroad.

Many people attributed the change in climate to Ronald Reagan's election as president of the United States. Gunshots and fireworks resounded on election night in the wealthy barrios of San Benito, Escalón and Flor Blanca. And Colonel Majano complained bitterly that rightists inside the government and out began to see themselves as "all powerful" with Reagan's landslide triumph.[9] A body was found on the streets of the capital, mutilated like so many others, but with a sign that read: "With Reagan, we will eliminate the miscreants and subversives in El Salvador and Central America."[10]

As the bodies of the five FDR leaders lay in state in the Metropolitan Cathedral, a powerful bomb exploded, blowing the coffins from their stanchions and sending pieces of limbs and wood into the air. The so-called Maximiliano Hernández Martínez Brigade had struck again.

The Lonely Road

The road from the airport to San Salvador is a lonely and scary ride. The airport is new, a belated product of Molina's National Transformation. It was opened precipitously in 1980 to allow the former airport to be used by the military. There is little around it save pasture and farmland. The building is marble, modern, resembling an air-conditioned mausoleum.

When the planes arrive, little buses ferry passengers to the capital. The trip is silent and tense. Preferably one is met at the airport by friends to share the lonely sojourn through army checkpoints along the road.

In the warm evening of December 2, 1980, Jean Donovan, a plump blonde woman, waited at the airport with her friend, Dorothy Kazel. Both were from Cleveland and now did relief work in the port city of La Libertad, Jean as a lay missioner and Dorothy as an Ursuline nun. They shared the same hard work, and, at the end of a day, a glass of Pilsener beer.

Not long before, Jean Donovan had revealed some of her anguish at what was happening to a friend: "The Peace Corps left today," she wrote, "and my heart sank low. The danger is extreme and they were right to leave. . . . Now I must assess my own position, because I am not up for suicide. Several times I have decided to leave. I almost could, except for the children . . . the poor bruised victims of adult lunacy."[11]

Now the two women awaited the return of their friends,

Sisters Ita Ford and Maura Clarke, from Nicaragua, where they had gone to attend a conference of the Maryknoll Order.

Ita Ford and Maura Clarke worked in Chalatenango province, where they distributed clothing and food to children and mothers displaced by the army's "clean-up" operations. Two weeks earlier, a note had been tacked to the pale green door of the stucco parish house in Chalatenango, where both women had small rooms. It read: "In this house are communists. Everyone who enters here will die. Try it and see." The two women ignored the note and continued to carry food and medicine to those in need, even into areas where the army was afraid to go.

The local military did not understand their work. Shortly before her death, Ita Ford told a journalist: "The colonel of the local regiment said to me the other day that the Church is indirectly subversive because it is on the side of the weak."[12]

At the airport, a group of Canadian religious people greeted Jean Donovan and Dorothy Kazel and headed down the road for San Salvador. Not much later they were stopped by uniformed security forces and searched at gunpoint. Earlier that afternoon, TACA airline's first flight from Managua to San Salvador had been boarded by three Salvadorean soldiers. Another Maryknoll nun, en route to Miami, was questioned twice by the stewardess about her destination at the request of the soldiers.

Later, a tape of a radio transmission intercepted after the arrival of that plane was given to Ambassador Robert White by a "high-ranking Christian Democrat." He said it was a military transmission. "No, she didn't arrive on that flight," a male voice said on the tape; "we'll have to wait for the next."[13]

Their plane touched down at 7 p.m. at the new airport. At about the same time at a movie house in Chalatenango, an unknown man approached one of the parish staff who worked with Ford and Clarke. According to the priest of the sisters' parish, Father Efrain López, the man showed him a sheet of paper with names on it and said, "Here is a list of people we are going to kill—and today, this very night, we will begin." Ford and Clarke were on the list.[14]

At the airport, the four women set off toward San Salvador in the white Toyota van that belonged to Kazel and Donovan. At about 10:30 p.m., campesinos near the village of Santiago Nonualco, about a half-hour's drive from the airport in the opposite direction from the capital, saw the van pass their houses. Then they heard a short burst of machine-gun fire, followed by three or four single shots. The van returned the way it had come. Frightened, the campesinos closed the doors of their houses and waited till morning.

The next day, December 3, the Toyota van, its license plates removed, was found burned along the airport road. Earlier that morning, a milkman had discovered the bodies of four women and reported it to the authorities. National Guardsmen and several civilians arrived and prepared a common grave. The justice of the peace drove up to authorize the burials, recording them as "unknowns."

December 4, a Catholic priest from Santiago Nonualco called Church authorities to report that several of his parishioners had seen soldiers burying four women who looked like foreigners. Ambassador White, church workers, the local and foreign press rushed to the gravesite to witness the exhumation of the bodies. Each of the four women had been shot at least once in the head. One was found with her pants on backward. Two had no underwear.

As Ambassador White surveyed the grisly scene, he was heard to mutter: "This time they won't get away with it." Then as a group of National Guardsmen walked menacingly toward him and his aide, he asked, "Are they coming to get us?"[15]

Insufficient Evidence

The murders immediately made headlines around the world. Memorial masses were held and church leaders in the United States began to channel the public's outrage into acts of protest against U.S. policy. A banner inside the historic San Francisco cathedral read: "U.S. Dollars Kill U.S. Nuns."[16]

At the funeral in Chalatenango, where Ita Ford and Maura Clarke were buried, Peter Hinde, an American priest, told a reporter: "I hope this incident will continue to have repercussions world-wide, especially in the United States, to compensate for the ten thousand dead and the support given by our government."[17]

And the acting archbishop of San Salvador, Monseñor Rivera y Damas, was shaken from his position of even-handed condemnation of violence to make one of his strongest statements: "The Church is persecuted because she tells the truth that shakes up the powerful. . . . Although those directly responsible for this persecution try to hide their guilt, denouncing the violence slickly as a battle between the far right and the far left, nevertheless . . . it has been evident that the majority of the persecution has been carried out by security forces and paramilitary organizations. Because of this we reject those versions which would hold other social groups responsible."[18]

The carefully crafted façade that hid the junta's role in the repression was violently torn away. Under heavy pressure from the public, President Carter ordered the suspension of $25 million in economic and military aid to the junta and dispatched a fact-finding mission led by William D. Rogers, a former State Department official, and William Bowdler, assistant secretary of state.

One week later, on December 13, the fact-finding team reported back to the president: they had found no "direct evidence" linking the killings to government officials or to "high echelons" of the security forces. There was, however, circumstantial evidence that the security forces were involved. Rogers told reporters he was satisfied that the Salvadorean authorities would conduct a thorough investigation.

That same day in El Salvador a major restructuring of the government was announced, following eight days of intense negotiations between the army and the Christian Democrats. Colonel Majano, the idealistic reformer, was out; Colonel Abdul Gutiérrez, commander-in-chief of the armed forces since May, was promoted to vice-president as well; and Napoleón Duarte was named president of the junta, now trimmed to four members.

Before the week was out, $25 million in economic aid was on its way to El Salvador. The State Department explained that it was "critically needed to maintain the Salvadorean economy," and that the junta's reorganization could bring "greater efficiency and a stronger, more unified civilian control over the government." The suspension of military aid, however, would be maintained pending further progress in the investigations into the December 2 killings.

On April 29, 1981, six months after the killings, six National Guardsmen were arrested. Ambassador White, by then out of a job, told John Dinges of Pacific News Service that Salvadorean authorities knew within days of the murders the names of soldiers who manned the roadblocks from the airport. They could have arrested the men immediately. White told Dinges: "I seriously doubt that there are only six Guardsmen involved. If there were, there wouldn't have been enough incentive for the cover-up to have taken place. An arrest of six enlisted men to allay public opinion is a very simple thing to accomplish. . . ."[19]

Significantly, the arrested Guardsmen include a sergeant, Luis Colindres Alemán, and a colonel, José Moreno Canjura.[20] In addition to the cover-up alluded to by Ambassador White, the clearly premeditated nature of the murders suggests that orders came from "higher up." According to recent press reports, for example, Sergeant Colindres Alemán ordered the Guardsmen to dress in civilian clothes before driving to a specific spot on the highway to await the church women's van. Later, the rapists and murderers returned to the airport for a celebratory drink.[21]

The Fig-Leaf President

In a ceremony full of pomp and ironies, Napoleón Duarte was inaugurated as El Salvador's new president on November 21, 1980. Speaking to a stony-faced officer corps Duarte told of his pride at being the first civilian president in fifty years, although he wished that he had come to power by electoral means. As he received the congratulations of his friends and associates, a military man approached him and said, "We finally have given you your presidency."

It was an historic day for the son of a tailor and poor campesina: graduate of Notre Dame; successful businessman; co-founder of El Salvador's Christian Democratic Party; mayor of San Salvador; presidential candidate; president. A remarkable career.

But despite the presidential sash, the editorials proclaiming Duarte "the new hope" for his country, the talk of moderation's triumph over extremism, nothing had changed in El Salvador. Napoleón Duarte had no power. He was there to lend respectability to the blood-stained junta. But Gutiérrez—with García behind him—still controlled the army. As one of Duarte's friends remarked, "He is president at last, which he has wanted to be all his life. And he must want it obsessively to take it now."[22]

Overture to Uprising

The number of skirmishes between the Salvadorean army and the guerrillas of the FMLN increased after the inauguration. In Morazán province, a bearded army lieutenant observed that his patrols had fought with guerrillas every day during the first two weeks of December. Two days before Christmas, two of his soldiers were killed and two wounded. A Lieutenant Galdamez, leading a search-and-destroy mission in Usulután province, boasted, "We are in the final phase of annihilation. They aren't guerrillas. They don't have an ideology; they aren't fighting for a cause. They are bandits."[23]

During the month of December, the FMLN occupied forty-two towns, carried out twenty-three ambushes and thirty-eight attacks on military posts.[24] On December 12, the FMLN issued a communiqué: "The military commands coordinated by the Front have received instructions to concentrate their potential fire power. All military units and militia must take combat positions in the barrios, *colonias,* cantons, guerrilla fronts, highways, etc. . . Await the orders of the DRU, your General Command."[25]

At the U.S. embassy on 25th Avenue in San Salvador, Ambassador Robert White watched the growing power of the military and the oligarchy and the changing signals from Washington. He knew his name was reported to top a list of career diplomats soon to be removed for nonconformity with

Reagan's right-wing views. White's subtle and delicate strategy to strengthen Duarte at the center and isolate the left was fast unraveling. A strange new fear that being a U.S. citizen no longer gave one automatic protection settled over the embassy community. John Sullivan, a freelance journalist from New Jersey, disappeared in late December. And then in January the violence struck very close to home.

On the front page of the *New York Times* a headline: "Two Americans Slain in Salvadoran City, Aided Land Reform." It was a tragic twist to a tale of deep frustration. Michael Hammer and Mark Pearlman had worked on the agrarian reform program for the American Institute of Free Labor Development (AIFLD). Together with Rodolfo Viera, head of the Agrarian Reform Institute (ISTA) and the Salvadorean Communal Union (UCS), they were shot in the coffee shop of the Sheraton Hotel.

The Sheraton International sits on the slopes of one of the volcanoes that surround San Salvador. It is a favorite hangout for the wealthy, one of the few places where they can go and feel safe. It is said that for every car in the parking lot, there is a second for the bodyguards. Security is impenetrable. Yet two men had walked calmly into the hotel at about 11:30 p.m. on January 4, drawn pistols and killed the three men, then walked out.

Members of the junta predictably blamed the left. But less opportunistic voices noted that it would have been impossible for the left to penetrate security so easily. It had to be an inside job.

As the investigation proceeded, two theories were put forth. One laid the blame on the oligarchy, hurt by the agrarian reform. The other theory was based on the fact that Viera and his principal assistant, Leonel Gómez, were both very critical of the junta. Viera was said to have threatened to resign if the repression against ISTA technicians and members of the UCS continued, and if the reform were not given more official support. To those who recognized the usefulness of the agrarian reform illusion, the loss of UCS support would be a terrible blow. They may have decided to eliminate both Viera and Gómez in order to preserve the program's image. Michael Hammer was square-faced, with a dark mustache and broad shoulders, just like Gómez. According to this theory, he was the wrong man, shot instead of the Salvadorean.

In April 1981 two men were arrested for the murders, Hans Christ and Ricardo Sol Meza, both of whose families had lost lands to the agarian reform. Evidence was insufficient to bring them to trial. But by then Robert White was no longer ambassador, talk of agrarian reform and Duarte had dropped to a whisper, and a full-scale war was underway.

CHAPTER VIII

"Our Mountains Are the People"

"Things will be white hot in El Salvador by the time of Reagan's inauguration," warned Fermán Cienfuegos, one of the five principal commanders of the FMLN.[1] By early December 1980 the FMLN/FDR had agreed to a common battle plan. Victory seemed within reach. Ronald Reagan would face a *fait accompli*.

The January offensive came as no surprise, then. The junta awaited it; the outgoing Carter administration hoped they would be out of office when it came; and the Reaganites wondered whether El Salvador might not already be lost.

Even the precise timing was known a few days beforehand, when battle plans for the offensive fell into the junta's hands. But the revolutionary forces were undaunted. Optimism infused their ranks and rebel communiqués sometimes called it the "final offensive" of the Salvadorean people. There were even disputes among the various organizations of the FMLN/FDR over the government they would establish and who would be in it. Later, the FMLN/FDR admitted they

183

had suffered from *triunfalismo*—the belief that victory was certain.

The offensive began on January 10, 1981—and in those first heady days, it seemed that the FMLN/FDR had not exaggerated its prospects. The provincial capital of San Francisco Gotera in Morazán fell to the FMLN; a massive attack was launched on the garrison in Chalatenango. In Santa Ana, the country's second largest city, the garrison revolted, its commander was executed and one company crossed over to the rebels' side after blowing up the munitions stockpile.

The installations of the Salvadorean air force were attacked and important equipment was destroyed. The city of Metapán in Santa Ana province fell to the FMLN. Roughly two-thirds of the country was the scene of major military actions.

For a people's army that never before had attempted national, coordinated action, the offensive was extraordinary. Estimates of the guerrillas' strength ranged from 4,000 to 6,000—many of them fresh recruits with no prior experience in conventional battle. The local militias added another 5,000 fighters, whose tasks were to protect local populations and take part in local actions. The enemy numbered 20,000—including the regular army and all the security forces combined.

In El Salvador, the mountains and jungles commonly associated with guerrilla warfare are scarce. It is impossible to walk in the *campo* without running into at least a small cluster of homes. Nonetheless, the guerrillas launched their offensive from secure encampments in the countryside. A local militia member, "Isabél," explained how: "The enemy can be twenty meters from a training center, yet he doesn't find it. He can organize combing operations from La Unión, in the east, to Santa Ana, in the west, and never come upon a single one of our training camps. He doesn't find them because our people are with the revolution and know how to protect their fighters."[2]

During the January offensive and after, peasants sacrificed to provide the guerrillas, *los muchachos,* with tortillas and beans; they hid arms and medicines in their huts; and, young and old, they kept track of the army's movements as they plowed their fields or brought their produce to market. "Our mountains are the people," say the guerrillas in explaining their ability to survive.

In the cities, especially San Salvador, the FMLN's infrastructure was far more fragile, given the tremendous difficulty of organizing under the nose of the enemy. By the time of the offensive, the popular organizations had been forced underground and many members had left the city to join the people's army. Yet even in the capital itself, FMLN camps, housing 100 guerrillas or more, were hidden in the dense barrios of the poor. They were protected by local lookouts and supplied with food by the barrio dwellers—even as the army patrolled the streets in armored cars and helicopters flew constantly overhead.

Ten days into the offensive, U.S. press reports confirmed the FMLN's advances: "Salvadorean Rebels Given Military Edge"; "Salvadorean Army Shows First Signs of Strain"; "Rebels Roam Unmolested in Salvadorean Town." Sensing their own proven strength, the FMLN/FDR announced their willingness to seek a political solution to the conflict to avoid further bloodshed. They proposed a dialogue with the United States—"the power behind the Salvadorean throne"—and not with the junta directly. "We want to talk to the owner of the circus, not to the acrobats," said Guillermo Ungo, the new president of the Democratic Revolutionary Front.[3] But nothing came of their proposal.

By the end of January, the tide began to turn against the FMLN. The inexperience of new fighters, and the still imperfect coordination among five guerrilla armies, testing the recent establishment of a unified command, took its toll on the FMLN columns in the countryside. "People weren't trained to know where the bullets were coming from," said an FMLN commander. "The transition from leading commando units to full-size columns, from guerrilla tactics to full-scale battles, was much more difficult than we had imagined."

The scarcity of weapons was another problem. Battlefield reports indicated the presence of sophisticated weapons alongside antique relics. Militia members often had no weapons at all. Francis Pisani of *Le Monde* wrote that "Sixty-odd guerrilla fighters at San Lorenzo had between them a single bazooka and an automatic rifle, which had been taken from the Salvadorean army only a few days earlier. . . . Some of the guerrilla fighters on the slopes of San Vicente volcano were armed with pistols, rifles, machetes and even slings. The regular guerrillas had FAL [Belgian] automatic rifles."[4] Compounding the problems of fighting a war with ill-equipped troops, FMLN spokespersons in Mexico City charged that troops from Honduras and Guatemala were providing air and ground support to Salvadorean units.

In the towns and cities, the rebels could not maintain their presence without inviting bombings and heavy civilian casualties. San Francisco Gotera was abandoned after eight days, and a "tactical retreat" was ordered from most other towns. But perhaps most critical to the offensive's loss of momentum was the FMLN's failure to carry it to the capital. There, a general strike had been timed to coincide with military actions. But revolutionary forces in San Salvador were much weaker than the FMLN had imagined.

The General Strike

In Nicaragua, the general strike linked to the Sandinistas' final offensive in June 1979 had been supported by factory owners and workers alike. The risks the strikers took were great, but in no way comparable to the situation faced by San Salvador's workers in January 1981. To strike was to declare one's loyalties. The oligarchy stood united. The labor movement had been severely weakened in the months preceding the offensive by a series of arrests. Then, days before the offensive, the army assaulted a safehouse in the capital, arresting several key leaders and capturing plans for military actions. The junta knew the countdown: 4,000 government troops were kept in San Salvador, despite the need for reinforcements in the *campo*, waiting for the FMLN's first move.

The guerrillas' failure to mount diversionary military actions in the capital meant that heeding the call to strike was tantamount to suicide for the city's unarmed workers. Even so, twenty-six factories were struck on the first day, and

20,000 public employees walked out on January 15.[5] They paid the consequences after the strike petered out. Army lists of "subversives killed in combat" included the names of several union leaders known to have been jailed during the strike.[6]

"They Gave a War and Nobody Came"

San Salvador was the tribunal from which the U.S. press and embassy judged the January offensive. There they saw only the feeble and repressed general strike, and an occasional FMLN squadron in the streets. They saw nothing of the war in the countryside and by February, most journalists had concluded that the war was over. "Leftists Routed," said the headlines. "They gave a war and nobody came," said the caustic Ambassador White.

The FMLN/FDR had oversold the offensive and paid a high price for their *triunfalismo*. It would take several months for the U.S. press to rediscover the war and reassess the FMLN's strength. But during the months of February and March, some reporters ventured beyond the safe haven of the capital. They learned that it was possible to walk for hours through terrain controlled by the FMLN. They saw underground hospitals and primitive munitions factories. They visited guerrilla camps, still intact, and were told that the FMLN was assessing its errors and reformulating its strategy for the months ahead. Most importantly, they saw the army only near its garrisons in the towns and cities. Large sectors of the countryside belonged to the FMLN.[7]

According to FMLN commander Joaquín Villalobos, this was the most significant achievement of the January offensive: the passage from political control of certain zones in the countryside to military control as well.[8] The guerrillas thus had a rear guard within the national territory—secure areas in which to train new recruits, care for the wounded and plan coordinated attacks. Now any time the army tried to move within the FMLN zones of control, the guerrillas were ready for them.

But the FMLN knew by March that the enemy went

beyond the corrupt and undisciplined ranks of the Salvadorean armed forces. The war had entered a new phase—
one in which the United States played a very direct role.

Carter's Last Stand

Ronald Reagan, plagued by a trigger-happy image during the electoral campaign of 1980, was right when he said,
"I didn't initiate the El Salvador thing. I inherited it."[9]

Three days before leaving office, Jimmy Carter decided
he could no longer afford to be righteous. He had promised
the families of Ita Ford, Maura Clarke, Jean Donovan and
Dorothy Kazel that no further aid would be released to El
Salvador until those deaths were solved. But the FMLN's
offensive had upped the price of that promise. Carter ordered an emergency airlift of helicopters, artillery pieces,
infantry weapons and ammunition to El Salvador—$5 million
in "lethal" aid covered by a contingency fund that allowed
the president to bypass Congressional authority over military
aid. Another $5 million in "non-lethal" aid was also released.
One high-level official in the State Department—one of the
architects of Carter's policy on human rights—was rumored
to be on the verge of resigning. But for three more days, he
reportedly said, what the hell?

In a pattern that would become familiar in the Reagan
days ahead, Carter based his policy reversal on administration claims that "captured documents" had revealed the guerrillas were receiving "arms, ammunition, training and political
and military advice [from] Cuba and other Communist nations."[10] The documents were not made available for public
perusal. But the allegations were strengthened by a timely
report from El Salvador: five small boats had landed at Cuco
Beach, near the Gulf of Fonseca and Nicaragua, bearing 100
well-armed guerrillas. According to Defense Minister García,
a fierce battle had taken place and 50 invaders were dead on
the beach. Ambassador White, a long-time opponent of "lethal" aid to the junta, said the invasion had changed his mind.
Nicaragua was involved. Send in the guns.[11]

Later, after journalists traveled to Cuco Beach and found

no bodies or evidence of Nicaraguan involvement, U.S. officials in El Salvador said that White may have "overemphasized" the alleged invasion; that the evidence was no longer as "compelling."[12] No matter. The M-16s, the grenade launchers, the helicopters were already in place, and the way was paved for Ronald Reagan to send more.

No More Preconditions

Since October 1979, Jimmy Carter had felt obliged to justify U.S. support for the junta by citing its efforts to reform the oligarchic structures of Salvadorean society. But each wave of resignations by respected civilian leaders, each massacre of peasant farmers, and each body found with tied thumbs and missing limbs frustrated his efforts to affix a centrist label to a government that would not behave. Carter thought he could blackmail the army into obedience by promising shiny tanks and guns in exchange for restraint and a few reforms. But it was Carter who ultimately paid the ransom.

Enter Ronald Reagan, who quickly dropped all pretense of tying aid to reform. His secretary of state, Alexander Haig, had a theory that would justify any amount of U.S. aid on national security grounds alone: the Russians are intent on swallowing Central America, making use of their Cuban surrogate in the region. The FMLN are "terrorists," with international ties. Therefore El Salvador is an East-West battlefield, a test of American resolve, a place to "draw the line."

Suddenly the domestic causes of unrest were secondary or nonexistent. The nature of the junta, the army, the fate of the agrarian reform, were irrelevant to U.S. policy. All that mattered was the nature of the alternative: a potential beachhead for the Soviet Union in Central America, together with Nicaragua, Cuba, Grenada—a threat to the security of the United States. Next we'll be fighting at the Rio Grande.

But Haig's views were in sharp contrast to the European evaluation of events. Germany, Sweden, Austria, Spain— these governments were unimpressed, even alarmed, by this warmed-over rhetoric from Cold War days. They continued to emphasize the domestic causes of El Salvador's unrest, to send aid to the new Nicaragua, and actively support the FDR and its proposal for negotiations to end the conflict.

Mexico was even less receptive. According to Haig's theories, Mexico, with its newly discovered oil fields, was a prime target of Soviet designs on the hemisphere—the next domino, if El Salvador and Guatemala were to fall. It was embarrassing that President López Portillo refused to share these fears. He continued to insist that Mexico's best defense against revolutionary contagion was stability to the south, and that could be achieved only by erasing the domestic causes of discontent.

In the United States, the memory of Vietnam was still very fresh—and strengthened by Reagan's choice of a general for secretary of state. Alexander Haig thought the Vietnam war could and should have been won. Could he now be trusted not to seek vindication by plunging the United States into another long and losing war?

Reagan's policies were in trouble, and he needed to back up his conspiracy theory with proof—something bigger than a rowboat invasion at Cuco Beach—to get military aid past Congress and stop European allies from flirting with the FDR. By February 1981, the administration had built what it thought was an air-tight case.

A Textbook Case

It started with leaks to the *New York Times* and lightning trips to Europe and Latin America to share the "evidence" with friendly governments. Eighteen pounds of documents had been captured from guerrilla hideouts, implicating the entire Eastern bloc, "Arab radicals," Vietnam, Ethiopia, Cuba and Nicaragua in El Salvador's proxy war. At a press conference on February 17, a gloating Secretary Haig vowed to stop the flow of arms, even if it meant going to "the immediate source of the problem—and that is Cuba."[13]

Three days later, the State Department released a white paper on El Salvador, stating that "the insurgency . . . has been progressively transformed into a textbook case of indirect armed aggression by Communist powers."[14] Captured documents, the white paper alleged, showed that Shafik Handal, secretary general of El Salvador's Communist Party, had made a shopping trip through Eastern Europe, the Soviet Union, Ethiopia and Vietnam. A document said to have been drafted by Handal himself showed that each country on his route promised to support the rebels with arms, military supplies and money—except the Soviet Union, which promised only an airline ticket to his next destination. As a result of Handal's efforts, more than 200 tons of weapons had been smuggled into El Salvador through Cuba and then Nicaragua.

Leaders of the FMLN/FDR in Mexico immediately called the documents a fake, stating that the guerrillas fight with weapons purchased on the black market or captured from the enemy. But every major newspaper in the United States reprinted the white paper as gospel. Secretary Haig said it was time to shake the "Vietnam syndrome" that had paralyzed U.S. policy since the early 1970s, and Congressional leaders quickly obliged. Senator Charles Percy, chairman of the Senate Foreign Relations Committee, agreed to "draw the line" in El Salvador even while admitting that members of the junta are "as unpopular with their own people as was Vietnam [sic]."[15]

A few lone voices challenged the authenticity of the documents, citing past CIA attempts to forge evidence where it did not exist.[16] Some pointed to the inconsistencies between the white paper's portrait of guerrillas armed to the teeth and battlefield reports in January describing antiquated Mausers and a scarcity of weapons. Others recalled the two white papers on Vietnam which (investigations revealed only much later) had merely provided the public, press and part of Congress with a rationale for policy that had been put in place months before.

And if there were outside aid to the guerrillas? How was that different from U.S. aid to the junta? The State Department's distinction was simple: aid to a revolutionary movement is immoral and conspiratorial, while aid to "an established government" is a legitimate and disinterested act. That the government in question came to power by coup d'état, and rules by terror, is irrelevant. (So was the distinction, when policymakers began discussing U.S. military aid to the defeated UNITA forces in Angola—guerrillas trying to overthrow an "established government.")

Within days of the media blitz that surrounded the administration's claims, the National Security Council approved plans to send $25 million in fresh military aid to the junta; $63 million in economic aid; and fifty-six advisers— strike that, "trainers"—to teach Salvadoreans how to use their new weaponry: Green Berets to train a new "quick reaction force" of 2,000 men; counterinsurgency experts to help plan the war; helicopter and intelligence specialists, and more.

At the embassy in San Salvador, a successor to the deposed ambassador, Robert White, was carefully chosen: Deane Hinton had served as director of the U.S. Agency for International Development (AID) in Guatemala from 1967 to 1969, during the height of the counterinsurgency war assisted by American Green Berets. He then moved to the U.S. embassy in Chile, during the campaign to destabilize the Allende government. Hinton was and is one of the few Reagan appointees with experience in Latin America—and the situation in El Salvador called for an expert.

Ghosts of Vietnam

But the road to intervention in El Salvador was not as smooth as the administration expected it to be. Secretary Haig was dismayed by the Europeans' cool reaction to his envoys; the Socialist International continued to press for negotiations with the rebels; and President López Portillo of Mexico had the audacity to state that Cuba was Mexico's beloved friend.

As for the U.S. public, there was little enthusiasm for another war in a godforsaken country that few people could find on a map, but where, it was said, "vital U.S. interests" were at stake. President Reagan said the 56 advisers would not go out on combat missions, but many remembered that the first 500 in Vietnam were technically "civilians." He said he foresaw no need for U.S. ground troops—but neither had

Eisenhower, Kennedy or Johnson. The Vietnam analogy haunted the administration, and by March, letters to the White House were running ten to one against military aid to the junta.[17]

Opposition to Reagan's policies toward Central America was well organized by the spring of 1981. A new generation of activists had joined with veterans of the Vietnam protests to create a Committee in Solidarity with the Salvadorean People (CISPES) in October 1980. By May, more than 200 chapters across the United States were organizing teach-ins and marches and lobbying campaigns.

The voice of Monseñor Romero—and the deaths of four American women—had galvanized churches of all denominations into active protest against U.S. policy. A student in the solidarity movement was shocked when he went home for Easter break to a Polish suburb of Chicago: "I hadn't been able to talk politics with my parents for years," he said. "But there they were, studying El Salvador in Bible classes and organizing candlelight vigils in memory of the archbishop's murder."

In Boston, a group of nuns and priests sat down in the offices of Speaker of the House Tip O'Neill. Archbishop James A. Hickey of Washington D.C. told Congress, in the name of the Catholic bishops of the United States, that the sending of U.S. advisers was "risky to the point of reckless."[18]

Congress could hardly ignore the deluge of letters from constituents. Slowly, the shadow of the white paper began to recede and congresspeople began to talk about violations of the War Powers Act, requiring the president to consult with Congress before sending U.S. military personnel into combat areas. Representative Clarence Long of Maryland reminded his colleagues that he was the only member of Congress whose son fought in Vietnam. He did not want other sons to fight in "another Vietnam."

Embarrassed by the backlash, the administration clumsily tried to downplay the issue and push El Salvador to the back pages once again: "Our impression is that this story is running about five times as big as it really is," a senior State Department official told reporters—adding that the administration would like reporters to write less about El Salvador and more about other issues.[19] Perhaps spurred by this rebuke, some journalists began to reexamine the origins of the El Salvador "story." That in itself soon made front-page news.

The White Paper Has Holes

A June 8 headline in the *Wall Street Journal* asked a question: "Tarnished Report?"—then beneath it, "Apparent Errors Cloud U.S. 'White Paper.' "[20] One day later, the lead paragraph in a *Washington Post* report read as follows: "The State Department's white paper on El Salvador, published in February, contains factual errors, misleading statements and unresolved ambiguities that raise questions about the administration's interpretation of participation by communist countries in the Salvadorean civil war."[21]

The gist of both these articles was that the sweeping conclusions of the white paper were not substantiated by a careful reading of the documents themselves. For example, the summary had cited 800 tons of weapons pledged to El Salvador by the socialist bloc, and 200 tons delivered by the time of the January offensive. Not true. The documents indicated that at most 10 tons had made it across the border. Nowhere was there even a mention of 200 or 800 tons.

Jon Glassman, the State Department official said to have discovered and deciphered the documents, tried to explain some of the discrepancies to Jonathan Kwitny of the *Journal:* the statistics on arms shipments came not from the documents, he said, but from "extrapolations" on reports of air and truck traffic in the region. There were "guesses" and "errors"—such as attributing authorship to Shafik Handal of the incriminating documents on arms aid to the guerrillas. And there were "embellishments" that conveniently linked the FMLN to the administration's bogeymen around the world. The white paper, for example, describes a meeting between Salvadoreans and the Palestinian leader, Yasir Arafat. "Arafat promises military equipment, including arms and aircraft," according to the white paper. But the document includes only a parenthetical reference: "On the 22nd there was a meeting with Arafat."[22] Nothing more.

The State Department defended its conclusions, despite these exposés, citing "still-secret sources" that would confirm its claims. But the exposures added a new element to the analogy between El Salvador and Vietnam; the government's credibility was badly shaken, casting doubt on the authenticity of the documents themselves.

No Easy Victory

The loud drum-beating strategy of Secretary Haig had backfired, along with attempts to manipulate the press; not only the public but the media was at long last skeptical of official claims. And by the summer of 1981, it was slowly dawning on the administration that the war in El Salvador would not be short. Haig had expected more of the Salvadorean army, and less of the guerrillas. Easy in, easy out— a cheap victory for the administration's anti-Soviet battle worldwide and a feather in his cap.

But El Salvador today is not Guatemala, or Bolivia, or Venezuela of the late 1960s, where counterinsurgency worked well against small guerrilla bands. In El Salvador, the electoral struggles of the 1960s, the protests and base communities and land seizures of the seventies had made struggle a tradition and fermented the revolution. The people saw no alternative by 1981 but to fight; they had nothing more to lose.

In such conditions, counterinsurgency means a war against the people and the army's tactics are designed accordingly. "Special war," as the FMLN commander Salvador Cayetano Carpio, has called it, means "the extermination of the population in order to deprive the movement of its life blood." On its search-and-destroy missions, allegedly designed to "separate the fish from the water," the army does not distinguish between armed guerrillas and the peasantry at large; the victims are usually women, children and the elderly. "The result of this inhuman war," said Carpio in a recent interview, "is the depopulation of entire areas. Even someone who is hardened to seeing people suffer so much is struck by how many compañeros are lost and how many children are murdered. One of my strongest recollections from my visits to the war zones are the enormous stretches where villages are completely overgrown with weeds. Beautiful little houses left behind. You can see the care the peasants used to put into their homes. All this, all of it, covered with weeds. All the furniture, whatever these humble peasants had, thrown out and burned. And most of the houses burned. Dozens and dozens of villages like this, over a huge area. This is what explains the great number of refugees, about 500,000 of them in El Salvador and neighboring countries."[23]

While the army's tactics are murderously effective against the civilian population, they consistently have failed to crush the guerrilla columns of the FMLN. Newspaper reports increasingly evoke memories of Vietnam: the guerrillas seem to "melt away" as the army approaches; their camps "spring back to life" once they leave. Each time the army claims to have "cleaned up" an area, the guerrillas make a mockery of their claims by staging ambushes or the temporary occupation of towns. In Morazán, after one much publicized sweep by the army in August 1981, the FMLN came back to occupy the town of Perquín for nine days. And from "somewhere in El Salvador," *Radio Venceremos* broadcasts news of the war to the entire country, while the army searches in vain for transmitters.

"One of the strengths of the revolutionary movement," says Cayetano Carpio, "is its presence throughout the country. The army finds itself completely circumscribed in its operations. It can't move about freely in most regions because of the threat of ambushes everywhere. The troops therefore get confined to fixed bases. If it weren't for helicopters, these forces couldn't be sustained." Carpio calls helicopters "the guts of this kind of war." They ferry the elite Aclacatl Brigade, trained by U.S. advisers as a quick-reaction force, into combat zones that the regular army is reluctant to enter. They also are mounted with machine guns, and there have been repeated reports of choppers firing at civilian populations—once, at least, with U.S. military and civilian officials aboard.[24]

But in August 1981 Ambassador Deane Hinton had to

admit that all ten choppers supplied to the Salvadorean army by the United States had been knocked out of commission by guerrilla ground fire; there were problems with spare parts for repairs.[25] Official sources reported that casualties within the army were as high as 12 percent for the first six months of 1981.[26] And the junta was again pleading for more U.S. aid.

By late summer it was clear that quick victory for either side was a mirage and that the Salvadorean army, by itself, did not have the means, the men or the capacity to win the war. The United States sent four more helicopters in August, without announcing the shipment publicly, but still it was not enough.[27] Ronald Reagan had promised to bring the advisers home quickly, but now he had to send an additional team to assemble and test fly the choppers.

The Salvadorean economy was a bottomless pit that millions of U.S. aid dollars could never fill: $144 million were sent in fiscal 1981, but many more millions had been taken out of the country by the fleeing oligarchs investing in Miami condominiums. Twenty-five percent of the country's power grid was knocked out in August by the FMLN, leaving entire cities in darkness for weeks at a time. Duarte took a portable generator along to press conferences and speeches. Warehouses full of crops ready for export were burned to the ground and bridges were bombed throughout the country.

Ambassador Hinton told reporters, somewhat apologetically: "The army can't defend anything all the time. [They] have 10,000 or 12,000 men, and there are an estimated four to six thousand guerrillas in action. In Malaya [in the 1950s] the British had a ten-to-one advantage and it took them four to five years to defeat the rebels there."[28] It would be a long war.

The Mexico-French Declaration

On August 28, 1981, Mexico and France, now led by a Socialist president, Francois Mitterand, issued a joint declaration that sent shock waves through the diplomatic community. The declaration recognized the FMLN/FDR as "a representative political force" that must take part in future negotiations to end the conflict. It also called for a restructuring of El Salvador's armed forces before "authentically free" elections could be held there. The declaration was clear testimony to the FMLN's advances on the battlefield and to the FDR's success in winning international support.

The Reagan administration immediately scurried to offset the impact of the Mexican-French initiative, encouraging a counter-declaration from Guatemala, Chile, Argentina, Paraguay, Venezuela, Bolivia, Colombia and the Dominican Republic. Their statement accused Mexico and France of "interfering in the internal affairs of El Salvador." But that was all that Washington could extract. There was no statement of support for the junta from this potpourri of nations, all dependent on the United States for aid and arms.

The Salvadorean junta started its own public relations campaign. Napoleón Duarte came to New York to address the General Assembly of the United Nations. With a surprisingly straight face, he said that "El Salvador's problems must involve only Salvadoreans," and then flew to Washington to lobby for more helicopters, communications gear, trucks—and $300 million in economic assistance. Duarte did not ask for more advisers, however, insisting that Salvadoreans wanted to be self-reliant.[29]

On his ten-day tour of the United States in September 1981, Duarte was accompanied by Colonel Vides Casanova, head of the National Guard and a man tightly linked to the death squads.[30] Vides Casanova made sure that Duarte never departed from his script. He rejected any negotiations or dialogue with "organized armed sectors" and told the U.S. press that the Salvadorean army is "obedient." But from New York to San Francisco, Duarte was pursued by demonstrators and plagued by embarrassing questions concerning the deaths of the four American women. Six soldiers arrested for the crime in April 1981 had still not been charged, nor had their names been made public. It was unlikely they would ever be brought to trial. Duarte told the National Press Club in Washington that if the suspects were presented to the judge, the judge might be threatened.[31]

His meetings with senators and congresspeople, his appearances on television talk shows, and his speech to the United Nations brought little comfort to Duarte's cause. On September 23, 1981, the Senate imposed conditions on further military aid to the junta that stipulate that President Reagan must certify, twice a year, that El Savador's junta is making progress in human rights and political reforms; that it is making "good faith efforts" toward investigating the American deaths, before U.S. aid can be released.

At the United Nations, in December 1981, a strong resolution was passed condemning the junta's violations of human rights and calling for a negotiated end to the war. France, Greece, Algeria, Yugoslavia and West Germany had lobbied strongly for the resolution, and only Turkey and the United States, alone among the NATO powers, voted to oppose it.

The call for negotiations was echoed in newspaper editorials in the United States and, increasingly, the Reagan administration was seen as the major obstacle to an end to the bloodshed taking a toll of 1,000 lives a month by the end of January 1981.[32]

But the administration had backed itself into a corner. By declaring El Salvador a test of American resolve, by escalating the war into a confrontation between East and West, it had left itself no room for graceful concessions or reassessments of the political costs of U.S. involvement. European allies were betting on the other horse; Latin American countries, even those antagonistic to the revolutionary cause, were loath to support a policy of direct U.S. intervention. And opposition at home was surprisingly strong.

Elections as a Way Out

In July 1981 Thomas Enders, assistant secretary of state for inter-American affairs, made a speech to the World Affairs Council that signaled a change in the administration's strategy for selling the war. Enders made the usual references to external threats "so close to our shores," but the tone was less hysterical than the ravings of Alexander Haig. And the main portion of his speech was given over to a discussion of what he called a political solution to the conflict. "For just as

the conflict was Salvadorean in its origins," said Enders, caus-
ing eyebrows to rise, "so its ultimate resolution must be Salvadorean."[33]

The heart of this new strategy was to propose elections
as a way out of El Salvador's "vicious circle" of violence. Two
elections were planned: one in March 1982 to a Constituent
Assembly that would draft a new constitution, followed by
presidential elections in 1983. "All parties that renounce violence," said Enders, "should be encouraged to participate in
the design of new political institutions and the process of
choosing representatives from them." He specifically mentioned two legally registered parties in El Salvador—Ungo's
National Revolutionary Movement and the electoral vehicle
of the Communist Party, the Nationalist Democratic Union—
and invited them to test their strength with ballots instead
of bullets.

The strategy behind the elections proposal is simple: it
is designed to encourage divisions within the FMLN/FDR;
defuse criticism from Europe and Latin America; portray
the United States as a catalyst of democratic change; and,
most importantly, buy time for the war effort that will defeat
the guerrillas once and for all.

But the strategy hasn't worked. All member organizations
of the FMLN/FDR have refused to participate in the "electoral
farce." The Salvadorean Bar Association has stated that fair
elections would be impossible "under the current political
conditions," and Bishop Rivera y Damas, acting archbishop
of San Salvador, has accused the junta of imposing "an almost
massive level of repression in the rural areas" and a "selective"
campaign of violence in the cities. Such conditions, he said,
"would make it appear that elections alone are not the desired
solution for the simple reason that elections and war are
different problems."[34] Typical of European sentiments is the
reaction of Pierre Schori, international secretary of Sweden's
Social Democratic Party: "Elections with death lists of the
opposition—you might as well hold them in the cemeteries."[35]

Indeed, the notion of free elections in a country with no
freedoms is preposterous and cynical. El Salvador's independent press has been extinguished; critics of the junta
must flee the country to voice their opinions; people involved

in refugee work and human rights investigations, including judges appointed by the junta, are routinely assassinated. Can the United States really expect opposition leaders to campaign, when six leaders of the FDR were kidnapped, tortured and murdered in November 1980? Can it really expect people to lay down their arms and trust in the willingness of the army to accept the people's verdict?

The answer is that neither the United States nor the junta expects any of the above. Instead, they offer only more of the same: more helicopters, more advisers, more bloodshed and a meaningless exercise in elections to cover it all under a sheath of democratic choice. Who are the candidates in the 1982 elections? The names should ring a bell: former Major D'Aubuisson, the man believed to have masterminded the assassination of Monseñor Romero; retired General "Chele" Medrano, the man who founded ORDEN. Both have formed their own parties to compete with two more parties representing conservative business sectors and, on the other end of the spectrum, the Christian Democrats. The army, under Colonel García, has grouped itself around the Party of National Conciliation (PCN), its traditional war-horse.

Meanwhile, the FMLN/FDR continue to press for negotiations with the junta. They have set no preconditions for beginning the talks; they have asked that other governments take part as witnesses; and once the repression and the war have ended, they see elections as essential to establishing a genuine democracy. But the FMLN/FDR have few illusions about the prospects of negotiating with an army still firmly backed by the United States. "Negotiations don't automatically mean solutions," says Carpio. "To negotiate is to negotiate, to disagree. Each side has its point of view and sometimes they are uncompromising points of view. It's a very complex process that many people do not understand. But two things must be emphasized about the possibility of negotiations in El Salvador: the irreversible determination on the part of the revolutionary forces to fight to the end, if necessary, to guarantee the interests of the Salvadorean people and, at the same time, their flexibility and willingness to negotiate in order to arrive at a just outcome worthy of our people."[36]

Stalemate Can Be Fatal

If the Reagan administration continues to reject negotiations and support the junta's intransigence, there is no end to the war in sight. And most sources now agree, at least in private, that the guerrillas have the upper hand. Secretary of State Haig called it a "stalemate" in November 1981, and remarked that stalemates can be fatal.[37] According to the *Washington Post*, the FMLN now controls an estimated one-quarter of the national territory.[38] And the guerrillas no longer predict quick victories, but they are confident that the tide has turned definitively in their favor.

The country is now divided into three different "fields of struggle": first, the FMLN's zones of control, or "liberated territories," which include strings of guerrilla camps that control the surrounding areas and provide protection to the peasant population; second, the areas dominated by the FMLN but where the army and related paramilitary forces still have a scattered presence; and third, areas of the country, particularly the cities, where the army's presence has forced the opposition to devise underground forms of resistance.

In the liberated territories, the government in San Salvador doesn't exist. Local officials haven't been heard from since they all fled to the garrisons for protection and, in some areas, people have elected their own local governments.

"Throughout these liberated territories," according to Cayetano Carpio, "there are certain villages or clusters of houses or stretches of a few miles where members of the paramilitary force, ORDEN, still live, or where army patrols of anywhere from fifty to seventy soldiers can still be found. But these people don't dare to carry out any offensive operations. They are completely isolated for miles and miles around. All roads have been cut, and there is no electricity or anything. The soldiers keep functioning only by helicopters since they have no other way of moving. Then you encounter a vast stretch of land where only the guerrillas and the people live, roaming freely from one area to another. They still take military precautions, of course, against enemy ambushes which can still occur."

In the "disputed areas," the situation is more complex.

The population is divided into two groups: those who live in the vicinity of the many guerrilla camps that exist throughout the central part of the country; and towns nearby where the army has stationed paramilitary troops from ORDEN or military patrols with their families. These are the most treacherous areas for the guerrillas and the peasantry, and one of the FMLN's primary goals today is to convert these areas into "liberated zones."

In the large cities the government has attempted to create showcases for the rest of the world, using brutality to enforce a climate of "business as usual." There is therefore little evidence of opposition activity, aside from the constant power blackouts and the clandestine distribution of mimeographed sheets. "Right now it would be a mistake to plan [demonstrations] because of the intense repression," said Carpio. "So in the cities there seems to be passivity in the sense that you find less activity compared to several years ago. But this doesn't tell you anything about the morale of the people or about the levels of organization that aren't visible. Appearances should not be confused with reality."

The FMLN/FDR maintains that the process of consolidating and expanding the liberated territories will proceed, alongside efforts to prepare for popular insurrections in the cities. The longer the war goes on, they say, the more their ranks will swell with the victims of the army's atrocities.

What are people fighting for in El Salvador, and what do they see as their future? There are no simple answers. But perhaps a closer look at life in the liberated zones will provide some insights into the changes envisioned by the FMLN/FDR, into the reasons people still say they prefer "to die quickly fighting than to die slowly starving."

Life in the Liberated Zones

On the cusp of a tree-covered hill in northern El Salvador stand several dozen mud-and-stick huts, gathered haphazardly around what tries to be a square. It is almost dusk and a group of people are gathered around a flag pole as the flag of the FMLN is raised. Their almost tuneless voices break the evening silence.

> Revolución o Muerte
> Es una diaria consigna
> Es la consigna del pueblo
> Es el destino de todos

> Revolution or Death
> It is the daily cry
> It is the slogan of the people
> It is the destiny of all.

Life in the liberated zones is very basic. The areas have no electricity; they never did. Roads in and out have been mined. Water comes from streams and rivers and springs. "Revolutionary crops" are sown for basic subsistence and to feed *los muchachos;* but often they are burned when the army passes through.

The FMLN does not try to hold these areas when attacked by the army. Rather they gather the people in the zone together, and lead them through the army's encirclement to safety. Once the children and old people are safe, the guerrillas return to engage the enemy in battle. And once the army leaves, they lead the people back to pick up the pieces of their lives.

People stay in these war zones because, ironically, it is safer there than in any other part of the country. Before the FMLN established these zones of control, and before the war even, daily life was the constant dread that the National Guard might appear and drag off one's spouse; or the landlord that rented the land might rape one's daughter. Now the young men and women of the FMLN protect them from all that.

Very few outsiders have visited the liberated zones. The trip there is fraught with danger. But a composite picture can be drawn from the accounts of several journalists, American and European, who visited the zones on separate occasions between March and November of 1981.[39] Invariably they were struck by the harsh conditions of life, but they were also impressed by the ingenuity employed to cope with them.

To those who knew El Salvador "in the old days" the contrasts are startling. Before, life in the *campo* consisted of long hours in the field—first tending to the landlord's crops, and then, with what time was left, to the tiny parcels that the campesinos rented in exchange for their labor. When the landlord or the National Guard was not around, ORDEN watched over the land. And at night, and on Sundays, the campesinos drowned their sorrows and fears in *aguardiente*; they beat their wives; fought with their neighbors in drunken, machete brawls.

Today, in the liberated pockets controlled by the FMLN, people still work from dawn to dusk. They grow sorghum, corn and rice—collectively or, more often, on individual plots. But they work to feed themselves and their families, and to sustain the war. The ORDEN people have fled to the protection of National Guard outposts in the depopulated towns. And there is no drunkenness, no liquor at all. The FMLN forbids it within its ranks. Security dictates a constant state of alert for all.

Some villages are only a few kilometers from the nearest refugee camp. Anyone could walk over there at any time. But many prefer to stay—out of political commitment, or out of a more basic desire for security. The refugee camps are invaded periodically by the army; men and boys are taken away and never seen again. The FMLN teaches the people in the villages to resist and stay alive.

In each community there is usually a small house where a dozen or so guerrillas live. It is like a fort and a central command that stays in contact with the FMLN camps in the area. In addition to the small core of seasoned fighters, there is the local militia—young men and women from age 16 to 24, who are responsible for the security of the village. They are poorly armed. Some train only with sticks. But they volunteer for the most dangerous patrols. "The junta's soldiers are on strange terrain in these areas, and they are always afraid. But the village is the militia members' home. They are defending their mothers, their children," said an American observer on the scene. "Their morale is incredibly high."

Everyone in the community has a task, in addition to tending the fields. One area of work is called "*ingeniería*"

*Above: hospital in a
liberated zone.*

*Right: guerrillas in training
in liberated zone.*

*Facing page: members of
the local militias of the
FMLN, Chalatenango
province.*

H.E. Mattison

Rick Reinhard

Below: Salvador Cayetano Carpio, one of five principal commanders of the FMLN.

Facing page top: army regulars and their mutilated victims in Chalatenango province.

Facing page bottom: a refugee camp at La Virtud, Honduras.

(engineering). It means recovering bombs that are dropped by the army but fail to explode, then taking the shells apart and repacking them into homemade bombs. Others in *ingeniería* dig the trenches, the hiding places, the tunnels.

In one area, villagers had erected a "fish factory" near a stream which is dammed save for a small opening. As the fish leap through the opening, they land on a board beside the stream and immediately are taken to fires along the bank. There they are smoked, and readied for the backpacks of the people's army.

The older men and women build furniture for the huts or tend to the infants. Youngsters toss tortillas or gather wood for the fires. And women are encouraged to take on tasks that break the bounds of their traditional roles in society. "We have some women who join us as cooks," one guerrilla explained. "But they soon realize that they have opportunities to do other things. They become combatants, or medics, or leaders."[40] A woman standing nearby nods her agreement. She has been trained as a combat engineer and now is in charge of fortifications for ten guerrilla camps.

The number of women in arms varies from one place to another. In areas where the popular organizations once were strong, where there is a long history of struggle, and where, perhaps, there are more women from the cities, women's participation tends to be greater. But everywhere, the old patterns of *machismo* are coming apart. Men do not brag of their conquests any more, or fight with other men over nothing. "The organization wouldn't take my husband in," said one woman, "because he used to drink and beat me. I was a member of the organization before he was."

New Priorities

The FMLN says the tasks of "reconstruction" have not yet begun in the liberated zones; the struggle for the bare necessities of life is still too hard. But despite the very great limitations on human and material resources, new priorities have been established and small steps taken toward addressing the most urgent needs of the community. Health and education head the list.

One area visited by reporters had only one doctor to treat the wounds of FMLN fighters and serve the community at large. But he started a barefoot doctors program in the village, training young people with at least a second-grade education to recognize malaria, typhoid and different infections. They now treat routine emergencies, set breaks, pull molars and the like.

Everyone in the village attends classes in first aid and basic hygiene. The purpose, explains the doctor, is to show people that doctors are not magical creatures that have the secret key to their needs.

A village in another province has one doctor and a surgeon who commutes between an FMLN field hospital and an eighteen-bed facility in the village itself. Amputations are done with a Swiss army knife and without the benefit of morphine. The doctors say they have treated campesinos who arrive in the village with blotch-burn marks, the sign of white phosphorous bombing.

Just as most people in the liberated zones had never been treated by a doctor before, most of the children had never been to school. They were too far away, or the children were needed in the fields. Now the children sit outdoors, or under thatched roofs, on wooden logs, stretching to see over the heads of those in front. There are too many pupils and not enough teachers to go around. The blackboard is an old painted door, and sticks scratch the earth in lieu of pens and paper.

The "superintendent of schools" in one liberated zone is a 48-year old nun, Sister Rosa, who walks thirty-five kilometers a week to visit schools in four different villages. In perfect English, she tells a reporter that she taught school in New Jersey for twenty years, but the last nine months in her own country have been "the most meaningful" of her life.

Sister Rosa talks with sadness about the children's anxiety. Two schools have had to be moved several times to evade the army. The teachers are poorly trained; they should be students themselves. But education for adults is still a luxury. Most cannot read or write.

Political education is also a priority in the liberated zones, but it is voluntary, by all accounts, and received with mixed reviews. Some people say they have trouble understanding the students or city-types that come to the villages to talk about imperialism or socialism or democracy. Others seem remarkably well informed, given the isolation of these zones, about Nicaragua's agrarian reform, or the latest installment of U.S. aid to the junta. *Radio Venceremos* is the villagers' only source of news, and guerrilla couriers arrive periodically to replenish their supply of batteries.

Breaking Through the Lines

Life is precarious in the liberated zones. At any moment militia patrols may come back with news that the army is on its way. Then mortar fire; the drunken voices of ORDEN people, who lead the army into the zones as the soldiers move cautiously through the underbrush. Overhead whir the Huey helicopters, Vietnam-surplus, firing indiscriminately into the trees. The leaves rattle as if with rain.

One American lived through such an operation. "First the guerrillas broke through the army's encirclement. They opened a little hole in the lines and we all crawled through on our bellies. The woman next to me had her jaw blown off."

It seems like an interminable journey to safety. Mothers half smothering their infants to keep their cries from alerting the army; elderly men and women running to catch up with the others, and the militia closing up in the rear. "Why don't they send the civilians—at least the elderly—to the refugee camps?" the American asks. "They choose to stay," he is told. "And we are glad. *Necesitamos el calor de las masas*. We need the warmth of the masses. It reminds us whom we are fighting for."

Once the civilians are safely out of the battle zone, the FMLN returns to fight in earnest, wasting no bullets, frustrating the army with their elusive tactics and detailed knowledge of the terrain. Finally the army leaves, often inventing success stories and body counts to justify their departure. And the villagers return. The army has burned their huts and torched the fields. What little livestock they had is dead. But they begin anew; digging up the food they have hidden away, sowing the fields. One man in the village has survived thirteen such operations. He explains why he stays: "Well, compañero, I'm an old man already. I'm thirty-two. What we're fighting for, those who will reap the benefits, are the children."

Some people in the liberated zones talk about a socialist tomorrow. Others say they are not sure what that means, and they refer to the Bible, to loving one's neighbor and working together as equals, as their vision of the future. Or they talk about Nicaragua, and what they hear is happening there in the countryside and in the schools. And some don't talk about the future at all. They just treasure their temporal safety from the National Guard, the landlord, the neighbor who belongs to ORDEN. And they talk about what it means to live as a community and trust one another. "*Los muchachos* made it possible."

For Isabél, a Refugee

Here in our cramped Solidarity office
on Clark Street, you are safe.
The child's breath a single flute note,
humming your pulse,
raising your breast in waves
that roll the sleeper away, away.
Her tiny hand a fist grip
even in your arms, even here.

We are relieved when you remember to talk, mer-
ciful as family chatter at my father's wake,
hovering, desperate comfort, above an abyss.
You recite a litany of terror
It was our blood, you whisper,
on their boots, tracked through the campo,
bleeding us over the land.
Careful butchers, to tie our thumbs
behind our silent backs.

Then exile and Honduran camps
where disease and hunger coil
like coyotes ready to spring.
Five, ten funerals a week
always children, asleep in coffin cradles,
luminous in candle flames and wildflowers,
annointed in tears and sorrow songs.
We are peasants who endure.

By morning light the men
planted a green necklace of corn
around the hills' charcoal throat.
Somos los trabajadores.
Women told the children
God burned life into the soil,
and stayed with them,
passing 5,000 across the border,
safe under the guerrillas arc,
whose arms opened
the mountains and rivers dark doors,
swift and sure as the
hands of God on the Red Sea.

I will see my land again
when the revolution triumphs.
That soil which holds forever
in its dark blood womb
the bones of Farabundo Martí
and all the fallen ones.
Every seed that swings
a green shoot skyward, defies despair.
We will harvest
a nation from a graveyard.
With every murder,
they grow another revolutionary
sweet and defiant as corn.

—Renny Golden
Chicago Religious Task Force on
El Salvador/Central America

CHAPTER IX

The Wider War

A likely article in the New York Times, *some day in the not-too-distant future: Washington—President Reagan announced today he had ordered fourteen American gunships to take up positions in the Gulf of Mexico, off the coasts of Guatemala, Nicaragua and Honduras, to enforce a quarantine against arms shipments from Cuba to Nicaragua.*

"We are moving to curb Communist interference in a tragic, rapidly spreading conflict in the Central American region," said President Reagan in a brief statement. "As a result of continued provision of arms from Cuba through Nicaragua to pro-communist guerrillas in El Salvador, Guatemala and Honduras, violence has engulfed these countries and now, war has broken out between Nicaragua and Honduras. We believe that naval control of the arms flow is a necessary step to prevent further escalation and to re-establish peace quickly."

Under the South Atlantic Command, the fourteen ships will remain until further orders patroling in a chain from northern Guatemala to the coast of Costa Rica. Up to now, U.S. military involvement in the region was limited to supplying military aid and advisers.

The president said the United States had not provided support to the army of approximately 2,000 rebels, including Nicaraguan exiles opposed to the Sandinista junta as well as Honduran soldiers, which crossed the border into Nicaragua last Thursday. The rebels engaged in combat with the Sandinista army in at least three villages in western Nicaragua. Reports that fighter jets belonging to the Honduran army had bombed the dense jungle in the area to aid the incursion could not be verified.

In response to questions, the president said, "The democratically elected government of Honduras has faced repeated provocation from the Nicaraguan junta." He added that no commitment of U.S. combat troops to Central America is contemplated at this time.

Following the president's statement, a high-ranking State Department official said in a briefing that the administration would push for quick action in the Organization of American States for a Central American peace-keeping force drawn from several Latin American countries. Both Argentina and Venezuela have already expressed their willingness to participate with troops.

[In Nicaragua, Defense Minister Humberto Ortega declared a war emergency and ordered a full-scale mobilization of the 60,000-strong militia reserves.]

Turning to the inside, one might also find an article describing the largest army offensive to date in El Salvador, involving 4,000 men, artillery and extensive air support against rebel positions in Morazán province. One might learn that Argentina is supplying logistical and intelligence support to the offensive, and is considering sending several crack battalions if the Salvadorean junta requests such aid. And in Guatemala, insurgents have launched their most daring action yet, against military garrisons in five provinces, in the latest chapter in that country's increasingly bloody civil war.

Part of a futuristic nightmare? Or the rhetoric of the Reagan administration put into practice? The logic of that rhetoric contains a built-in escalation clause: if El Salvador is only one battle in a larger war against Soviet designs, then the "El Salvador Solution" must be applied to Guatemala as well, where insurgents are only steps behind their Salvadorean counterparts in their capacity to threaten a ruthless regime. If Somoza was first on the Soviet "hit list," and if Nicaragua now serves as a "foothold" to spread revolutionary fires, then the defeat of U.S. policy toward Nicaragua must not be regarded as irreversible. And if Cuba is the most dangerous source of unrest in the region, then Cuba must be dealt with as well. As Secretary of State Haig has stated, "We must go to the source."

There is no question that Washington will try to avoid the commitment of U.S. combat troops in Central America. But it has many options short of that—all of which spell greater U.S. involvement in a regionalized conflict that could dwarf Vietnam as an American trauma.

Already there is considerable coordination among the armies of El Salvador, Guatemala and Honduras. High-level talks among the three governments have established an informal alliance designed to help the Salvadorean army confront future FMLN offensives.[1] Banned from sending military aid to Guatemala, under the provisions of a human rights rider to the Foreign Assistance Act, and facing growing domestic opposition to continued aid to El Salvador, the Reagan administration is sending arms and advisers to Honduras for the fight against "regional subversion." Honduras already has the strongest air force in Central America. Now its army is being groomed for a regional role in a conflict that could very well pit Honduran troops against Nicaragua's seasoned army and local militia. Border clashes have occurred with growing frequency since early 1980.

Countries in the Southern Cone of Latin America consider themselves experts in the art of counterinsurgency. Relations between the governments of El Salvador and Guatemala, on the one hand, and Chile and Argentina, on the other, have never been more cordial. Argentina provided $15 million in economic aid to El Salvador in 1981, and diplomatic and military sources in Argentina have acknowledged that Argentina is providing six-month training courses for Salvadorean intelligence officers, focusing on problems of organization, infiltration and interrogation.[2]

Argentina's new president, General Leopoldo Galtieri, is known to be greatly concerned about El Salvador as "a key point for the continental balance." In an interview published several months before his new appointment, Galtieri was asked: "[Is] the Argentine Army . . . thinking of sending more personnel than usual to El Salvador? Galtieri: "In principle we are not thinking of that." Question: "But you do not think of it as a crazy idea...?" Galtieri: "I will not think of it as a crazy idea if it is requested by the Government of El Salvador."³

Meanwhile, the *New York Times* reported on November 5, 1981, that Secretary of State Haig has asked for contingency plans from the Pentagon for possible military action in El Salvador and against Cuba and Nicaragua. "Officials said that examples of requests for Pentagon studies were phrased in terms of 'Show me what U.S. forces could do if there were a decision to blockade Nicaragua or launch certain types of operations against Cuba.' "

"The officials said," the article continued, "that several Latin American countries had been contacted at high levels in government and the military and asked if they might join in any kind of military operations. The officials did not say or did not know what the responses were . . ."⁴

Haig may be blustering and bluffing, but as Cayetano Carpio of the FMLN said recently, "When the sickness of militarism runs so deep, the worst insanities can happen."⁵ A closer look at the situation in three key countries in Central America—Honduras, Nicaragua and Guatemala—underlines the potential consequences of greater direct or indirect U.S. involvement in Central America's war.

HONDURAS: THE NEW REGIONAL GENDARME

The borders of three countries come together near the dusty town of Nueva Ocotepeque in Honduras. Despite the lack of amenities, it is a perfect meeting place for officers from Honduras, Guatemala and El Salvador, the "iron triangle" of Central America. There they discuss plans to coordinate military strategy, to aid one another against "communist subversion" and keep tabs on neighboring Nicaragua. El Salvador and Guatemala boast the largest armies in the region, but Honduras is clearly the key partner in this new alliance—the only one not fully absorbed by the fight against revolutionary forces within its own borders. Honduras is still comparatively tranquil; its army can look outward.

Until recently, Honduras fit the stereotype of a "banana republic" to a tee: second only to Haiti in per capita poverty; chronically unstable, with 150 governments in 160 years; ruled by a notoriously corrupt set of generals; and catering to the whims of Standard Fruit and United Brands. Washington virtually ignored the country and its neighbors privately mocked its army's resounding defeat in the 1969 war with El Salvador.

But then came the demise of Anastasio Somoza in Nicaragua, the strongman of the region, its pillar of stability. Somoza had actively promoted CONDECA (the Central American Defense Council) and gone to the aid of dictators in distress (as in the case of El Salvador's Sánchez Hernández in 1972). Without him, and with revolutionary movements threatening the stability of El Salvador and Guatemala, U.S. policymakers began the search for a new steadfast ally in the region. It didn't take long. Costa Rica has no army; Panama's Omar Torrijos had supported the Sandinistas and was talking to the FMLN/FDR; Honduras was their only choice.

In 1980, Congress approved $53.1 million in economic aid to Honduras and $3.9 million in military aid—making it second only to El Salvador as the largest recipient of U.S. aid, despite a sparse population of 3 million. Military aid to Honduras included mortars, grenade launchers, M-16s, communications gear, training for Honduran officers—and, on *loan* to the Honduran government and therefore not included in the aid total, ten HUEY helicopter gunships for a country not at war.[6] By the spring of 1980, there were 37 U.S. advisers in Honduras, but few people in the United States even noticed.[7] It was easier to slip them into Honduras than El Salvador, but their function was the same.

John Bushnell, President Carter's assistant secretary of state, told Congress that military aid to Honduras was essential to its new "geopolitical role," and to the U.S. effort to halt the flow of arms to El Salvador's FMLN. The helicopters would be used to patrol the border areas. "We predict that the conflict with El Salvador will diminish quickly," he said, "and that, when this happens, the helicopters will be returned to the United States."[8] The advisers were needed to accompany the choppers.

In 1981 the Reagan administration raised the military aid total to Honduras to $8.8 million, with another $10.7 million authorized for fiscal 1982. This amounts to more military aid in just one year than Honduras received in all the years between 1950 and 1979.[9]

The payoff for U.S. policy in the region has been substantial since the aid faucet to Honduras was opened full force in 1980. During Carter's last year in office, the Honduran army turned its eyes southeast to El Salvador, where the army's efforts to "clean up" the northern provinces were an embarrassing failure. And since the Reagan administration broadened the scope of U.S. designs for the region, Honduras has turned to the southwest—to help Alexander Haig carry out his promise to "do something about Nicaragua." With domestic pressures at home to curb U.S. involvement in El Salvador, and keep "hands off" Nicaragua, the Reagan administration is deftly using Honduras as its proxy—and still, few people have taken note.

Burying the Hatchet

In 1980, the Carter administration and the Salvadorean junta alleged that the FMLN had established guerrilla bases in the demilitarized zones between Honduras and El Salvador. This stretch of land, three kilometers deep into each country, was a reminder of the border issues still in dispute since the 100-hours' war in 1969, and the OAS was still nominally in charge of making sure that neither army entered the zone. The Salvadorean army had been conducting clean-up operations there for months, but coordinated efforts with the Honduran armed forces would facilitate their task.

There was still bad blood between the two armies and border negotiations had been deadlocked for eleven years.

But suddenly, at a meeting in Miami in April 1980, shortly after the U.S. Congress approved the aid package to Honduras, there was a breakthrough. Honduras dropped its long-standing condition that the border line be finalized before relations could be mended. And five months later, in November 1980, a peace treaty was signed, with much fanfare, that simply outlined a procedure for future border talks while restoring full diplomatic and economic relations.

Most importantly, the peace treaty paved the way for greater military coordination between El Salvador and the newly armed Honduras. On both sides of the border, soldiers were lectured on the need for brotherly cooperation, the need to bury the hatchet lest the communist menace triumph and spread. As early as May 1980, one month after the Miami talks, armies on both sides began joint maneuvers, known as "sandwich operations." The first of these, the massacre at the Sumpul River, caught hundreds of Salvadoreans in the pincers of two armies. Honduran soldiers stood on the river bank separating the two countries and forced the desperate refugees back into the firing range of their Salvadorean brothers.

Coordination between the two armies has continued since that massacre. On March 16, 1981, the Salvadorean air force dropped bombs on 8,000 refugees attempting to cross the Lempa River into Honduras, and Honduran soldiers blocked their escape route.[10] Some two hundred peasants, mostly women and children, drowned or were killed.[11]

But even for the refugees who make it to Honduras alive, the peace treaty has meant continued persecution or death. Honduras has allowed Salvadorean air force planes to fly raids over its territory; Salvadorean soldiers and members of ORDEN regularly conduct tent-to-tent searches in the refugee camps, seizing those suspected of guerrilla ties. In late November 1981, 1,000 Salvadorean troops crossed into Honduras to comb the camps that now harbor more than 20,000 Salvadorean refugees. At La Virtud, one of the largest camps, raiders rounded up twenty refugees at gunpoint, tied their thumbs behind their backs in typical deathsquad fashion, and marched them out of the camp. According to Ingemar Cederberg, director for northern Latin

America for the United Nations High Commissioner for Refugees, Honduras' failure to protect the refugees is a violation of the U.N. Convention on the Status of Refugees and of "moral, international obligations."[12]

Eyes on the Other Border

In stark contrast to the plight of Salvadorean refugees, Nicaraguan exiles have found a hospitable new home in Honduras. Remnants of Somoza's National Guard, plus some new converts to their cause, are allowed to train on Honduran soil for the "liberation" of their homeland. They are also allowed, and actively encouraged, to launch nighttime raids across the border, attacking frontier posts and Sandinista patrols. Hundreds of Nicaraguans have been killed in these raids, including many young *brigadistas* teaching literacy classes in remote areas near the border. According to Nicaraguan Defense Minister Humberto Ortega, Honduran reconnaissance planes have violated Nicaraguan airspace and army patrols have covered the retreat of *somocista* raiders.[13]

There have also been direct clashes between the two armies, along the 1,000-mile border. The Honduran army's weekly television program has repeatedly focused on the border incidents, exhorting the population to prepare to defend the homeland.

Room for Second Thoughts

But the Honduran army is not united in its willingness to do the U.S. bidding in Central America. Both the FMLN/FDR and the Sandinista government in Nicaragua have the sympathy of broad sectors of the Honduran population. Nicaragua's army and militia are nothing to scoff at, and the Hondurans can ill afford a replay of 1969, another blow to the army's prestige. Most importantly, the comparative tranquility of political life in Honduras cannot be expected to last. While there is no significant guerrilla movement to date, Honduras has some of the most highly organized trade union and peasant organizations in Central America; the economy is in deep trouble; and the recent elections offer no guarantees against growing unrest.

Jimmy Carter used the carrot of U.S. aid to pressure for a return to civilian rule in Honduras. The military had been in power for eighteen years, and the ruling general, Policarpo Paz García, was notoriously corrupt and a drunkard to boot. To make Honduras a more palatable ally in the region, and to preempt the growth of an armed opposition, Carter succeeded in pushing for constituent assembly elections in April 1980 and presidential elections in November 1981. The November race offered an exceedingly narrow range of choices, and both major candidates, of the Liberal and National Parties, had to promise the army a substantial voice in government before being approved.

The victor in November was Dr. Roberto Suazo Córdova, a conservative lawyer and Liberal Party candidate, but most observers believe that real power still resides in the army. The problems faced by the new government are serious. A secret study prepared in late 1981 by the Superior Council of the Honduran armed forces forecast that "a general disillusionment will set in from the sixth month of the new government when the Liberals cannot fulfill the expectations awakened among the electorate." The study concluded that "if anarchy and subversion" proliferate—perhaps a reference to land invasions in November 1981, involving over 4,000 peasants—the armed forces may face the choice of installing either "a revolutionary military government with broad popular support" or "a civilian-military dictatorship of the extreme right."[14]

Whether the army will try to sublimate domestic unrest by provoking a war with Nicaragua, or whether they will resist U.S. pressures and focus on domestic concerns, is a matter of much debate, and conflicting interests, in Tegucigalpa, Washington, San Salvador and Managua.

NICARAGUA: TURNING BACK THE CLOCK

Mornings before work or on weekend afternoons—once a week—thousands of volunteers gather in Managua's many open fields. Practicing with old World War I rifles, or wooden make-believe ones, they learn to march, to run with a rifle, to hug the ground, to shoot straight. The new recruits of the Sandinista Popular Militia tease each other lightly as they form into practice squads, taking particular aim at the veteran guerrilla fighters among their ranks. "Hey, compañero, did you come just to get off all that weight you've put on with your soft desk job?" The laughter isn't because they don't feel the gravity of the situation, but because they do.

It was only two and a half years ago that Nicaraguans finally drove Somoza and his National Guard from the country—at a cost of 40,000 dead, an equal number of children orphaned, 100,000 wounded. Homes, factories, schools, roads, croplands, whole cities were destroyed. And now Nicaraguans are preparing to fight once again.

When asked, they aren't sure where the invasion will come from, but they are sure it will come. It might involve just the paramilitary groups, training abroad in Honduras and the United States. Or it might include the Honduran army itself. Some are convinced the United States will intervene directly.

The Reagan administration has made no secret of its desire to turn back the clock in Nicaragua and "roll back" the revolution. At first the pretext was arms shipments to El Salvador's guerrillas. While never proven, these allegations prompted the February 1981 cut-off of further U.S. economic aid to the Nicaraguan government. Then came the Haig hyperbole of "totalitarian rule" in Nicaragua, the Soviet beachhead theory and claims that Nicaragua was arming itself to take over the isthmus.

A major aim of U.S. pronouncements was to rob Nicaragua of important allies in Latin America and Europe. But it hasn't worked. President López Portillo of Mexico has consistently denounced U.S. policy toward Nicaragua: "Amid falsehood and sophistry we have reached the extreme in which the campaign against Nicaragua is carried out in the name of democracy. It is no small paradox that the destruction of a democratic regime is proposed in order to save it from future risks or that an attempt is made to create a chain of peripheral dictatorships to maintain the welfare of the central democracies."[15]

European leaders, including Willy Brandt, Olof Palme of Sweden, French President Mitterand and Felipe González of Spain, formed the International Committee for the Defense of the Nicaraguan Revolution, and European governments and Mexico have sent substantial economic aid to Nicaragua. Even Venezuela, a steadfast ally of the United States in matters concerning El Salvador's junta, has made it clear to Washington that it opposes any military actions aimed at Nicaragua.[16]

But the administration appears to be proceeding with its plans to destabilize the Sandinista government. One aspect of U.S. policy is aimed at the Achilles' heel of the revolution— Nicaragua's war-ravaged economy. In addition to cutting off all economic aid to the government, and pressuring allies and multilateral agencies to do the same, the administration has suspended wheat exports to Nicaragua; it has warned that Nicaraguan beef exports to the United States will be cut off if Nicaragua goes ahead with plans to purchase breeding stock from Cuba; and it has threatened to stop exporting resins needed in Nicaragua's plastics plants, presumably because Nicaragua might sell its surplus to Cuba.

At the same time, the United States has sustained the flow of economic aid to sectors in Nicaragua opposed to the revolution, including the Superior Council of Private Enterprise (COSEP) and the conservative and smallest trade union federation, the National Confederation of Labor (CNT).

But economic strangulation is not an end in itself. It presupposes that persistent economic hardship will erode political support for the Sandinistas. The threat posed by Nicaragua to "stability" in the region is not a military one: it is the potential success of its literacy campaign, its agrarian reform, and other measures aimed at redistributing wealth and bettering the lot of its people. Henry Kissinger's 1970 cable to then U.S. ambassador to Chile, Edward Korry, comes to mind: "Once Allende comes to power in Chile we will do all in our power to condemn Chile and Chileans to the utmost deprivation and poverty; a policy designed for a long time to come to accelerate the hard features of a communist society in Chile."[17] Socialism can't be allowed to work.

But the Reagan administration has not stopped at economic measures. By allowing Nicaraguan exiles to train in Florida and California, the administration has signaled its support for freelance attempts to overthrow the Nicaraguan government, and holds the door open to coordination between these miniscule groups and a broader U.S. effort. In answer to Reagan's lame explanation that these groups are training on private property and are therefore untouchable, Commander Daniel Ortega of Nicaragua asked "How would the American government react if suddenly in Nicaragua . . . it should occur to some ranch owner to loan his property to train Puerto Ricans to fight for the independence of their country?"[18]

U.S. military aid and encouragement to Honduras now presents the most immediate threat to Nicaragua's sovereignty. But the administration has also explicitly refused to rule out direct U.S. actions against Nicaragua. According to a December 1981 report in the *Boston Globe,* it was decided at a National Security Council meeting to "press covert action in Nicaragua and El Salvador to infiltrate hostile elements both to gain intelligence and try to destabilize their effectiveness; [to] intensify public relations efforts at home and abroad to provide heretofore classified details on what the Soviets, Cubans and Nicaraguans are doing in Central America to create a climate of opinion in which stern action later might be supported; [and to] instruct the Pentagon to work up very specific contingency plans on such things as quarantines, blockades and military exercises .... "[19]

GUATEMALA: THE NEXT TO GO

Guatemala—the name once evoked kaleidoscopic travel poster images: Mayan temple ruins straining through jungle overgrowth to touch the sun; placid Indian women weaving brilliant shawls and intricate tapestries; towering white cathedrals, tributes in Baroque stucco to this imperious seat of Central American colonial rule.

Today, grisly images intrude: a 55-year old village woman, tortured and shot for denying knowledge of her son's whereabouts; "disappeared" nuns and priests in numbers rivaling El Salvador's assault on the Church; 300 deaths a *week*, according to the latest reports, and incontrovertible proof that the government is to blame. The Guatemalan generals seek no excuses; they are doing their job; they offer no concessions in exchange for arms; and the Reagan administration isn't asking for any.

Guatemala is now routinely referred to as the next "El Salvador," only bloodier. Eighty percent of its children suffer from malnutrition; 30 percent of the labor force is unemployed; 90 percent of its rural populace can't read or write. And while the bottom 10 percent of the people make do with 0.5 percent of the land, the top 10 percent prosper on 82 percent of the land.[20] Military rule has been the norm, almost without interruption, since the CIA engineered the overthrow of Jacobo Arbenz in 1954 and helped to undo his reforms.

Guatemalan generals have smothered any attempt at reform or fair elections. They have murdered peasants, trade unionists, teachers, students and journalists—and consciously they have targeted the moderate center of Guatemalan politics, to preempt any notion of replacing the army with a "lesser evil," Salvadorean style. Nearly eighty Christian Democrats have been murdered since April 1980; Alberto Fuentes Mohr, leader of the Social Democratic Party, and Manuel Colom Argueta of the United Revolutionary Front (FUR), were murdered in 1979.

Not surprisingly then, the Guatemala guerrilla movement has grown into a powerful force over the last decade, capable of mounting major attacks on towns and garrisons and carrying out diversionary maneuvers in the border region with El Salvador. By so doing they have kept the Guatemalan army tied down and unable to intervene against the FMLN. The four main revolutionary forces include the Guatemalan Workers Party (PGT); the Rebel Armed Forces (FAR); the Guerrilla Army of the Poor (EGP); and the Revolutionary Organization of People in Arms (ORPA). Each is strong in different regions; their increasingly coordinated actions now cover half of the country, including the most densely populated zones and those of greatest economic importance.[21]

Most threatening to the generals is the incorporation of Guatemala's Indian population into the guerrillas' ranks. Until recently, the country's 4 million Indians (out of a total population of 7 million) were described as stoically resigned to their appalling poverty. No one says that anymore. Not since the massacre of 114 Kekchi Indians, demonstrating in 1978 in a town called Panzós for the return of their lands. Not since 75,000 sugar workers, predominantly Indians, staged a paralyzing strike in February 1980 on Guatemala's southern coast. And not since the Indians have participated in armed takeovers of towns and farms, communicating the ideas of their revolution in their own languages, of which there are twenty-two.

Guatemala's trade union movement, along with other sectors of the urban opposition, must now operate primarily underground. The elections scheduled for March 1982 are being boycotted by all parties but the far right. Even the Christian Democrats have joined the boycott; they took part in the municipal elections of 1980, but since suffered too many deaths in their ranks. Increasingly, the struggle against military rule is an armed struggle—in terrain far more favorable to guerrilla warfare than El Salvador's dense *campo*. Guatemala is five times the size of El Salvador; it has extensive semi-tropical forests and vast empty spaces. And like the FMLN, the merging guerrilla armies of Guatemala have the support of a people with nothing more to lose, and everything to fight for.

A Shameless Alliance

The Reagan administration cannot very well deny reports of government complicity in Guatemala's brutal violence. (Amnesty International has reported unequivocally that the death squads operate under the direct supervision of the president, General Lucas García.) But a shameless alliance has nonetheless been struck between the Guatemalan right and the Reaganites.

U.S. economic interests in Guatemala are substantial. Some 190 U.S. firms and affiliates have operations there, more than in any other Central American country, and U.S. oil companies are now exploring the newly discovered jungle fields in Petén province. But the tightest bond between the Guatemalan generals and oligarchs and the new team in Washington is an ideological one. They share the same theories of outside subversion and dominos in line; the same rationalizations for dispensing with human rights and human life, in the name of "national security" in Guatemala and at home. Guatemala's insurgents are now routinely described by State Department officials as "Cuban-supported Marxist guerrillas," as they gear up for persuading Congress to rescind its ban on military aid to regimes with records of gross violations of human rights.

Already the Reagan administration has managed to slip supplies to Guatemala through the back door. On June 5, 1981, the administration approved the commercial sale of $3.2 million in trucks and jeeps to Guatemala, claiming they were for "non-military" uses. In July, sixteen Guatemalan military officers were brought to the United States for pilot training. The State Department has insistently tried to get clearance for shipping spare helicopter parts to Guatemala, but efforts thus far have been blocked by the House Foreign Affairs Committee.[22]

Meanwhile, the State Department says it is using "quiet diplomacy" to encourage changes in Guatemala. But each day the United States sinks one more inch into the quagmire of a Central American war.

NOBODY'S BACKYARD

Our ministers accredited to the five little republics . . . have been advisers whose advice has been accepted virtually as law. . . . We do control the destinies of Central America and we do so for the simple reason that the national interest absolutely

dictates such a course. . . . Until now Central America has always understood that governments which
we recognize and support stay in power, while those
we do not recognize and support fall.
—State Department memorandum, 1927 [23]

For over a century the United States has asserted its
right to determine events in its own "backyard," the thirty-
odd republics of Latin America and the Caribbean, for the
sake of its own "national security." The right to keep hostile,
foreign powers out of the hemisphere was asserted in the
Monroe Doctrine in 1823. But in fact, the United States has
used the threat of "outside subversion," or "foreign ties," to
discredit indigenous movements and justify open and covert
intervention in the domestic affairs of other nations: marines
landing on the shores of Santo Domingo in 1965; CIA monies
channeled to Chile to subvert an elected government.

Central America is only the latest chapter in a long history of attempts to deny the right of self-determination to
the peoples of the hemisphere; to subordinate their interests
to the geopolitical needs of Washington and the economic
interests of a wealthy few.

Official explanations of the stakes in El Salvador and
Central America speak of the strategic importance of pro-
tecting shipping lanes and the Panama Canal, access to the
oil fields of Mexico and Guatemala. Not to be too brazen, the
United States bases its right to these resources not on self-
interest, but on the need to keep them from the other side—
as if, were the "enemy" to win, all of Central America would
be handed to the Soviet Union on a silver platter, as a staging
ground for war on the United States.

What the Reagan administration fails or refuses to understand is that people fighting today in El Salvador and
Guatemala, those who fought yesterday in Nicaragua, are
not about to exchange one form of domination for another.
They are fighting precisely to recover the independence lost
since colonial times; the right to decide their own future.

Ironically, U.S. dominance in Central America surely
will persist even if opposition movements triumph. A case
in point is Nicaragua, which has doggedly tried to maintain

good relations with the United States and successfully has renegotiated terms of investment with U.S. corporations. The economy of Nicaragua is too weak, too dependent on outside aid and investment to contemplate an intentional break with the United States, even as the new government tries to reduce that dependence by seeking diverse sources of assistance in Latin America, Europe and the socialist bloc. The same holds true for El Salvador, where the FMLN/FDR have repeatedly declared their desire to establish good relations with the United States. No revolutionary movement in Central America looks to the Soviet Union as their sugar daddy for the future, since that country could ill afford to support another economy in the region. Revolutionaries are not unrealistic, nor are American corporations that, by and large, have accepted the new terms of their presence in such countries as Angola and Nicaragua.

Still less convincing is the Haig-style argument that U.S. intervention in Central America can be justified by a desire to save the hemisphere from "totalitarian rule." One need only cite U.S. support for military dictatorships in Chile, Argentina, Brazil and Bolivia to expose the hypocrisy of such statements. But more significantly, one should examine both the history and programs of the revolutionary forces now contending for power in Central America. It is true, as Jeane Kirkpatrick, U.S. Ambassador to the United Nations, likes to point out, that the peoples of Central America have had little or no experience with democracy.[24] They have lived under dictatorships since most of them can remember. But it does not follow that they are unprepared for it; or disdain it; or that there is something inherent in the "Latin style" that makes it impossible. Rather democracy is what the struggle is all about. And perhaps we in the United States will have much to learn from the experiments that unfold in Central America.

The experience of the popular organizations in El Salvador is key to the creation of a genuinely participatory system. Before the war, before the need to go underground and take up arms, members of the popular organizations tasted what democracy might mean—a direct say in the definition of priorities, in the choice of leaders, in the setting of goals and strategies. They experienced the difficult process of reconciling the interests and views of diverse sectors: peasants and factory workers, teachers and bus drivers, Christians and Marxists. All were given a voice; they intend to use that voice to shape El Salvador's future.

The program for a Democratic Revolutionary Government in El Salvador, put forth by the FMLN/FDR, reflects the class and political diversity that characterizes the revolutionary movement today. It also reflects the reality of a poor country, whose wealth has been plundered for centuries and whose economy cannot be changed overnight. The program pledges to respect human rights, to protect political pluralism, and to create a mixed economy with key sectors under public control. Undoubtedly there will be conflict once victory is won; differences as to the pace and depth of change. Capitalism has not been kind to the people of El Salvador. Socialism means different things to different sectors of the opposition. But as the FDR's president, Guillermo Ungo, has said, "I can't predict what will happen in the year 2,000, but right now the FMLN/FDR are united in their desire to end the war and shape a new future."

Washington's War

Washington's war on El Salvador is an ideological one that pins labels on people to hide their humanity and divides the world into a bi-polar model. This book has been about people. A similar book could be written about people in Guatemala, Honduras, Nicaragua. Each would contain its own special history and heros. But the basic themes would be the same: economic exploitation of the many by the few; the use of military force to control or destroy any movements toward change; U.S. support for those armies and governments; and the sad realization that armed struggle is perhaps the last hope.

In El Salvador, it is a hope that grows. On January 27, 1982, the FMLN destroyed 6 U.S.-supplied helicopters and damaged 22 warplanes in a daring attack on the military airport outside San Salvador. "We are losing the fight with the guerrillas in the countryside," Napoleon Duarte admitted in February.

Both Duarte and Minister of Defense García stress that increased U.S. military aid is essential to their government's survival—an opinion that U.S. officials and Congressional delegates share. U.S. officials also know that the size of the Salvadorean army must be doubled, possibly tripled, as Duarte has said, if it is to defeat the revolutionary forces. Salvadorean soldiers are now taking a crash course at Fort Benning, Georgia to overcome a serious shortage of officers. Another whole battallion is being trained at Fort Bragg, North Carolina. But this will not resolve the problem of winning new recruits into the army—a process that increasingly takes the form of forced roundups in the cities and villages, netting fourteen and fifteen year old boys, and poses a growing problem of desertion from the army's ranks. Non-American diplomats see—and state plainly—that the Salvadorean government cannot win without foreign troops, "from the United States or someone," as one of them put it.

Recognizing the lack of support at home for sending U.S. troops, the Reagan administration has denied any plans to do so, while refusing to "rule it out." Meanwhile, aid and training continue. In February 1982, President Reagan signed an executive order releasing an additional $55 million in defense equipment to El Salvador, to be drawn, under emergency procedures, from Defense Department stocks, and without congressional approval. Military aid figures for fiscal 1982 are upgraded on an almost weekly basis, while figures for economic assistance continue to rise astronomically. All this has been justified by a transparently subjective certification procedure, in which President Reagan assured Congress that El Salvador's military-civilian junta is making "a concerted" effort to protect human rights, that it has achieved "substantial control" over its security forces, and that it is making "continuing progress" in carrying out political and economic reforms.

There is no end to the war in sight. And in this war, as in other struggles for economic and social change in the hemisphere, the United States is on the wrong side. All of us will pay for what the U.S. government is doing in El Salvador. We are paying now: with tax dollars to buy helicopters that fire on peasant populations and to save an oligarchic economy from collapse; with the growing discontent throughout a land where the spiritual wounds of Vietnam have only now begun to scar over. Someday the young men and women who cannot get jobs because the administration phased out federal training programs, who cannot get an education because of cutbacks in student loans and assistance to public schools, who lose their jobs because their unions were broken or never formed, may pay with their blood abroad.

We have tried to tell the story of the women and men of El Salvador who have given their lives and of their lives to create a more just, equitable and democratic society in their country. Their sacrifice is awesome, their courage an example. But Americans have known virtually nothing of that courage and of our complicity in its repression. The images of Latin America, projected on the pages of newspapers or television screens, are beset with stereotypes that politicians, corporations and the media have created to deny us an understanding of the history, traditions and culture of the 250 million people who inhabit the rest of the hemisphere.

To win basic rights, to organize, to be secure from police attack, to bargain collectively, to have shelter, food, clothing, an education—for these the Salvadorean people have never stopped fighting. It should not be hard for us to identify with their determination and recognize that there—as here—those rights are never secure. We remember the bloody battles for the right to unionize, to make civil rights a reality, or abortion legal and safe. Once these victories seemed forever. No more.

Nor should it be difficult to reject the terror and barbarism of the Salvadorean armed forces: children impaled on the machetes of the National Guard; corpses beheaded and left lying on the streets; the skull of a man split open, a leaflet he was distributing stuffed in the wound; a woman raped by an entire platoon and then murdered, acid poured over her face to reveal death's hideous skull. It is meant to silence, this terror. But for the good burghers of El Salvador and their military watchdogs, death is not enough. There is dismemberment, desecration, dehumanization—all to restore the silence of the graveyard of 1932.

But silence can no longer be bought in this fashion. For every two who creep terrified into the darkness, there is one who says "no more." Their numbers now have grown to include the majority of El Salvador's people. Only this, and not the unproved allegations of outside aid, can explain the ability of the FMLN to challenge the combined might of two governments, El Salvador's and our own.

To sympathize with this struggle, or to feel revulsion at the murders done in our name and paid for by our taxes, is not enough. As Arnoldo Ramos, spokesperson for the FDR, observed at a massive rally in protest against U.S. aid to El Salvador, the people of the United States have been called upon twice in one generation to stop their government's destruction of another people. As in Vietnam, so in El Salvador, it must be done again.

The longer we remain horrified but silent, the more we allow the Reagan administration to believe in its "mandate"— interpreted as the right to punish the poor, the unemployed, the working class, the elderly at home; and to rebuild the American empire at the expense of peoples struggling for a more dignified life abroad. *We* must stop the war in El Salvador, the plans to sabotage the victories of the Nicaraguan revolution, the attempts to quietly support a genocidal government in Guatamala. It is a question of national pride.

Not the pride of a president and his ministers for whom the word means "being tough" toward a country with a population 45 times smaller than that of the United States. That is the bully's pride. Not the pride of ensuring the national security of the United States by trampling on the rights of others to determine their own future. That is no security at all. The present policies of the Reagan administration make "anti-Americanism" in the third world a self-fulfilling prophecy. Only by actively dissenting from those policies can we hope to erase the equally insidious stereotypes of Americans that exist abroad, and build on a national heritage that began with revolution and believes in social justice.

Roque Dalton, the great Salvadorean poet, whose work and example have greatly inspired this book, wrote of the awakening of the Salvadorean people from their sleep of the "half-dead." May his words by a reveille to our own awakening:

The dead are more insolent than ever.

It used to be easy:
we gave them a starched collar a flower
we placed their names on an honor roll:
the length and breadth of our land
the illustrious shades of yesteryear
the monstrous statue.

The cadaver signed on memory's dotted line
joined the rank and file once more
and marched to the beat of our worn out music.

But what are you gonna do
the dead
just ain't what they used to be.

These days they get ironic
ask questions.

Seems to me they're starting to figure out
that they are the majority.

—The Warrior's Rest
Roque Dalton

Epilogue: The 1982 Election and After
(2nd Edition)

* On March 27, 1982, under the intense scrutiny of the international press, El Salvador elected a Constituent Assembly. Its tasks were to prepare a new constitution and to enact legislation during the transition from rule-by-junta to elected government. Since 1981, Washington had urged this scenario as a way to improve the country's international image, and the Salvadorean military, José Napoleón Duarte and the Christian Democrats supported it enthusiastically. Oligarchic and business interests were at first suspicious; but wooed by the U.S. embassy, they entered the political fray through the old "official" National Conciliation Party (PCN); the National Republican Alliance (ARENA), a new extreme right-wing party with strong support from the traditional oligarchy; the Salvadorean Popular Party and two smaller political organizations. The Reagan administration pulled out all of the stops to promote the election. Presidential pronouncements and regular press briefings were buttressed by officially sanctioned delegations of dignitaries and specialists who had worked on U.S.-sponsored elections in Vietnam. Even the CIA contributed a special invisible ink to prevent double voting.

* Although U.S. Ambassdor Deane Hinton tried to cajole some of the organizations of the FMLN/FDR into participating in the election, none of them did so. They explained that the electoral machinery was still in the hands of those forces which had been responsible for 50 years of fraud. The military's assurances that it would respect the results were no more credible in 1982 than in any previous election. Moreover, all the FMLN/FDR leadership was on a "traitors' list," prepared in 1981 by the Salvadorean armed forces. In the climate of official terror that prevailed in El Salvador, participation threatened not only their own lives but those of their potential supporters. They refused to legitimate a process whose intent was not to determine the people's will but to refurbish the image of the Salvadorean government and discredit the insurgency.

* How many turned out to vote on March 27 was a subject of rejoicing, dismay, suspicion—and controversy. The government claimed 1.5 million, a figure higher than that estimated by some State Department officials for the entire electorate. The prestigious Central American University in San Salvador charged that given the time that it took to cast each ballot, nowhere near that number could have voted during the period that the polls were open. It reported claims by unnamed diplomats that participating parties, the armed forces and the U.S. embassy had made a "pact" to maintain the proportions that each party had won but to increase the total vote cast. All three vehemently denied the charges.

* But, even given a fraudulent official count, the turnout was still larger than anyone expected. Why? Voting their class interests, the wealthy and many of the middle class wanted a restoration of the old order, the abolition of the junta's reforms and elimination of the "subversives"—no matter what the cost. Other people voted because the election was sold as the way to end the war. The repression had closed all peaceful channels of political expression. These were the votes of the frustrated and the exhausted, anxious to say that, above all else, they wanted peace. But many people voted simply out of fear.

233

* Voting is compulsory in El Salvador. Two weeks before the election, General García said that those who did not vote would be committing an "act of treason." Each ballot was marked with a number corresponding to the name of the voter. The boxes into which the voter slipped the thin, translucent paper ballots were clear plastic. And, most importantly, election officials stamped the national identity cards of all who appeared at the polls. That card—the *cedula*—is required everywhere, everyday, in El Salvador, when you are stopped on a street corner by the National Guard or getting your paycheck from the boss. Without the appropriate mark the certainty is that you broke the voting law, and the presumption is that you are a guerrilla or a sympathizer.

* The big winner in the election was former army major Roberto D'Aubuisson and his newly created ARENA party. Although the party won only 25% of the vote, D'Aubuisson quickly formed an alliance with the other business-oriented parties of the right and took majority control of the Constituent Assembly.

* The big losers in the elections were José Napoleón Duarte and the Christian Democrats. With the discreet support of the U.S. embassy and more overt backing from moderate sectors of the armed forces, they had expected victory—despite an intensely vicious campaign against them by D'Aubuisson and ARENA. They won about 35% of the vote. Anxious to create an international image of national unity, the embassy and key sectors of the armed forces twisted arms to secure a place for the Christian Democrats in the new government. D'Aubuisson's price was that Duarte return to private life. An uneasy truce was made and the Christian Democrats got several lesser ministries. But, by September 1982, thirteen Christian Democrats had been murdered. Upon the death of the thirteenth, Duarte finally accused D'Aubuisson of "indirect" responsibility in the crime.

* The FMLN/FDR response to the election was confused and confusing. They offered voters no viable alternative to participation—short of armed struggle. They disagreed among themselves and gave multiple and contradictory instructions to potential supporters. Culminating a two-month campaign, an election offensive demonstrated their increased military strength in the eastern part of the country. But in San Salvador, where much of the Salvadorean army and international press were concentrated, their efforts seemed ineffectual.

* Under U.S. pressure and against the wishes of ARENA, the Constituent Assembly elected Alvaro Magaña, a banker with strong ties to the military, as interim president. Magaña claimed no long-term pretensions to power, representing himself as an administrator of the transition. Then, defying the embassy, the Constituent Assembly gutted the agrarian and banking reforms.

* The March elections resolved nothing. The war goes on. International human rights organizations still denounce abuses by the Salvadorean military and para-military forces. The bodies still appear in the streets. Still, the late night knock, the screams, the blood, the death. Again the Reagan administration certifies to Congress that protection of human rights is improving. Reform, according to Washington, marches on. U.S. economic aid keeps the Salvadorean economy alive; U.S. military aid keeps the Salvadorean army fighting. Washington still wants a victory in El Salvador. Even if it has to ignite all of Central America to get it.

Footnotes

I. Where Coffee Is King

1. David Browning, *El Salvador: Landscape and Society* (Oxford: Clarendon Press, 1971) p. 14.

2. Quoted in *ibid.*, p. 7.

3. For data on land concentration and forms of ownership, see Eduardo Colindres, *Fundamentos Economicos de la Burguesia Salvadoreña* (San Salvador: UCA Editores, 1977).

4. Rafael Guidos Vejar, *El Ascenso del Militarismo en El Salvador* (San Salvador: UCA Editores, 1980); Rafael Menjivar, *Formacion y Lucha del Proletariado Industrial Salvadoreño* (San Salvador: UCA Editores, 1979); Browning, *op. cit.*

5. Browning, *op. cit.*, citing Government Report, September 9, 1879, p. 204.

6. *Ibid.*, p. 216.

7. The World Bank, *World Development Report, 1980* (Washington D.C.: World Bank, 1980); U.N. Economic Commission for Latin America, *Statistical Summary of Latin America 1960-1980* (New York: United Nations, 1979); Amnesty International, *El Salvador: General Background* (London: Amnesty International, 1977) pp. 1-3; Melvin Burke, "El Sistema de Plantacion y la Proletarizacion del Trabajo Agricola en El Salvador," *Estudios Centroamericanos* (San Salvador: UCA) no. 335/336 (September-October 1976) pp. 473-487.

8. Comment made by Salvadorean woman, San Salvador, 1969.

9. Quoted in Lilian Jimenez, *El Salvador: Sus Problemas Socio-Economicos* (Havana: Casa de las Americas, 1980) p. 119.

10. Theodore Roosevelt relied on the Monroe Doctrine to announce a new policy of military intervention in Central America, based on the need to combat the instability of governments in the region through the presence of U.S. troops.

11. Guidos Vejar, *op. cit.*, chapter III, part A.

12. Thomas Anderson, *Matanza: El Salvador's Communist Revolt of 1932* (Lincoln: University of Nebraska Press, 1971) chapter II; Menjivar, *op. cit.*, p. 49.

13. Anderson, *op. cit.*, p. 35.

14. Guidos Vejar, *op. cit.*, p. 102, citing Ernesto Richter, *Proceso de Acumulacion y Dominacion en la Formacion Socio-Politica Salvadoreña* (San Jose, Costa Rica: SCUSCA, 1976) p. 47.

15. Anderson, *op. cit.*, p. 51.

16. *Ibid.*, pp. 52-53, citing Gustavo Pineda, "La Tragedia Comunista de 1932," *Diario de Hoy*, January 18, 1967.

17. *Ibid.*, p. 70, citing *Diario de Hoy*, February 4, 1967.

18. *Ibid.*, p. 61.

19. Roque Dalton, *Las Historias Prohibidas del Pulgarcito* (Mexico City: Siglo XXI, 1974) pp. 125-126.

20. Anderson, *op. cit.*, pp. 83-84, citing National Archives, Record Group 59, file 816.00/828, Major A.R. Harris, December 22, 1931.

21. *Ibid.*, p. 136.

22. *Ibid.*, p. 126, citing Pineda, *op. cit.*, February 10, 1967.

23. Jimenez, *op. cit.*, p. 121.

24. Dalton, *op. cit.*, pp. 119-120.

25. *Ibid.*, p. 126.

II. Great Expectations

1. William Krehm, "Democracies and Tyrannies of the Caribbean," unpublished English ms., chapter I, p. 15. In Spanish, William Krehm, *Democracia y Tiranias en el Caribe* (Buenos Aires: Editorial Palestra, 1959).

2. *Ibid.*, chapter II, p. 6.

3. *Ibid.*, chapter I, p. 10.

4. For a brief summary of the Communist Party's argument, see Rafael Menjivar, *Formacion y Lucha del Proletariado Industrial Salvadoreño* (San Salvador: UCA, 1979) pp. 88-90.

5. Federico Gil, Enrique Baloyra and Lars Schoultz, "The Failure of Democratic Transition in Latin America: El Salvador," unpublished manuscript (December 1980) p. 21.

6. *Ibid.*, pp. 33-34. The most significant party at this time was the Party of Renovation (PAR), representing a small, liberal sector of the elite. In 1950, the PAR obtained a respectable 43% of the presidential vote, but that showing was reduced to a mere 3% by the 1956 race.

7. Salvador Cayetano Carpio, *Secuestro y Capucha* (San Jose, Costa Rica: EDUCA, 1979) p. 24.

8. Thomas Anderson, *The War of the Dispossessed: Honduras and El Salvador 1969* (Lincoln: University of Nebraska Press, 1981) p. 28.

9. *Wall Street Journal*, March 13, 1961.

10. The three civilian members of this junta were Dr. Rene Fortin Magaña, Dr. Ricardo Falla Caceres and Fabio Castillo. Fortin Magaña dropped out of political life for twenty years and returned in

1981, leading a conservative, business-oriented party created to participate in the 1982 elections; Fabio Castillo was the presidential candidate of the Party of Renovation (PAR) in the 1967 elections and now is in the leadership of the Central American Revolutionary Workers Party (PRTC).

11. Fabio Castillo, Testimony Before the Subcommittee on International Organizations, *Human Rights in Nicaragua, Guatemala and El Salvador: Implications for U.S. Policy*, U.S. House of Representatives, 94th Congress, 2nd Session, June 8-9, 1976 (Washington D.C.: U.S. Government Printing Office, 1976) p. 47.

12. For more detailed information on the U.S. role in Guatemala's 1954 coup, see: Suzanne Jonas and David Tobis, *Guatemala* (New York: NACLA, 1974); and Stephen Kinzer and Stephen Schlesinger, *Bitter Fruit: The Untold Story of the American Coup in Guatemala* (New York: Doubleday and Co., 1982).

13. *Wall Street Journal*, March 13, 1961.

14. Thomas Anderson, *Matanza* (Lincoln: University of Nebraska Press, 1971) p. 157.

15. Between 1950 and 1969 U.S. sales of military equipment and materiel totaled $1.4 million, the bulk of that money spent in the 1960s. Grants to the Salvadorean military totaled $4.3 million and $2.9 million was spent on military training. U.S. Department of Defense, Defense Security Agency, *Foreign Military Sales and Military Assistance Facts* (Washington D.C.: U.S. Government Printing Office, 1979).

16. Hector Dada Hirezi, *La Economia de El Salvador y la Integracion Centroamericana 1945-60* (San Salvador: UCA Editores, 1978).

17. OECD, *Stock of Private Direct Investments by D.A.C. Countries in Developing Countries, End 1967* (Paris: OECD, 1972); U.S. Department of Commerce, *Foreign Investment of the United States* (Washington D.C.: U.S. Government Printing Office, 1953).

18. "Central America: Patterns of Regional Economic Integration," *Bank of London and South America Review* (June 1979) pp. 340-342.

19. Harald Jung, "Class Struggles in El Salvador," *New Left Review* (London) no. 122 (July-August 1980) p. 8, citing Melvin Burke, *The Proletarianization of Agricultural Labor in Latin America: The Case of El Salvador*, mimeographed, 1976, p. 45; and International Labor Office, *Year Book of Labor Statistics* 1970, (Geneva, 1970) pp. 82 ff, and *ibid.*, 1978, pp. 78 ff. Manufacturing workers, as a percentage of the economically active population in El Salvador, actually dropped from 13% in 1961 to about 10% a decade later. International Labor Office, *op. cit.*

20. Anderson, *War of the Dispossessed, op. cit.*, p. 32.

21. For information on AIFLD activities in Latin America, see: Victor Reuther, *The Brothers Reuther and the Story of the UAW: A Memoir* (Boston: Houghton Mifflin, 1976); Philip Agee, *Inside the Company: CIA Diary* (New York: Bantam/Stonehill, 1975); and the following issues of the *NACLA Report on the Americas*: "Smoldering Conflict: Dominican Republic, 1965-75" (Vol. IX, no. 3); "Argentina: AIFLD Losing its Grip" (Vol. VIII, no. 9); and "Chile: The Story Behind the Coup" (Vol. VII, no. 8).

22. William C. Doherty, Jr., "U.S. Labor's Role in El Salvador," *AFL-CIO Free Trade Union News*, Vol. 36, no. 2 (February, 1981).

23. For a history of AIFLD involvement in the peasant movement in El Salvador, see Carolyn Forche and Philip Wheaton, *History and Motivations of U.S. Involvement in the Control of the Peasant Movement in El Salvador* (Washington D.C.: EPICA, 1980).

24. For an informative account of this period, and the Christian Democratic Party, see Stephen Webre, *Jose Napoleon Duarte and the Christian Democratic Party in Salvadoran Politics: 1960-1972* (Baton Rouge and London: Louisiana State University Press, 1979).

25. Anderson, *War of the Dispossessed, op. cit.*, p. 93.

26. *Ibid.*, p. 141.

III. The Writing on the Wall

1. A fourth party, the Salvadorean Popular Party, founded in the mid-sixties after a split in the PAR, also ran a candidate in the elections representing middle-sized business interests.

2. Fabio Castillo, Testimony Before the Sub-Committee on International Organizations, *Human Rights in Nicaragua, Guatemala and El Salvador: Implications for U.S. Policy*, U.S. House of Representatives, 94th Congress, 2nd Session, June 8-9, 1976 (Washington D.C.: U.S. Government Printing Office, 1976) p. 43.

3. *Ibid.*

4. *Ibid.*

5. How Duarte lost his fingertips is a subject of some controversy. He told *New Yorker* correspondent Tom Buckley, in 1981, that he was injured in a construction accident in Venezuela. Former friends and associates, however, confirm our version, claiming that Duarte himself blamed the army's brutality in 1972, but changed his story when he stepped into the junta to share power with the army.

6. Mario Menendez, "Interview with Salvador Cayetano Carpio," *Granma*, English language edition (Havana), March 23, 1980.

7. Menendez, "Interview with Salvador Cayetano Carpio, Part II," *Granma*, English language edition (Havana), March 30, 1980.

8. Menendez, "Interview with Joaquin Villalobos," *Granma*, English language edition (Havana), May 18, 1980.

9. Alberto Arene, "Las Multinacionales y el Desfalco de la Economia Nacional," *Boletin de Ciencias Economicas y Sociales* (San Salvador) July-August, 1978, p. 22. A 1974 study showed that foreign capital was involved in at least half of all Salvadorean businesses, usually in joint-venture arrangements. *Ibid.*, citing "Las Inversiones Extranjeras," presented by the Institute for Economic Research, University of El Salvador, to the Second National Congress of Professionals of the Economic Sciences, San Salvador, October 1974.

10. *Women's Wear Daily*, March 3, 1980, p. 1.

11. Quoted in Lilian Jimenez, *El Salvador: Sus Problemas Socio-Economicos* (Havana: Casa de las Americas, 1980) p. 142.

12. FAPU, "Lo que el Pueblo Debe Saber sobre ORDEN," *Polemica Internacional* (San Salvador) February 1980, p. 28.

13. Eduardo Galeano, "Days and Nights of Love and War," *NACLA Report on the Americas*, Vol. 15, no. 5, 1981, pp. 24-25.

14. Menendez, "Interview with Joaquin Villalobos," *op. cit.*

15. Amnesty International Memorandum, "Students Who Disappeared During Dispersal of July 30, 1975 Street Demonstration, San Salvador, El Salvador"; Appendix to *Human Rights in Nicaragua, Guatemala and El Salvador: Implications for U.S. Policy, op. cit.*, p. 168.

16. Melvin Burke, "El Sistema de Plantacion y la Proletarizacion del Trabajo Agricola en El Salvador," *Estudios Centroamericanos* (San Salvador: UCA Editores) no. 335/336 (September-October 1976) p. 476.

17. *Ibid.*, p. 481.

18. *Ibid.*, p. 476.

19. Interview with General Jose Alberto Medrano by Richard White, San Salvador, July 23, 1980, quoted in Robert Armstrong and Philip Wheaton, "Reform and Repression: Policy of the United States in El Salvador," *A Report on the Meeting of the Permanent Tribunal of the Peoples on the Violation of Human Rights in El Salvador*, Mexico City, February 9-11, 1981 (Washington D.C.: CISPES, 1981) p. 117.

20. *Ibid.*

21. Quoted in Alain Gheerbrant, *The Rebel Church in Latin America* (London: Penguin Books, 1974) p. 255.

22. Quoted in Cornell Capa and J. Mayone Stycos, *Margin of Life* (New York: Grossman Publishers, 1974) p. 149.

23. Alan Riding, "In El Salvador, 'The Peasants Live Like Serfs 400 Years Ago,'" *New York Times*, August 27, 1975.

24. Navidad Campesina, Aguilares, December 21, 1975, cited in *Rutilio Grande* (San Salvador: UCA Editores, 1978) p. 87.

25. Homily at Apopa, February 13, 1977. Cited in *Rutilio Grande*, *op. cit.*, p. 108.

26. Riding, "El Salvador's Landowners Relax After Reform Scare," *New York Times*, April 8, 1977.

27. Anderson, *War of the Dispossessed: Honduras and El Salvador 1969* (Lincoln: University of Nebraska Press, 1981) p. 148.

IV. A Madness Seized the Land

1. All material on the elections, unless otherwise noted, comes from *The Recent Presidential Elections in El Salvador: Implications for U.S. Foreign Policy*, Hearings Before House Subcommittees on International Organizations and on Inter-American Affairs, March 9 and 17, 1977 (Washington D.C.: U.S. Government Printing Office, 1977).

2. Georgie Anne Geyer, "From Here to Eternity," *Washington Post*, September 10, 1978.

3. *The Recent Presidential Elections, op. cit.*

4. Latin America Bureau, *Violence and Fraud in El Salvador* (London: Latin America Bureau, 1977) p. 21.

5. Material on the death of Father Rutilio Grande comes from William J. O'Malley, S.J. *The Voice of Blood* (Maryknoll, N.Y.: Orbis Books, 1980).

6. El Salvador followed Argentina, Brazil, Chile and Uruguay in turning down U.S. assistance which, according to a law signed by President Ford in 1976, was linked to the recipient country's human rights conditions. Guatemala took similar action the following day. U.S. military aid to El Salvador in this period amounted to about $2.5 million annually, most of it in low interest credits for purchase of U.S. equipment. The aid also included $600,000 in training grants for the Salvadorean armed forces. *Journal of Commerce*, March 18, 1977; and *Washington Post*, March 19, 1977.

7. Placido Erdozain, *Archbishop Romero* (Maryknoll, N.Y.: Orbis Books, 1981) p. 1.

8. *Ibid.*, p. 18.

9. Amnesty International, "Background to Rural Problems in El Salvador," translation of selections from interviews with campesinos

describing repression in the Aguilares area of El Salvador in May 1977, AI Index No. AMR 29/11/77, mimeograph (London: Amnesty International, September 17, 1977).

10. *Ibid.* See also, Erdozain, *op. cit.*, pp. 24-25.

11. *Religious Persecution in El Salvador,* Hearings Before the House Subcommittee on International Organizations, July 21 and 29, 1977 (Washington D.C.: U.S. Government Printing Office, 1977).

12. Alan Riding, "El Salvador Moves to Suppress Unrest," *New York Times,* May 3, 1978.

13. Amnesty International, *El Salvador: Campaign Booklet* (New York: Amnesty International, October 1978) p. 7.

14. Erdozain, *op. cit.*, p. 28.

15. Karen DeYoung, "Church Demands Change in El Salvador," *Washington Post,* August 5, 1978.

16. Riding, "El Salvador's Dissidents Disappointed at U.S. Silence," *New York Times,* May 8, 1978.

17. Riding, "El Salvador Moves to Suppress Unrest," *op. cit.*

18. Tom Fenton, "Empty Belly Makes Salvadorean Peasant a 'Red,'" *Miami Herald,* April 27, 1978.

19. R. Sandoval, "What Cannot Be Forgotten," in *El Salvador Reports* (New York: CAVHRES) Vol. II, no. 3, December 1978, p. 6.

20. FAPU, "Lo que el Pueblo Debe Saber sobre ORDEN," *Polemica Internacional* (San Salvador), February 1980, pp. 24-25.

21. Marlise Simons, "Sunday Mass Becomes Challenge to Military," *Washington Post,* December 19, 1978.

22. Riding, "El Salvador's Dissidents," *op. cit.* In early May, 1978, the State Department dispatched two deputy assistant secretaries of state, Mark Schneider and Sally Shelton, to look into the charges of human rights abuses. Their report was critical of the Romero government and doubted its capacity to reform itself. To show displeasure, the Carter administration abstained on a loan application that the Romero government was pursuing at the World Bank, which nonetheless was approved. Further efforts by State Department moderates to impose sanctions failed.

23. Jon Sobrino, "Monseñor Romero y la Iglesia Salvadoreña, Un Año Despues," *Estudios Centroamericanos,* no. 389/340 (March 1981) pp. 132-133.

24. Mario Menendez, "Interview with Salvador Cayetano Carpio," *Granma,* English language edition (Havana), March 30, 1980.

25. Simons, "Sunday Mass," *op. cit.*

26. Erdozain, *op. cit.*, p. 48.

27. Comision de Derechos Humanos (CIDH), *Informe Sobre Derechos Humanos en El Salvador* (San Jose, Costa Rica: CIDH, 1979) p. 58.

28. *New York Times*, May 6, 1979.

29. Recounted by eyewitness Gene Palumbo, present at the ceremony.

30. *Miami Herald*, February 11, 1979.

V. In Search of a Center

1. Alan Riding, "U.S., Wary After Rebellion in Nicaragua, Weighs How to Act in El Salvador," *New York Times*, September 17, 1979.

2. Viron Vaky, "Central America at the Crossroads," Testimony before the House Committee on Foreign Relations, September 11, 1979.

3. Riding, "Salvadoran Police Fire on Protestors," *New York Times*, September 15, 1979.

4. "Proclama de la Fuerza Armada de El Salvador," *Estudios Centroamericanos*, no. 372/373 (October-November, 1979) pp. 1017-1018.

5. Interview with Colonel Adolfo Majano, December 1981.

6. Laurie Becklund, "Salvador Balancing Act," *Los Angeles Times*, November 1, 1979 (emphasis added).

7. Becklund, "Junta Quiets the Thunder of Revolution," *Los Angeles Times*, October 26, 1979.

8. Amnesty International, "Report on El Salvador," in *Amnesty International Report 1980* (London: AI Publications, 1980) p. 133.

9. *Ibid.*

10. Riding, "New Junta in El Salvador Says It Will Recognize Cuba," *New York Times*, October 19, 1979.

11. Interview with Dr. Guillermo Ungo, July 1980.

12. For a discussion of the Communist Party's arguments for participating in the first junta, see Mario Menendez, "Interview with Shafik Jorge Handal," *Granma*, English language edition (Havana), June 1, 1980.

13. Riding, "Salvadoran Junta Tells of Plans," *New York Times*, October 17, 1979.

14. Ana Guadalupe Martinez, *Las Carceles Clandestinas de El Salvador* (San Salvador, 1978).

15. Riding, "Salvadoran Women Plead for Word on Missing Sons," *New York Times*, October 20, 1979.

16. Shirley Christian, "Junta Trying to Make Friends with Its People," *Miami Herald*, December 15, 1979.

17. Amnesty International, *op. cit.* p. 137.

18. Interview with Colonel Adolfo Majano, December 1981.

19. Becklund, "Salvador Junta Unable to Keep Reform Promise," *Los Angeles Times*, November 15, 1979.

20. Interview with Dr. Guillermo Ungo, July 1980.

21. *Washington Post*, October 9, 1980.

22. Menendez, "Interview with Shafik Jorge Handal," *op. cit.*

23. "El Gabinete de Gobierno, Magistrados de la Corte Suprema de Justicia y Funcionarios de Instituciones Autonomas, se dirigen a las Fuerzas Armadas por intermedio del COPEFA," *Estudios Centroamericanos*, no. 375/376 (January-February 1980) pp. 117-119.

24. "Renuncia de Algunos Ministros y Subsecretarios del Estado," *ibid.*, pp. 120-121.

25. Menendez, "Interview with Shafik Jorge Handal," *op. cit.*

26. *Miami Herald*, January 25, 1980.

VI. Ten Bodies a Day

1. *Miami Herald*, February 17, 1980.

2. Karen DeYoung, "U.S. Weighs A Military Role in El Salvador," *Washington Post*, February 14, 1980.

3. According to Hector Dada, Christian Democratic member of the first and second juntas, in testimony before the Permanent Tribunal of the Peoples in Mexico City, February 1981, the acting U.S. ambassador to El Salvador in early 1980, Mr. James Cheek, advised the government to undertake a "clean counterinsurgency war."

4. *Miami Herald*, February 16, 1980.

5. Homily of February 17, 1980, in IEPALA, *Monseñor Oscar Romero: "Cese La Represion!"* (Madrid: Editorial Popular, IEPALA, 1980) pp. 142-143.

6. *New York Times*, editorial, February 22, 1980.

7. DeYoung, "U.S. Weighing Military Role," *op. cit.*

8. Interviewed in December 1981, Colonel Majano claimed that he forced D'Abuisson to resign after the October coup.

9. "Carta de Renuncia de Hector Dada Hirezi a la Junta Revolucionaria de Gobierno," *Estudios Centroamericanos*, no. 377/378 (March-April 1980) pp. 377-378.

10. "Carta de Renuncia de Miembros de la Dirigencia del Partido Democrata Cristiano," *Ibid.* pp. 378-379.

11. Roy Prosterman, Jeffrey Riedinger, Mary Temple, "Land Reform and the El Salvador Crisis," *International Security* (Cambridge, Ma.) Summer 1981, Vol. 6, no. 1, p. 58; citing C.L. Sulzberger, "Vietnamizing the Peace," *New York Times*, February 17, 1972.

12. For more details on these financial reforms, see *Wall Street Journal*, March 10, 1980.

13. *Miami Herald*, March 1, 1980.

14. Prosterman *et al.*, *op. cit.*, p. 61 citing ISTA statistics.

15. For critical analyses of the agrarian reform, see: Laurence R. Simon and James C. Stephens, Jr. *El Salvador Land Reform: Impact Audit, 1980-81* (Boston: OXFAM-America, 1981); and collection of articles offering different assessments of the land reform in Gettleman, Lacefield *et al.*, eds., *El Salvador: Central America in the New Cold War* (New York: Grove Press, 1981). According to the OXFAM Report, only 9% of permanent crops (of which coffee comprises over 90% of the value) are grown on farms larger than 1,235 acres, but over 63% are grown on farms smaller than 500 acres.

16. The OXFAM Report disputes the junta's claims as to the number of beneficiaries of the reform. According to OXFAM, Phase I of the land reform benefits only permanent resident laborers on the expropriated estates, whose numbers have been drastically reduced over the past fifteen years because of greater capital investment in agriculture. In addition, the timing of Phase I further reduced the number of beneficiaries. OXFAM cites a U.S. AID study of the agrarian reform, which states that "...the intervention process took place during a period of low labor demand, and because in many cases temporary workers do not live on the haciendas [the beneficiary population was reduced]. The result was that in some takeovers at the time of intervention only the management and permanent workers [e.g., tractor drivers, mechanics, bookkeepers, etc.,] were on the farms...The net result in many cases was that the already privileged few were incorporated in the associations and the associations' poor majority of workers were left wondering when the reform would encompass them." U.S. AID, *Agrarian Reform Organization*. Annex IIA *A Social Analysis*, p. 28. Quoted in OXFAM, *op. cit.*, p. 35. (On May 14, 1980, Colonel Jaime Abdul Gutierrez announced that there would be no more reforms carried out beyond Phase I and Phase III of the agrarian reform; the fears of Phase II landowners were allayed.)

17. Amnesty International, "Report on El Salvador," in *The Amnesty International Report 1980* (London: AI Publications, 1980) p. 135.

18. Alan Riding, "Salvadoran Army Steps Up Drive Against Leftists," *New York Times*, March 12, 1980.

19. Resignation letter of Jorge Alberto Villacorta, Undersecretary of Ministry of Agriculture and Livestock, March 26, 1980. Reprinted in OXFAM, *op. cit.*, pp. 29-30.

20. *Miami Herald*, March 11, 1980.

21. Riding, "The U.S. Role in El Salvador," *New York Times*, March 13, 1980.

22. Homily of March 23, 1980, in IEPALA, *op. cit.*, pp. 199-205. For a very moving eyewitness account of the archbishop's last sermon in the cathedral, see Thomas E. Quigley, "Remembering a Bishop," *The Witness* (Amber, Pa.), Vol. 63, no. 9 (September 1980) pp. 10-12.

23. Jorge Lara-Braud, "'El Pueblo Unido Jamas Sera Vencido,'" in *Christianity and Crisis* (New York), Vol. 40, no. 8 (May 12, 1980) p. 114.

24. *Ibid.*

25. *New York Times*, March 30, 1980.

26. *Ibid.*

27. "Testimony of the Ecclesiastical Delegates at the burial of Monseñor Oscar Arnulfo Romero in relation to the events which occurred during the funeral," March 30, 1980 (mimeo).

28. Interview with Enrique Alvarez Cordova, July 1980.

29. *Miami Herald*, April 18, 1980.

30. Prosterman *et al.*, *op. cit.*, p. 66.

31. For an extensive account of Operation Phoenix see Noam Chomsky and Edward S. Herman, *The Washington Connection and Third World Fascism* (Boston: South End Press, 1979) pp. 322-328 and accompanying footnotes.

32. *Miami Herald*, August 1, 1980.

33. *Miami Herald*, May 3, 1980.

34. Roy Prosterman, "El Salvador's Land Reform—the Real Facts and the True Alternatives," in Gettleman, Lacefield *et al.*, eds., *op. cit.*, pp. 174-175.

VII. The War Is On

1. Christopher Dickey, "Suspects in Plot Freed in El Salvador," *Washington Post*, May 15, 1980.

2. Interview with Colonel Adolfo Majano, December 1981.

3. Interview with Father Rafael Moreno, May 1980.

4. Socorro Juridico, *El Salvador: Del Genocidio de la Junta a la Experanza de la Lucha Insurreccional* (San Salvador: Arzobispado de San Salvador, 1981) p. 9.

5. David Blundy, "Victims of the Massacre that the World Ignored," *The Sunday Times* (London) February 22, 1981.

6. Recorded by an author, San Jose, Costa Rica, June 1980.

7. Interview with Ruben Zamora, July 1980.

8. Dickey, "Arrest of Leftists Blunts Hopes of Salvador Accord," *Washington Post*, November 29, 1980.

9. For Majano's reaction to events in Washington, see Dickey, "Killings Signal Shift to Right in El Salvador," *Washington Post*, November 29, 1980.

10. Robert Armstrong, "Salvador's Right Hails Reagan," *Guardian*, November 19, 1980, citing wire services reports.

11. Jean Donovan, letter to a friend.

12. Interview with Ita Ford, November, 1980, conducted by David Helvarg.

13. Lawyers Committee for International Human Rights, *A Report on the Investigation of Four American Churchwomen in El Salvador* (New York), September 1981, p. 18, citing John Dinges, "New Evidence on Missionaries' Deaths in Salvador Suggests Official Plots," Pacific News Service, July 1, 1981.

14. Dinges, *op. cit.*

15. *Daily News* (New York), December 5, 1980.

16. Marjorie Hyer, "Four Murders Trigger U.S. Catholic Protests," *Washington Post*, December 10, 1980.

17. "Two Murdered American Nuns Buried in Salvadoran Town," *New York Times*, December 7, 1980.

18. Colman McCarthy, "Service in El Salvador," *Washington Post*, December 14, 1980.

19. Dinges, *op. cit.*

20. Lawyers Committee for International Human Rights, *op. cit.*, p. 17, citing *Washington Post*, May 27, 1981.

21. Warren Hoge, "Judge in Salvador Frees One of Six in Nuns' Deaths," *New York Times*, February 14, 1982.

22. Bob Levin with Beth Nissen, "Storm Over El Salvador," *Newsweek*, March 16, 1981.

23. "Deserted Villages are Testimony to Salvador's Woe," *New York Times*, December 22, 1980.

24. Centro Universitario de Documentacion e Informacion (CUDI), "Panorama General del Mes de Diciembre," *Balance Estadistico*, Vol. 1, no. 6, p. 10.

25. FMLN Communique, December 12, 1980, cited in Centro Universitario de Documentacion e Informacion, *op. cit.*, p. 11.

VIII. "Our Mountains Are the People"

1. Alan Riding, "Salvadoran Rebel Predicts Final Push," *New York Times*, December 27, 1980.

2. Mario Menendez, "Interview with Farabundo Marti Military Commission," *Granma*, English language edition (Havana), April 27, 1980.

3. Marlise Simons, "El Salvador's Guerrillas Call for Peace Negotiations with U.S.," *Washington Post*, January 15, 1981.

4. Francis Pisani, "Where El Salvador's Guerrillas Get Arms," *Manchester Guardian/Le Monde Weekly*, March 8, 1981.

5. *Journal of Commerce*, January 15, 1981.

6. Alma Guillermoprieto, "Central America at Boiling Point," *Manchester Guardian/Le Monde Weekly*, February 1, 1981.

7. See, for example, the four-part series in the *Boston Globe* by Alex Drehsler, March 8-11, 1981. In March and April 1980, a group of foreign journalists spent five weeks with the FMLN in Morazan province. Their findings included, "demoralization within the army; difficulties for the military in taking positions and dislodging the guerrillas; and growing incorporation of the people into the guerrillas and an increase in their military capabilities." See *El Dia*, April 24, 1981, as cited in *Intercontinental Press*, June 1, 1981, p. 579. Our analysis is based as well on interviews with journalists and photographers in the field during February-March 1981.

8. Joaquin Villalobos, *Acerca de la Situacion Militar en El Salvador*, pamphlet published by the General Command of the FMLN, July 1981.

9. Karen DeYoung, "White Hand of Terror," *Mother Jones*, Vol. VI, no. 5 (June 1981), p. 28.

10. Christopher Dickey, "Salvadoran Military Begins Training with U.S. Weapons, Advisers," *Washington Post*, January 25, 1981.

11. Juan M. Vasquez, "Salvador Junta Wins Battle; War in Doubt," *Los Angeles Times*, January 23, 1981.

12. Dickey, "Salvadoran Troops Move into the Countryside," *Washington Post*, January 20, 1981.

13. See excerpts of February 17 briefing by Secretary of State Haig to representatives of NATO and other countries, *New York Times*, February 21, 1981.

14. Juan de Onis, "U.S. Says Salvador is 'Textbook Case'," *New York Times*, February 20, 1981; see also, U.S. Department of State, *Communist Interference in El Salvador: Documents Demonstrating Communist Support of the Salvadoran Insurgency*, February 23, 1981: U.S. Department of State, Bureau of Public Affairs, *Special Report No. 80: Communist Interference in El Salvador*, February 23, 1981.

15. Don Oberdorfer, "Salvador Is 'the Place to Draw the Line' on Communism, Percy Says," *Washington Post*, February 20, 1981.

16. Ex-CIA agents were among the most vocal critics of the State Department's white paper on El Salvador. See: Warner Poelchau, editor, *White Paper Whitewash: Interviews with Philip Agee on the CIA and El Salvador* (New York: Deep Cover Books) June 1981; and Ralph McGehee, "The CIA and the White Paper on El Salvador," *The Nation*, April 11, 1981. For an analysis of U.S. press treatment of the "captured documents," see: Jonathan Maslow and Ana Arana, "Operation El Salvador," *Columbia Journalism Review* (New York), May-June 1981.

17. Edward Walsh, "Reagan Gets First Public Opinion Backlash," *Washington Post*, March 27, 1981.

18. Juan de Onis, "Reagan Aides Meet Sharp Attack in House," *New York Times*, March 6, 1981.

19. John M. Goshko, "State Department Shifts, Seeks to Cool Off Salvador Publicity," *Washington Post*, March 13, 1981.

20. Jonathan Kwitny, "Tarnished Report? Apparent Errors Cloud U.S. 'White Paper,'" *Wall Street Journal*, June 8, 1981.

21. Robert G. Kaiser, "White Paper on El Salvador is Faulty," *Washington Post*, June 9, 1981.

22. *Ibid.*

23. Interview with Salvador Cayetano Carpio, conducted by the Center for the Study of the Americas (Berkeley, California), December 1981.

24. Oberdorfer, "U.S.-Supplied Copter Fires on Salvadoreans," *Washington Post*, October 27, 1981.

25. Dickey, "El Salvador Could Get Aid Boost," *Washington Post*, August 21, 1981.

26. Guy Gugliotta and Shirley Christian, "Salvador War: Both Sides Are All Punched Out," *Miami Herald*, October 16, 1981.

27. Gerald F. Seib, "El Salvador Gets More U.S. Helicopters," *Wall Street Journal*, August 26, 1981.

28. Dial Torgerson, "Consolidating Hold on Village," *Los Angeles Times*, August 20, 1981.

29. Bernard D. Nossiter, "Salvador Chief Rejects Talks Unless Rebels Disarm," *New York Times*, September 20, 1981.

30. On April 29, Army Captain Ricardo Alejandro Fiallos told a House subcommittee that he fled his country in December 1980, after receiving anonymous death threats for having spoken out against military atrocities against the civilian population. "It would be a grievous error," Fiallos testified, "to believe that the forces of the extreme right...operate independent of the security forces. The simple truth is that...acts of terrorism credited to these [death squads] such as political assassinations, kidnappings and indiscriminate

murder are planned by high-ranking military officers and carried out by members of the security forces.

"Whom do I refer to when I say 'high-ranking military command'?" Fiallos went on to identify all the top-level military commanders in El Salvador, including Colonels Jaime Abdul Gutierrez, Guillermo Garcia, Reynoldo Lopez Nuila, head of the National Police, Francisco Moran, head of the Treasury Police, and Eugenio Vides Casanova, head of the National Guard. See "Central America Watch," *The Nation*, May 16, 1981.

31. Mary McGrory, "Our Recent Past is Haunting Duarte's Efforts to Win Friends," *Washington Post*, September 24, 1981.

32. Hugh O'Shaughnessy, "El Salvador Faces Prospect of a Long Drawn-out War," *Financial Times*, December 17, 1981.

33. Thomas O. Enders, "El Salvador: The Search for Peace," U.S. Department of State, Bureau of Public Affairs, Current Policy No. 296 (July 1981).

34. "Central America Watch," *The Nation*, May 30, 1981 and *New York Times*, December 7, 1981.

35. Simons, "Negotiations Remain Elusive," *Washington Post*, June 4, 1981.

36. Interview with Cayetano Carpio, *op. cit.*

37. Leslie H. Gelb, "Haig is Said to Press for Military Options," *New York Times*, November 5, 1981.

38. Guillermoprieto, "Salvadoran Left Reportedly Gains Ground," *Washington Post*, November 10, 1981.

39. Sources for information on life in the liberated zones include the personal account of Philippe Bourgois, a Ph.D. candidate at Stanford University, who was caught in an army search-and-destroy mission and spent two weeks fleeing the army with a group of Salvadorean villagers in the liberated zones; interviews with Jon Snow, a correspondent for British Independent Television News, who made two trips into the liberated zones between March and November, 1981; interviews with photographers and documentary film makers. Published accounts of life behind the lines include the four-part series by Alex Drehsler, *op. cit.*; Leo Gabriel, "El Salvador: Report from the Liberated Zones," *Liberation News Service*, No. 1013 (May 15, 1981); an extraordinary series by Raymond Bonner in the *New York Times* (January-February 1982) and by Alma Guillermoprieto in the *Washington Post* (January-February 1982).

40. Alex Drehsler, "Guerrillas Say Why They Fight," *Boston Globe*, March 10, 1981.

IX. The Wider War

1. Marlise Simons, "3 Armies Collaborate in Latin America," *Washington Post*, October 27, 1981.

2. *New York Times*, December 2, 1981.

3. U.S. Department of Commerce, *Foreign Broadcast Information Service: Daily Report, Latin America*, Vol. VI, no. 179 (September 16, 1981), p. B-1.

4. Leslie H. Gelb, "Haig is Said to Press for Military Options," *New York Times*, November 5, 1981.

5. Interview with Salvador Cayetano Carpio, December 1981.

6. *Miami Herald*, April 2, 1980.

7. Some sources estimated the number of U.S. advisers in Honduras, by Spring 1981, at 200 or more, with additional contingents of nonuniformed U.S. personnel in evidence at Tegucigalpa's luxury hotels. See "Central America Watch," *The Nation*, March 14, 1981.

8. John A Bushnell, "La Politica de los Estados Unidos en El Salvador y Honduras," *Relaciones Internacionales* (Costa Rica) Vol. 1, no. 1 (1980) p. 72.

9. U.S. Department of Defense, *Foreign Military Sales and Military Assistance Facts*, December 1980, p. 6; State Department information released to Congressional committees. For more information on the growing U.S military role in Honduras, see Raymond Bonner, "Green Berets Step Up Role in Honduras," *New York Times*, August 19, 1981.

10. David Blundy, "The Innocents Caught in Lempa River Massacre," *The Sunday Times* (London) April 26, 1981.

11. Bonner, "Salvadoran Refugees Suffer as War Spills into Honduras," *New York Times*, November 23, 1981.

12. *Ibid.*

13. *Latin America Weekly Report* (London) May 8, 1981.

14. Alan Riding, "Honduran Victor in Overture to Foes," *New York Times*, December 1, 1981.

15. Riding, "Mexican Assails U.S. on Nicaragua Views," *New York Times*, May 8, 1981.

16. Gerald F. Seib, "Venezuelan President, In Washington, Warns Against U.S. Latin Intervention," *Wall Street Journal*, November 20, 1981.

17. U.S. Senate, Select Committee to Study Governmental Operations, *Final Report Book IV: Supplementary Detailed Staff Reports on Foreign And Military Intelligence*, 94th Congress, 2nd Session, 1976, p. 127.

18. Jo Thomas, "Nicaraguan Junta Member Says U.S. Attitude is 'Disrespectful'," *New York Times*, April 21, 1981.

19. *Boston Globe*, December 4, 1981.

20. Jeremiah O'Sullivan-Ryan, "El rol de la informacion en la vida del agricultor de subsistencia: un estudio en el altiplano de Guatemala," *Estudios Centroamericanos*, no. 33 (June-July 1978) p. 508, and Monteforte Toledo, "Guatemala," p. 641.

21. For more information on the growth of Guatemala's guerrilla movement, see: Special Issue of *Green Revolution* (York, Pa.), Late Winter, 1981, devoted entirely to developments in Guatemala; Julia Preston, "Guatemala: the Muffled Scream," *Mother Jones*, Vol. 6, no. 9 (November 1981); and Marlise Simons, "Guatemala: The Coming Danger," *Foreign Policy*, no. 43 (Summer, 1981).

22. Cynthia Buhl, "Who Kept the Lid on Guatemala Aid?" *New York Times*, January 20, 1982.

23. Under Secretary of State Robert Olds, State Department Memorandum, 1927, quoted in Richard Millet, "Central American Paralysis," *Foreign Policy*, Summer 1980, p. 101.

24. See, for example, Jeane Kirkpatrick, "Dictatorship and Double Standards," in Gettleman, Lacefield *et al.*, eds., *El Salvador: Central America in the New Cold War* (New York: Grove Press, 1981), pp. 15-39; and Kirkpatrick, "The Hobbes Problem: Order, Authority and Legitimacy in Central America," paper presented at the December 1980 Public Policy Week of the American Enterprise Institute, Washington, D.C.

El Salvador's Political Map

Democratic Revolutionary Front (FDR)
Formed April 1980

Farabundo Marti National Liberation Front (FMLN)
Formed November 1980

Revolutionary Coordinating Council (Coordinadora)
Formed January 1980

Democratic Front
Formed April 1980

1. FPL (Popular Liberation Forces)
Formed 1970

Military arm: FAPL (Armed Forces of Popular Liberation)
Formed 1979

1. BPR (People's Revolutionary Bloc)
Formed 1975

Partial list of affiliated organizations:
-FECCAS (Christian Peasants Federation)
-UTC (Farmworkers' Union)
-ANDES (National Association of Salvadorean Educators)

1. MNR (National Revolutionary Movement)

2. MPSC (Popular Social Christian Movement)

3. UES (National University of El Salvador)

4. AGEUS (University. Students Associa-

2. RN (National Resistance) Formed 1975

Military arm: FARN (Armed Forces of National Resistance) Formed 1975

3. PRS (Party of the Salvadorean Revolution) Formed 1978

Military arm: ERP (People's Revolutionary Army) Formed 1971

4. PCS (Communist Party of El Salvador) Formed 1930

Military arm: FAL (Armed Forces of Liberation) Formed 1979

5. PRTC (Central American Revolutionary Workers Party) Formed 1979

---

2. FAPU (United People's Action Front) Formed 1974; reorganized 1976

Partial list of affiliates:

-MRC (Revolutionary Campesino Movement)

-FUERSA (United Front of Revolutionary Students-Salvador Allende)

3. LP-28 (People's Leagues—February 28th) Formed 1977

Affiliated organizations in the peasant, student, community sectors.

4. UDN (Nationalist Democratic Union) Formed 1969

Affiliates include:

-ATACES (Farm-workers Association)

-AES (High School Students Association)

5. MLP (Movement for Popular Liberation) Formed 1979

Affiliate organizations in the student sector

---

5. MIPTES (Movement of Independent Professionals and Technicians)

6. AEAS (Association of Bus Companies of El Salvador)

7. FENASTRAS (Federation of Salvadorean Workers)

8. FESTIAVTSCES (Federation of Food, Clothing and Textile Workers)

9. FSR (Revolutionary Union Federation)

10. FUSS (United Federation of Salvadorean Unions)

11. STISS (Union of Social Security Workers)

12. STIUSA (Union of United Industries Workers)

13. UCA (Catholic University "Jose Simeon Canas"); Observer status

APPENDIX 2

Platform of the
Democratic Revolutionary Front
(April, 1980)

The economic and social structures of our country—which have served to guarantee the disproportionate enrichment of an oligarchic minority and the exploitation of our people by Yankee imperialism—are in deep and insoluble crisis.

The military dictatorship is also in crisis, and with it the entire legal and ideological order that the oligarchic interests and the U.S. imperialists have defended and continue to defend, oppressing the Salvadorean people for half a century. Victims of their own contradictions, the dominant classes have failed due to the decisive and heroic action of the people's movement. It has been impossible to stave off this failure, even with the more and more brazen intervention of the United States in support of such efforts against the people.

Unswerving commitment to the interests and aspirations of the Salvadorean people by the revolutionary organizations has led to the deepening and strengthening of their roots among the vast toiling majority and the middle sectors. Hence the struggle for a free homeland, in which their vital needs and desires will be met, can be neither stopped nor diverted....

The revolution that is on the march is not, nor can it be, the work of a group of conspirators. To the contrary, it is the fruit of the struggle of the entire people—of the workers, the peasants, the middle layers in general, and all sectors and individuals that are honestly democratic and patriotic.

The most conscious and organized ranks of the Salvadorean people, now multitudinous, are fighting in a more and more broad and united way. The worker and peasant alliance—through its combativity, level of consciousness, daring, organization, and spirit of sacrifice for the sake of the people's triumph—has proven to be the most solid basis for guaranteeing the firmness and consistency of the entire liberation movement. Expressing the unity of the entire people, this movement unites the revolutionary forces and the democratic forces—the two great torrents generated by the long struggle carried out by the Salvadorean people.

The decisive task of the revolution on which completion of all its objectives depends is the conquest of power and the installation of a *democratic revolutionary government*, which at the head of the people will launch the construction of a new society.

Tasks and Objectives of the Revolution

The tasks and objectives of the revolution in El Salvador are the following:

1. To overthrow the reactionary military dictatorship of the oligarchy and Yankee imperialism, imposed and sustained against the will of the Salvadorean people for fifty years; to destroy its criminal political-military machine; and to establish a *democratic revolutionary government* founded on the unity of the revolutionary and democratic forces in the People's Army and the Salvadorean people.

2. To put an end to the overall political, economic and social power of the great lords of land and capital.

3. To liquidate once and for all the economic, political, and military dependence of our country on Yankee imperialism.

4. To assure democratic rights and freedoms for the entire people—particularly for the working masses, who are the ones who have least enjoyed such freedoms.

5. To transfer to the people, through nationalizations and the creation of collective and socialized enterprises, the fundamental means of production and distribution that are now hoarded by the oligarchy and the U.S. monopolies: the land held by the big landlords, the enterprises that produce and distribute electricity and other monopolized services, foreign trade, banking, and large transportation enterprises. None of this will affect small or medium-sized private businesses, which will be given every kind of stimulus and support in the various branches of the national economy.

6. To raise the cultural and material living standards of the population.

7. To create a new army for our country, one that will arise fundamentally on the basis of the People's Army to be built in the course of the revolutionary process. Those healthy, patriotic, and worthy elements that belong to the current army can also be incorporated.

8. To encourage all forms of organization of the people, at all levels and in all sectors, thus guaranteeing their active, creative, and democratic involvement in the revolutionary process and securing the closest identification between the people and their government.

9. To orient the foreign policy and international relations of our country around the principles of independence and self-determination, solidarity, peaceful coexistence, equal rights, and mutual respect between states.

10. Through all these measures, to assure our country peace, freedom, the well-being of our people, and future social progress.

The Democratic Revolutionary Government—Its Composition and Platform of Social, Structural, and Political Changes

The *democratic revolutionary government* will be made up of representatives of the revolutionary and people's movement, as well as of the democratic parties, organizations, sectors, and individuals who are willing to participate in the carrying out of this programmatic platform.

This government will rest on a broad political and social base, formed above all by the working class, the peasantry, and the advanced middle layers. Intimately united to the latter forces will be all the social sectors that are willing to carry out this platform—small and medium-sized industrialists, merchants, artisans, and farmers (small and medium-sized coffee planters and those involved in other areas of agriculture or cattle raising). Also involved will be honest professionals, the progressive clergy, democratic parties such as the MNR (National Revolutionary Movement), advanced sectors of the Christian Democratic Party, worthy and honest officers of the army who are willing to serve the interests of the people, and any other sectors, groups, or individuals that uphold broad democracy for the popular masses, independent development, and people's liberation.

All these forces are now coming together to make up a revolutionary and democratic alliance in which the political and/or religious beliefs of all are respected. The organized form to be taken by this voluntary alliance at the service of the Salvadorean people will be the result of consultations among all those who make it up.

Immediate Political Measures

1. A halt to all forms of repression against the people and release of all political prisoners.

2. Clarification of the situation of those captured and disappeared since 1972; punishment of those responsible (be they military or civilian) for crimes against the people.

3. Disarming and permanent dissolution of the repressive bodies— ANSESAL, ORDEN, National Guard, National Police, Treasury Police, and Customs Police, along with their respective "Special Sections"; of the Gotera "Counterinsurgency School"; the so-called Armed Forces Engineering Training Center in Zacatecoluca; of the cantonal and suburban military patrols; of the oligarchy's private paramilitary bands; and of all other kinds of real or nominal organizations dedicated to criminal action or slander against the people and their organizations. The current misnamed security bodies will be replaced by a civilian police force.

4. Dissolution of the existing state powers (executive, legislative, and judicial); abrogation of the Political Constitution and all decrees that have modified or added to it.

The *democratic revolutionary government* will decree a constitutional law and will organize the state and its activities with the aim of guaranteeing the rights and freedoms of the people and of achieving the other objectives and tasks of the revolution. In doing so, the *democratic revolutionary government* will adhere to the United Nations' "Universal Declaration of Human Rights."

The constitutional law referred to above will remain in force while the Salvadorean people prepare a new Political Constitution that faithfully reflects their interests.

5. Municipal government will be restructured so as to be an organ of broad participation by the masses in managing the state, a real organ of the new people's power.

6. The *democratic revolutionary government* will carry out an intense effort of liberating education, of cultural exposition and organization among the broadest masses, in order to promote their conscious incorporation into the development, strengthening, and defense of the revolutionary process.

7. The People's Army will be strengthened and developed. It will include the soldiers, noncommissioned officers, officers, and chiefs of the current army who conduct themselves honestly, reject foreign intervention against the revolutionary process, and support the liberation struggle of our people.

The new army will be the true armed wing of the people. It will be at their service and absolutely faithful to their interests and their revolution. The armed forces will be truly patriotic, the defenders of national sovereignty and self-determination, and committed partisans of peaceful coexistence among peoples.

8. Our country will withdraw from CONDECA (Central American Defense Council), from TIAR (Rio de Janeiro Inter-American Defense Treaty), and from any other military or police organizations that might be the instruments of interventionism.

9. The *democratic revolutionary government* will establish diplomatic and trade relations with other countries without discrimination on the basis of differing social systems, but based instead on principles of equal rights, coexistence, and respect for self-determination. Special attention will be paid to the development of friendly relations with the other countries of Central America (including Panama and Belize), with the aim of strengthening peace and upholding the principle of nonintervention. Close fraternal relations with Nicaragua will especially be sought, as the expression of the community of ideals and interest between our revolution and the Sandinista revolution.

Our country will become a member of the Movement of Nonaligned Countries and will develop a steadfast policy toward the defense of world peace and in favor of detente.

Structural Changes

The *democratic revolutionary government* will:

1. Nationalize the entire banking and financial system. This measure will not affect the deposits and other interests of the public.

2. Nationalize foreign trade.

3. Nationalize the system of electricity distribution, along with the enterprises for its production that are in private hands.

4. Nationalize the refining of petroleum.

5. Carry out the expropriation, in accord with the national interest, of the monopolistic enterprises in industry, trade, and services.

6. Carry out a thorough agrarian reform, which will put the land that is now in the hands of the big landlords at the disposal of the broad masses who work it. This will be done according to an effective plan to benefit the great majority of poor and middle peasants and agricultural wage workers and to promote the development of agriculture and cattle raising.

The agrarian reform will not affect small and medium landholders, who will receive stimuli and support for continued improvements in production on their plots.

7. Carry out an urban reform to benefit the great majority, without affecting small and medium owners of real estate.

8. Thoroughly transform the tax system, so that tax payments no longer fall upon the workers. Indirect taxes on widely consumed goods will be reduced. This will be possible not only through reform of the tax system, but also because the state will receive substantial income from the activity of the nationalized sector of the economy.

9. Establish effective mechanisms for credit, economic aid, and technical assistance for small and medium-sized private businesses in all branches of the country's economy.

10. Establish a system for effective planning of the national economy, which will make it possible to encourage balanced development.

Social Measures

The *democratic revolutionary government* will direct its efforts in the social arena toward the following objectives:

1. Create sufficient sources of jobs, so as to eliminate unemployment in the briefest possible time.

2. Bring into effect a just wage policy, based on:

    a. Regulation of wages, taking into account the cost of living.

    b. An energetic policy of control and reduction of the prices charged for basic goods and services.

    c. A substantial increase in social services for the popular masses (social security, education, recreation, health care, etc.).

3. Put into action a massive plan for construction of low cost housing.

4. Create a Unified National Health System, which will guarantee efficient medical service to the entire population (urban and rural). Preventive care will be the principal aim.

5. Carry out a literacy campaign that will put an end to illiteracy in the shortest possible time.

6. Develop the national education system so as to assure primary education to the entire population of school age and substantially broaden secondary and university education. Quality and scientific-technical diversification will be increased at all levels, and free education will be progressively introduced.

7. Promote cultural activity on a broad scale, effectively supporting and stimulating national artists and writers, recovering and developing the cultural heritage of the nation, and incorporating into the cultural assets of the broad popular masses the best of universal culture.

*   *   *

It is the unanimous opinion of the popular and democratic forces that only through realization of the measures contained in this platform can the profound structural and political crises of our country be resolved in favor of the Salvadorean people.

Only the oligarchy, U.S. imperialism, and those who serve their anti-patriotic interests are opposed to and are conspiring against these changes. Since October 15, 1979, various parties and sectors have vainly attempted to use the government to carry out a large part of the measures we propose without first overthrowing the old reactionary and repressive power and without installing a truly revolutionary and popular power. This experience has confirmed with full clarity that only the united revolutionary movement in alliance with all the democratic forces can carry out such a work of transformation.

The moment is approaching for this historic and liberating victory, for which the Salvadorean people have struggled and heroically shed so much of their blood. Nothing and no one will be able to prevent it.

For the unity of the revolutionary and democratic forces!

Toward the victory of the *democratic revolutionary government!*

APPENDIX 3

U.S. Military and Economic Aid

PRE-OCTOBER 1979

Military—1946-1979
Financial assistance for weapons, equipment, etc.............. $16.7 million
Training of officers and personnel (trained in Panama and the
United States in counter-insurgency, military intelligence,
basic combat)... 2,000 soldiers

Economic—1946-1975
Direct bilateral (government to government).................... $157.7 million
Multilateral (through international lending institutions)[1]......... $268.8 million
(grants and loans for agricultural development, food,
infrastructure, family planning and public health)

POST-OCTOBER 1979

Military
November 1979—Riot control equipment...................... $ 0.2 million
April 1980—Trucks, communications, night vision sights....... 5.7 million
January 1981—Ammunition, machine guns, grenades, grenade
launchers, flak jackets, helmets, helicopter training and
maintenance teams.. 5.0 million
March 1981—Training, communications, vehicles, arms,
ammunition, helicopters, refurbished air craft, uniforms........ 25.0 million
February 1982—Weapons, munitions, helicopters.............. 55.0 million
Fiscal year 1982 (estimated total)............................ 81.0 million
Training of officers and personnel, 1980-82.................... 1,900 soldiers
(this represents slightly less than 10 percent of the
Salvadorean armed forces)

Military-related
Economic Support Fund (actual expenditures, FY 1981)......... $126.5 million
Economic Support Fund (estimated total, FY 1982).............. 100.0 million
(a fund for selected countries of special political and security
interest to the United States. The money can be used for military
related public works or it can replace money already budgeted by
the recipient country, allowing the money it replaces to be used
for military purposes)

Economic
Direct bilateral (government to government)
Fiscal year 1980. .... $ 59.0 million
Fiscal Year 1981. .... 107.7 million
Fiscal Year 1982 (estimated). .... 91.2 million
Multilateral (through international lending institutions,[1]
U.S. government corporations[2])
Fiscal Year 1980. .... $119.0 million
Fiscal Year 1981. .... 122.5 million
Fiscal Year 1982 (estimated). .... 131.4 million
(grants and loans for public works, agrarian reform, food
and development projects)

U.S. Military Personnel in El Salvador
As of February 1982, there were 42 military personnel in El Salvador, according to the U.S. State Department. They included experts to assist the five Salvadorean regional commands in planning specific military campaigns; Green Beret counterinsurgency experts; training teams to improve the performance of El Salvador's navy and to teach the maintenance and use of U.S.-supplied helicopters; specialists in administrative, logistical and command functions; and the military group at the U.S. embassy.

Sources: U.S. Department of Defense, *Foreign Military Sales and Assistance* (Washington, D.C.: Government Printing Office, 1979); U.S. Agency for International Development, *Program and Projects for Latin America FY 1977* (Washington, D.C.: Government Printing Office, 1977); Michael Klare and Cynthia Arnson, *Supplying Repression* (Washington, D.C.: Institute for Policy Studies, 1977), p. 38; Cynthia Arnson and Delia Miller, *Update: Background Information on El Salvador and U.S. Military Assistance to El Salvador* (Washington, D.C.: Institute for Policy Studies, 1980-81), nos. 1-4; U.S. Defense Security Assistance Agency, March 1981; Center for International Policy, "Total Aid Package for El Salvador May Reach $523 Million, *AID Memo* (Washington, D.C.: Center for International Policy, April 1981); *AID Memo Update*, June 2, 1981; telephone update, Center for International Policy, February 10, 1982.

[1]E.g., International Monetary Fund, Inter-American Development Bank, World Bank, etc.

[2]E.g., U.S. Commodity Credit Corporation, Eximbank, U.S. Overseas Private Investment Corporation (OPIC), etc.

APPENDIX 4

Direct Foreign Investment in El Salvador*

(in chronological order)

SALVADOREAN RAILWAYS CO. LTD. (U.K.): Railway linking San Salvador-Sonsonate-Acajutla (1894). Nationalized in 1962.

CH. BUTTERS CO. LTD. (U.S.)/(1) **Butters Divisadero: gold mine (1901).** (2) **Butters Salvador Mines Co.**: San Sebastian gold mine (1908). Both sold in the 1920s.

ALL AMERICA CABLES (U.S.): Telegraph and telephone (190-). Nationalized in 1965.

INT'L RAILWAYS OF CENTRAL AMERICA (U.S.): (1) Acquired San Miguel-La Union railway (1912). (2) Built El Salvador-Guatemala railway (1929; $12 million investment).

CENTRAL AMERICA MINES (U.S.-Canada)/**Cia. Minera del Divisadero S.A.**: Potosi gold mine and acquired 50% interest in San Sebastian mine. (192--1939).

INT'L POWER CO. LTD. (Canada)/**Cia. de Alumbrado Electrica**: Lighting and electric power (1926-1977).

MONTE CRISTO MINING (U.S.): Gold mine (192-). Sold in 1969 to Canadian Javelin.

ANGLO—SOUTH AMERICAN BANK LTD. (U.K.): Branch bank in San Salvador (193-).

NEW YORK & HONDURAS ROSARIO MINING (U.S.)/**N.Y. & El Salvador Mining Co. Inc.**: Gold and silver mines (1946; $.1 million investment). Sold in 1953.

GENESCO (U.S.)/**Calzado Salvadoreño**: Shoe factory, San Salvador. Acquired minority interest (1953).

INTERCONTINENTAL HOTELS (U.S.)/**Hotel El Salvador Intercontinental**, San Salvador (1954; $3 million investment).

TOYO SPINNING CO. (Japan)/**Industrias Unidas S.A. (IUSA)**: Cotton textile plant in San Salvador. Joint venture with C. Itoh (1954; $2.4 million investment). Capacity increased 50%, 1971-1972. Employed 1,850 as of 1973.

INT'L BASIC ECONOMY CORP. (U.S.)/**Productores de CAFE S.A.;** Soluble coffee. 49% joint venture with Tenco and locals (1955; $1.3 million investment).

PACIFIC VEGETABLE OILS-P.V.O. CORP. (U.S.)/**La Fabril de Aceites**: Vegetable oils, animal feed plant in San Miguel, 51% joint venture (1955).

ABC (U.S.): Two TV stations (1956, 1959).

---

*This chart includes known direct foreign investments in El Salvador. It was prepared in March, 1980 by Marc Herold, from the *Multinational Enterprise Data Base* (Durham, N.H.: Economics Program, University of New Hampshire).

The parent company is listed first, followed by its local subsidiary and investment data. Unless otherwise indicated, all subsidiaries were established by the parent company. Location of subsidiary listed when available. Date in boldface is the date of the initial investment.

SEARS ROEBUCK & CO. (U.S.): Dept. store in San Salvador (**1956**).

STERLING DRUGS (U.S.)/**Drogueria Centroamericana S.A.**: Pharmaceuticals plant in San Salvador (**1957**).

PILLSBURY (U.S.)/**Molinos de El Salvador S.A.**: Mill for imported wheat. 10% joint venture (**1959**).

SHERWIN-WILLIAMS (U.S.) /**S-W de Centro America S.A.**: Paint factory. Minority interest joint venture (**1959**).

BRITISH-AMERICAN TOBACCO CO. (U.K.)/**Cigarreria Morazan**: large cigarette plant near Ilopango. Joint venture (**1959**; $7.2 million investment).

FOREMOST (U.S.)/**Empresas Lacteas S.A.**: Ice cream, milk and cheese plant. Acquired 60% interest (**1960**: $.3 million investment).

CANADIAN SHELL CO. (U.K.-Dutch)/**Refineria Petrolera Acajutla S.A. (RASA)**: 13,500 b/d refinery at Acajutla for Venezuelan oil. 30% joint venture with ESSO and Salvadorean government (**1960**; $3 million investment).

STANDARD OIL OF N.J.-ESSO* (U.S.)/**RASA**: See above. 65% joint venture with Shell and Salvadorean government (**1960**; $10 million investment).

ESSO (U.S.)/**Fertica S.A.**: Fertilizer plant at Acajutla. Major interest joint venture (**1962**; $5 million investment). Sold to GUANOMEX in 1970.

STANDARD BRANDS (U.S.)/**Pan American Standard Brands Inc.**: Baking powder, gelatins, mixes; San Salvador (**1962**).

UNILEVER (U.K.-Dutch)/**Industrias Unisolas S.A.**: Detergents, margarine. Joint venture with DeSola family (**1962**; $1 million investment).

PHELPS-DODGE (U.S.): Copper telephone wires, San Salvador. 50% joint venture with Salvadorean government (**1963**; $2.5 million investment).

WESTINGHOUSE ELECTRIC (U.S.): Motors, transformers, bulbs (**1963**; $1 million investment).

CHORI CO. LTD. (Japan)/**Confecciones Textiles Inter-Americanos S.A.**: Synthetic fibers. Joint venture (**1963**).

ALCOA (U.S.)/**Alcoa de Centroamerica S.A. (ALDECA)**: Aluminum shapes from imported ingot. Acquired 80% interest (**1963**; $.4 million investment).

SATOH AGRICULTURAL MACHINE CO. (Japan): Agricultural cultivators. Joint venture (**1963**).

PFIZER (U.S.): Pharmaceuticals plant. Joint venture (**1963**; $1 million investment).

IMPERIAL TOBACCO CO. LTD. (U.K.)/**Lea & Perrins**: Worchestershire sauce from imported ingredients. Major interest joint venture (**1963**).

PROCTOR & GAMBLE (U.S.)/**Folger y Cia.**: Coffee buyers and instant coffee (**1963**).

ATSA EXPORT-IMPORT INC. (U.S.): 2 large molasses storage terminals in Acajutla (**1964**; $.5 million investment).

FIRST NATIONAL CITY BANK (U.S.): Bank branch in San Salvador (**1964**).

FOREMOST(U.S.)/**Corp. Bonima S.A.**: Pharmaceuticals. Acquired 50% interest (**1964**).

KIMBERLY-CLARK (U.S.): Tissue plant in Santa Tecla. 60% joint venture (**1964**).

MONSANTO (U.S.): Insecticides from imported inputs. 50% joint venture (**1964**). Closed in 1967.

PHILLIPS N.V. (Dutch)/**IMPELCA S.A.**: Light bulbs, San Salvador (**1964**; $.56 million investment).

---

* ESSO is a major subdivision of Standard Oil of New Jersey.

LENOX (U.S.): Plastic dishes, San Salvador. Joint venture (**1964**; $.15 million investment). New plant built in 1968.

INT'L HARVESTER (U.S.): Truck, bus assembly, Santa Ana. Minority interest, joint venture (**1965**; $.4 million investment). Closed 1969.

SEKISUI CHEMICAL CO. LTD. (Japan)/**Industrias de Tuberia S.A. (INTUSA):** Plastic siding, tubing in San Salvador. Joint venture (**1965**).

CROWN ZELLERBACH (U.S.)/**Cartonera Centroamericana S.A.:** Cardboard containers from imported components. Minority interest, joint venture (**1965**).

MERCON A.B. (Sweden)/**Vidrieria de Centroamerica S.A. (VISCA):** Pressed and blown glassware. Joint venture (**1965**; $1.8 million investment).

AMERICAN STANDARD (U.S.)/**Ideal Standard:** Air conditioning equipment assembly, San Salvador. 80% joint venture (**1965**; $.15 million investment). Sold in 1972.

BEMIS (U.S.)/**Bemis El Salvador:** Multiwall bags, Santa Ana. 50% joint venture (**1966**; $.3 million investment.).

CHORI CO. LTD.(Japan)/**Industrias Sinteticas:** Synthetic fibers. Joint venture (**1966**; $1 million investment). $10 million expansion in 1978.

MANHATTAN INDUSTRIES CO. (U.S.)/**Gadala Maria Hermanos S.A.:** Men's shirts (**1966**). Added women's sportswear in 1968.

TEXACO (U.S.)/**Texaco Caribbean Inc.:** Lube oil blending in Acajutla (**1967**).

McCORMICK & CO. (U.S.): Teas and spices, San Salvador (**1968**; $.2 million investment).

CHASE INT'L INV. CO. (U.S.)/**Financiera de la Pequeña Empresa S.A.:** Financing firm. Acquired minority interest (**1968**).

———— (German)/**Implementos Agricolas Centroamericanos S.A. (IMCASA):** Agricultural tools, Santa Ana. 28% joint venture (**1969**).

U.S. STEEL (U.S.)/**Metales y Estructuras (METASA):** Galvanized pipes and forms, Acajutla. Acquired majority interest (**1968**).

B.F. GOODRICH (U.S.)/**Quimicas Goodrich de Centro America S.A.:** Polyvinyl chloride. 20% joint venture with INSAFI (**1969**; $4 million investment).

MOORE (Canada): Business papers, San Salvador. Acquired 49% interest (**1969**; $.1 million investment).

CANADIAN JAVELIN (Canada)/**Minas San Cristobal:** (1) Acquired old properties of Monte Cristo (**1969**). (2) Opened Los Encuentros gold mine in 1971.

UNILEVER (U.K.-Dutch)/**La Favorita S.A.:** Soap factory. Acquired in joint venture with DeSola family (**1969**).

WILLIAM UNDERWOOD CO. (U.S.)/**Productos Alimenticias Underwood (PAUCASA):** Deviled ham. (**196-**). Sold in 197-.

BAYER FOREIGN INVESTMENTS (Germany)/**Bayer Quimicas Unidas:** Chemicals.** 98% joint venture (**196-**; $2.4 million investment as of 1978).

CARGILL (U.S.): Animal feed products.** Joint venture (**196-**).

GUANOMEX (Mexico)/**Fertica S.A.:** Fertilizer plant, Acajutla. Acquired majority interest (**1970**).

WARD FOODS (U.S.)/**Atarraya S.A.:** Shrimp trawling and processing. Acquired majority interest (**1970**).

UNITED AIR LINES' WESTERN INT'L HOTELS DIV (U.S.)/**Hoteles S.A.:** Camino Real San Salvador. Joint venture (**1970**; $4.4 million investment).

———— (South Korea)/**Central American Tuna Freezing Co.:** Fish freezing facility in La Union. 50% joint venture (**1970**; $1 million investment).

** Products listed under Cargill and Bayer have not been confirmed by public sources.

KIMBERLY-CLARK (U.S.): Crepe papers at Sitio del Niño. 60% joint venture (**1971**; $3.2 million investment).

TAPPAN CO. (U.S.)/**Ideal Standard**: Air conditioning equipment assembly plant. Acquired 80% interest (**1972**).

————— (Japan)/**Cia. Textilera**: Textile plant, Santa Ana (**1972**).

ESSO, SHELL (U.S.)/**Refineria Petrolera Acajutla S.A.** (**RASA**): Asphalt plant in Acajutla. 95% joint venture with locals (**1972**; $1 million investment).

TEXAS INSTRUMENTS (U.S.)/**T.I. El Salvador Inc.**: IC, semi-conductors and calculators, San Bartolo (**1973**). Employed 1000 in 1974.

GUANOMEX (Mexico)/**Fertica S.A.**: Ammonium sulfate plant in Acajutla (**1974**; $6 million investment).

DATARAM CORP. (U.S.)/**Dataram Int'l El Salvador C.A.**: Computer memory cores, San Bartolo (**1975**). Employed 400 in 1976.

BANK OF AMERICA (U.S.) Branch in San Salvador (**1976**).

GUANOMEX (Mexico)/**Fertica S.A.**: Sulfuric acid plant in Acajutla. Majority interest (**1976**).

KAY ELECTRONICS (U.S.): Electronics assembly plant, San Bartolo. Joint venture (**1976**).

SHELL CHEMICAL (Dutch)/**Shell Quimica de El Salvador**: Insecticides, fungicides, herbicides. Joint venture (**1976**).

————— (German): Textiles. Joint venture (**1977**; $2.4 million investment).

BECKMAN INSTRUMENTS (U.S.)/**APLAR (El Salvador) S.A.**: Transistor assembly, San Salvador (**1978**).

AVX CERAMICS CORP. (U.S.): Ceramic capacitors, San Bartolo (**1978**; $3.2 million investment).

MAIDENFORM INC. (U.S.)/**Confecciones de El Salvador**: Lingerie (**197-**). Sold in 197-.

RAPID AMERICAN'S BEAU BRUMMEL DIV. (U.S.): "Aris Isotoner" leather gloves (**197-**).

Major Investments in Distribution Facilities

ESSO (U.S.)/**West India Oil Co.** (Central America): Oil distribution (**194-**).

BRISTOL MYERS (U.S.)/**Cia. B-M Centroamericana S.A.**: Drug distribution (**1963**).

RALSTON PURINA (U.S.)/**Purina El Salvador**: Chow warehousing, San Salvador (**1966**).

STANDARD OIL CO. OF CALIFORNIA (U.S.)/**Cia. Petrolera California-Chevron Ltd.**: Oil Distribution (**1969**).

SINCLAIR OIL CORP. (U.S.)/**Sinclair Caribbean Oil Co.**: Oil distribution (**196-**).

DOW CHEMICAL/**Dow Quimica Centroamericana S.A.**: Chemicals sales, San Salvador (**1970**).

MATUSHITA ELECTRICAL INDUSTRIAL CO. LTD. (Japan)/**Nacional de El Salvador S.A.**: Batteries, electrical goods, San Salvador (**1973**).

Selected Bibliography by Topic*

General Histories

General histories of El Salvador, or books on Central America with particularly useful sections on El Salvador, include the following:

Armstrong, Robert. "El Salvador: Why Revolution," *NACLA Report on the Americas*, Vol. XIV, no. 2.

Browning, David. *El Salvador: Landscape and Society* (Oxford: Clarendon Press, 1971).

Centroamerica hoy (Mexico City: Siglo XXI, 1975).

Chavarria Kleinhem, Francisco. "Fundamentos politicos, economicos y sociales de la evolucion y desarrollo del movimiento sindical en El Salvador," Ph.D. dissertation, University of Costa Rica, 1977.

Dalton, Roque. *Las historias prohibidas del pulgarcito* (Mexico City: Siglo XXI, 1980).

Guerra, Tomas. *El Salvador en la hora de la liberacion* (San Jose, Costa Rica: [no publisher listed]).

Guidos Vejar, Rafael. *El ascenso del militarismo en El Salvador* (San Salvador: UCA, 1980).

Jimenez, Lilian. *El Salvador: Sus problemas socio-economicos* (Havana: Casa de las Americas, 1980).

Menjivar, Rafael. *Formacion y lucha del proletariado industrial salvadoreno* (San Salvador: UCA, 1979).

————, *El Salvador: El eslabon mas pequeno* (San Jose, Costa Rica: EDUCA, 1980).

Pearce, Jenny. *Under the Eagle: U.S. Intervention in Central America and the Caribbean* (London: Latin America Bureau, 1981).

White, Alistair. *El Salvador* (New York: Praeger Publishers, 1973).

*Resource materials on El Salvador are often difficult to obtain. All titles listed in this bibliography are available for use at the NACLA library in New York.

Early History

Books covering the early history of El Salvador (1900-1950) include the following:

Anderson, Thomas. *Matanza: El Salvador's Communist Revolt of 1932* (Lincoln: University of Nebraska Press, 1971).

Arias Gomez, Jose. *Farabundo Marti* (San Jose, Costa Rica: EDUCA, 1972).

Krehm, William. *Democracia y tiranias en el Caribe* (Buenos Aires: Editorial Palestra, 1959).

Menjivar, Rafael. *Acumulacion originaria y desarrollo del capitalismo en El Salvador* (San Jose, Costa Rica: EDUCA, 1980).

Modernization

Books covering the modernization period in El Salvador (1950s and 1960s) include:

Anderson, Thomas. *War of the Dispossessed: Honduras and El Salvador, 1969* (Lincoln: The University of Nebraska Press, 1981).

Cayetano Carpio, Salvador. *Secuestro y capucha* (San Jose, Costa Rica: EDUCA, 1979).

Forche, Carolyn and Wheaton, Philip. *History and Motivation of U.S. Involvement in the Control of the Peasant Movement* (Washington, D.C.: EPICA, 1980).

Menjivar, Rafael. *Crisis del desarrollismo: Caso de El Salvador* (San Jose, Costa Rica: EDUCA, 1977).

Rowles, James. *El Conflicto Honduras-El Salvador* (San Jose, Costa Rica: EDUCA, 1980).

Webre, Stephen. *Jose Napoleon Duarte and the Christian Democratic Party in Salvadoran Politics: 1960-1974* (Baton Rouge: Louisiana State University Press, 1979).

Repression and Electoral Fraud

Sources on the intense repression and electoral fraud of the 1970s in El Salvador include:

House of Commons, *Human Rights in El Salvador* (London: Parliamentary Human Rights Group, 1979).

Latin America Bureau, *Violence and Fraud in El Salvador* (London: LAB, 1977).

Martinez, Ana Guadalupe. *Las carceles clandestinas de El Salvador* (San Salvador, 1978).

U.S. Congress, House, Subcommittee on International Organizations, *Human Rights in Nicaragua, Guatemala and El Salvador: Implications for U.S. Policy: Hearings on June 8 and 9, 1976.*

————, House, Subcommittees on International Organizations and on Inter-American Affairs, *The Recent Presidential Elections in El Salvador: Implications for U.S. Foreign Policy: Hearings on March 9 and 17, 1977.*

The Catholic Church in El Salvador

Publications focusing on the role of the Catholic Church in El Salvador inlcude:

Erdozain, Placido. *Archbishop Romero: Martyr of El Salvador* (Maryknoll, New York: Orbis Books, 1980).

Gheerbrant, Alain. *The Rebel Church in Latin America* (London: Penguin Books, 1974).

Lernoux, Penny. *Cry of the People* (Garden City, New York: Doubleday and Co., 1980).

O'Malley, William. *The Voice of Blood* (Maryknoll, New York: Orbis Books, 1980).

Romero, Oscar A. *"Cese La Represion!"* (Madrid: Editorial Popular, IEPALA, 1980). (A collection of Monseñor Romero's writings and homilies.)

Rutilio Grande (San Salvador: UCA Editores, 1978).

U.S. Congress, House, Subcommittee on International Organizations, *Religious Persecution in El Salvador: Hearings on July 21 and 29, 1977.*

1979 Coup and Aftermath

Analyses of the October, 1979 coup and the post-coup period include:

Armstrong, Robert and Shenk, Janet. "El Salvador: A Revolution Brews," *NACLA Report on the Americas*, Vol., XIV, no. 4.

Amnesty International, "Report on El Salvador," in *Amnesty International Report 1980* (London: AI Publications, 1980).

Gettleman, Marvin E.; Lacefield, Patrick; Menashe, Louis; Mermelstein, David; and Radosh, Ronald, editors. *El Salvador: Central America in the New Cold War* (New York: Grove Press, Inc., 1981).

Guerra, Tomas. *El Salvador: Octubre sangriento* (San Jose, Costa Rica: Centro Victor Sanabria, 1980).

Hadar, Arnon. *The United States and El Salvador: Political and Military Involvement* (Berkeley, Calif.: U.S.-El Salvador Research and Information Center, 1981).

Navarro, Vicente; Cox, Harvey; Petras James; and Wald, George. *A Report on the Meeting of the Permanent Tribunal of the Peoples on the Violation of Human Rights in El Salvador* (Washington, D.C.: CISPES, 1981).

Poelchau, Warner, ed. *White Paper Whitewash: Interviews with Philip Agee on the CIA and El Salvador* (New York: Deep Cover Books, 1981).

Revolt in El Salvador (New York: Pathfinder Press, 1980).

Shenk, Janet and Butler, Judy. "Central America: No Road Back," *NACLA Report on the Americas*, Vol. XV, no. 3.

Simon, Laurence and Stephens, James C. Jr. *El Salvador Land Reform: Impact Audit, 1980-81* (Boston: OXFAM-America, 1981).

Socorro Juridico, *El Salvador: Del genocidio de la junta a la esperanza de la lucha insurreccional* (San Salvador: Archdiocese of San Salvador, 1981).

U.S. Congress, Senate, Subcommittee on Foreign Relations, *The Situation in El Salvador: Hearings on March 18 and April 9, 1981.*

Wheaton, Philip. *Agrarian Reform in El Salvador: A Program of Rural Pacification* (Washington, D.C.: EPICA, 1980).

————, *The Iron Triangle* (Washington, D.C.: EPICA, 1981).

Periodicals in Spanish

Spanish-language periodicals with extensive coverage of El Salvador, and the publications of the Salvadorean opposition, include:

Boletin de Ciencias Economicas y Sociales, a monthly bulletin published by UCA, the Catholic University in San Salvador (Apdo. 668, San Salvador).

Estudios Centroamericanos, a bi-monthly journal published by UCA, with in-depth analyses of economic and political issues, plus an extremely useful "Documents" section (Apdo. 668, San Salvador).

Inforpress Centroamericana, a weekly publication with excellent information on the economies of Central America (9a Calle "A", 3-56, Z.1, Guatemala).

Orientacion, the weekly newspaper of the Archdiocese of San Salvador (Seminario San Jose de la Montaña, San Salvador).

Polemica Internacional, the official magazine of FAPU, the United People's Action Front.

Revista Farabundo Marti, a publication of the FPL, Popular Liberation Forces.

Revista Internacional de las LP-28, publication of the LP-28, People's Leagues-28th of February (Apdo. 19-520, Mexico D.F.).

Señal de Libertad, weekly publication of Radio Venceremos, the radio of the FMLN (Apdo. 7-907, Mexico D.F.)

Periodicals in English

English-language periodicals with extensive coverage of events in El Salvador include:

Central America Monitor, bi-weekly publication of Boston CISPES (Committee in Solidarity with the People of El Salvador). Synthesis of European, Latin American and U.S. press reports on Central America. (CISPES, 1151 Mass. Ave., Cambridge, MA 02138).

El Salvador Alert!, published by CISPES (P.O. Box 12056, Washington, D.C. 20005).

El Salvador Reports, a bi-monthly newsletter published between 1977 and 1979, by the Committee Against the Violation of Human Rights in El Salvador (CAVHRES), New York.

Institute for Policy Studies Resource Materials on U.S. Military Assistance in Central America, special publications from IPS (1901 Q St., N.W., Washington, D.C. 20009).

Latin America Weekly Report and *Latin America Regional Reports: Mexico and Central America,* published by Latin American Newsletters Ltd. (91-93 Charterhouse St., London EC1M 6HR, England).

The Nation magazine publishes a regular column, "Central America Watch;" see also a special reprint of *Nation* articles (1980-1981), *El Salvador: The Roots of Intervention* (Nation, 72 Fifth Ave., New York, NY 10011).

Newsletter of the Religious Task Force for El Salvador, focusing on human rights and church issues in El Salvador (1747 Conn. Ave., N.W., Washington, D.C. 20009).

Solidaridad, the International Bulletin of the Legal Aid Office, Archdiocese of San Salvador, bi-weekly in English and Spanish (Apdo. 06-294, San Salvador).

Update Latin America, bi-monthly publication of the Washington Office on Latin America (110 Maryland Ave., N.E., Washington, D.C. 20002).

Washington Report on the Hemisphere, bi-weekly publication of the Council on Hemispheric Affairs; important coverage of legislative developments concerning El Salvador (1900 L St., N.W., Suite 201, Washington, D.C. 20006).

Glossary

aguardiente: literally, fire water; very crude corn or cane liquor

barrio: neighborhood

bloque: literally, bloc; short name for the People's Revolutionary Bloc (BPR), pronounced blo-kay

brigadista: member of a brigade; in Nicaragua, teacher in the national literacy campaign

cacique: traditionally, chief of an Indian community; now generally, local leader

campesino/a: peasant, or anyone who lives off the land in the countryside

campo: rural countryside

cantones: small rural communities in El Salvador

caudillista: in the style of the *caudillo,* a personalist, demagogic political leader

Chepe Toño: refined cane liquor, consumed by the more affluent

chicha: home-brew liquor

chusma: the rabble

cipotes: Indian word for children

colon: the basic unit of Salvadorean currency, worth approximately U.S. $0.40 in early 1982

colonias: literally, colonies; in El Salvador, neighborhoods in large cities

colonos: rural workers employed full-time on the *fincas* and *haciendas*

compañero/a: male or female companion; associate; comrade

compa: diminutive of *compañero/a;* used by members of the revolutionary organizations of El Salvador as an affectionate term to address one another

Coordinadora: refers to the *Coordinadora Revolucionaria de Masas,* the Revolutionary Coordinating Council of the Masses, uniting all the popular organizations

ejido: form of community land-holding; in El Salvador, a communal land grant provided by the Spanish Crown

elote: Indian word for young corn

finca: a coffee plantation

foquismo: strategy for guerrilla warfare based on the establishment of guerrilla *focos,* or centers, in rural areas from which military actions may be launched

guayabera: loose-fitting jacket shirt worn for semi-formal occasions

hacendado: owner of a *hacienda*

hacienda: a large estate

indio: literally, Indian; often used by the privileged classes as a pejorative term for the poor *juventud militar*: the military youth or young officers, referring to the movement that inspired the coup of October 1979

machismo: cult of masculinity requiring men to be super-males

maiz: corn

matanza: literally, massacre; refers to the repression of 1932 in El Salvador

mesones: urban slum housing, where many families live around a common courtyard

milpa: a small corn field

muchachos: the boys, or boys and girls; in El Salvador, affectionate term used for the guerrillas

operación de limpieza: army clean-up operation

patrón: landowner or boss; used more generally by campesinos as a term of servile deference

pedacito de terreno: small piece of land

pupusa: a popular Salvadorean dish, made of cheese, beans or pork rind inside a corn meal tortilla

refresco: homemade fruit drink or soda

somocista: of or pertaining to Anastasio Somoza, former dictator of Nicaragua; a follower of Somoza

tamales: popular Salvadorean food made of corn meal and meat, wrapped in banana leaves

tierras comunales: communal lands granted by the Spanish Crown to Indian communities

triunfalismo: over-confidence; the belief that triumph is certain

tugurios: shanty town communities that surround San Salvador and other large cities

turcos: literally, Turks; pejorative term for people of Semitic origin living in El Salvador

Acronyms

AFP: Agence France-Presse
AID: Agency for International Development
AIFLD: American Institute for Free Labor Development
ANDES: National Association of Salvadorean Educators
ANEP: National Association for Private Enterprise
ANSESAL: secret command structure within the armed forces, suspected of coordinating the repression under presidents Molina and Romero
ANTEL: National Telecommunications Company in El Salvador
AP: Associated Press
BPR: People's Revolutionary Bloc
CGS: General Confederation of Trade Unions
CGTS: General Confederation of Salvadorean Workers
CISPES: Committee in Solidarity with the People of El Salvador
CNT: National Confederation of Workers (Guatemala)
CONDECA: Central American Defense Council
COPEFA: Permanent Council of the Armed Forces
CPS: Salvadorean Communist Party
CROSS: Salvadorean Committee for Trade Union Reorganization
DRU: Unified Revolutionary Directorate
ECLA: United Nations Economic Commission on Latin America
EGP: The Guerrilla Army of the Poor (Guatemala)
ERP: People's Revolutionary Army
FAPU: United People's Action Front
FAR: Rebel Armed Forces (Guatemala)
FARN: Armed Forces of National Resistance
FARO: Agricultural Front of the Eastern Region
FDR: Democratic Revolutionary Front
FECCAS: Christian Peasants Federation
FMLN: Farabundo Martí National Liberation Front
FRTS: Regional Federation of Salvadorean Workers
FPL: Popular Liberation Forces
FSLN: Sandinista National Liberation Front (Nicaragua)
FUDI: Independent Democratic United Front
FUR: Front of Revolutionary Unity (Guatemala)
FUSS: United Federation of Salvadorean Trade Unions
INSAFI: Salvadorean Institute for Industrial Development
ISTA: Salvadorean Institute for Agrarian Transformation
LP-28: People's Leagues, 28th of February
MERS: High School Students Revolutionary Movement
MIPTES: Independent Movement of Professionals and Technicians of El Salvador

MLP: Movement for Popular Liberation
MNR: National Revolutionary Movement
MPSC: Popular Social Christian Movement
OAS: Organization of American States
ORDEN: Democratic Nationalist Organization
ORIT: Inter-American Regional Workers Organization
ORPA: Revolutionary Organization of the Armed People
    (Guatemala)
PAR: Party of Renovation
PCN: Party of National Conciliation
PGT: Guatemala Workers' Party
PRI: Institutional Revolutionary Party (Mexico)
PRS: Party of the Salvadorean Revolution
PRTC: Central American Revolutionary Workers' Party
PRUD: Party of Democratic Unification
RN: National Resistance
TACA: name of El Salvador's airline
UCA: Central American University, José Simeon Cañas
UCS: Salvadorean Communal Union
UDN: Nationalist Democratic Union
UNO: National Opposition Union
UPI: United Press International
UPT: Union of Shantytown Dwellers
UTC: Farmworkers' Union
UR-19: Revolutionary University Students
YSAX: radio station of the Archdiocese of San Salvador

Index

About the Authors

Robert Armstrong lived in El Salvador from 1967 to 1969, as a member of the Peace Corps. He has written extensively on Central America for *NACLA's Report on the Americas* and the *Guardian*, and has been active in human rights and solidarity organizations concerned with El Salvador since 1977. A graduate of Denison University and Rutgers University Law School, he is currently a staff member at the North American Congress on Latin America in New York.

Janet Shenk is a graduate of Smith College and received her master's degree in economics from the New School for Social Research. She has travelled extensively in Central America and South America over the last ten years, and worked in Ecuador from 1971 to 1974 as a Fulbright fellow and consultant to Ecuador's Ministry of Economic Planning. She is currently on the staff of the North American Congress on Latin America.